PRAISE FOR BUSINESS Rx

"Goldstick's thorough analysis considers whether danger signs indicate a temporary setback or a more lasting sickness... Business Rx demystifies the turnaround process. Helping you to learn from your own company's experience as well as that of many other firms, it is the complete guide to measuring, maintaining, and improving business fitness."

-MacMillan Book Clubs, Inc.
December 1988

"Business Rx gives you solid information on the causes of failure, and a good dose of how to take positive action that can heal a troubled company. Along the way, Goldstick offers a few valuable insights."

-Success Magazine
July/August 1989

"...It (Business Rx) includes numerous stories and anecdotes that vividly reveal the emotional and psychological pressures that businessmen undergo when managing a company in financial trouble, along with advice on how to cope with these pressures... And if anything fails, Goldstick recommends... learn from your mistakes and get on with your life. A good prescription from the 'business doctor'."

-Memphis Business Journal
March 13-17, 1989

"Perhaps most useful in Goldstick's book is his 'Business Health Index'... Goldstick is wry and often witty. He favors aphorisms and epigrams to make his points: 'The way out is through the door. Why is it that no one will use this exit?'"

-High Technology Business
April 1989

"...offers practical advice and suggestions in a readable format. He [Goldstick] not only walks readers through a bankruptcy proceeding but also provides an excellent quiz to help rate a company's health."

-Los Angeles Times
May 26, 1989

"Goldstick's is a book with an unusual twist: he illustrates his points by using familiar characters, such as Wilie E. Coyote... It is an effective tool, and makes the book fun to read. Cliches aside, Business Rx is full of useful information, charts, tables, graphs, formulas and diagrams. This offering is useful, practical and unusual."

-Turnarounds & Workouts Magazine
June 15, 1989

ABOUT THE AUTHOR

Gary Goldstick is the founder and president of G.H. Goldstick & Company, a management consulting firm based in Bakersfield, California.

G.H. Goldstick & Co. specializes in the area of financially troubled companies, turnarounds, loan workouts and bankruptcies.

Goldstick has acted as Chief Executive Officer and/or managed the turnarounds of companies in various industries including electronics, oil refining, medical services, vegetable packing, construction, polystyrene manufacturing, cosmetics distribution, shopping centers, mining, etc. In addition, Goldstick has guided a number of firms through the bankruptcy process to achieve a confirmed plan of reorganization and he has served as a state court appointed receiver, bankruptcy trustee and assignee for the benefit of creditors in numerous insolvency proceedings.

Prior to establishing his firm, Goldstick held various positions in engineering management with several computer and aerospace firms. He founded an electronics manufacturing company and for several years served as its CEO.

Goldstick received his bachelor of arts and bachelor of mechanical engineering from the University of Pennsylvania. His masters in electrical engineering was received from the University of California at Los Angeles and his masters in business administration from Pepperdine University.

He has conducted numerous management seminars, appeared on national television and radio and frequently speaks to business and professional organizations.

He is a Certified Management Consultant and a member of the Institute of Management Consultants.

Additional copies of this book can be ordered by writing or telephoning:

G.H. Goldstick & Co.
200 New Stine Road, Suite 251
Bakersfield, CA 93309
(805) 835-0304

BUSINESS Rx

BUSINESS ℞

How to Get in the Black and Stay There

GARY GOLDSTICK

WILEY

JOHN WILEY & SONS

New York / Chichester / Brisbane / Toronto / Singapore

This publication is designed to provide accurate and
authoritative information in regard to the subject
matter covered. It is sold with the understanding that
the publisher is not engaged in rendering legal, accounting,
or other professional service. If legal advice or other
expert assistance is required, the services of a competent
professional person should be sought. *From a Declaration
of Principles jointly adopted by a Committee of the
American Bar Association and a Committee of Publishers.*

Library of Congress Cataloging in Publication Data

Goldstick, Gary.
  Business R$_x$.
  Bibliography: p.
  1. Small business—United States—Management.
2. Small business—United States—Finance. 3. Industrial
management—United States. 4. Business failures—
United States. 5. Success in business—United States.
I. Title.

HD62.7.G684   1988   658'.022   88-10813
ISBN 0-471-62553-1

Printed in the United States of America

10 9 8 7 6 5 4 3 2 1

To Carol—my wife and best friend.
She comforts me during the bad times,
she celebrates with me during the good times, and
she enriches my life with her exuberance, compassion, and affection.

PREFACE

From the errors of others, a wise man corrects his own.

PUBLILIUS SYRUS
C. 1ST CENTURY B.C.

This is a book about the health of your business: how to enhance it, protect it, and, when necessary, restore it. When you own or operate a business, trouble is always one step behind you, or right around the next corner. Sometimes trouble catches up with you and sometimes you turn the corner and run into it head-on.

The fact is, many seemingly healthy businesses are really not fit. If their managers knew what to look for, they might be able to avoid business illness—or at least minimize the damage.

In my work as a turnaround manager, I deal with "sick" companies at all stages of illness and recovery. As we attempt to work through the turnaround process, my clients often say, "Oh, if only I knew then what I know now!" Business failure can be a great learning experience.

It is, however, a very costly and painful one. It is possible to learn about keeping your business on track, being aware of problems and dealing with them, and coping with failure without having to lose everything you own. You don't have to jump off a cliff to know that the landing will be rocky.

This book offers you some insight into what happens when businesses get sick, and how everyone—employees, creditors, the executives/owners—can and should react. More important, it shows you how to assess your company's fitness, identify symptoms, and prevent minor ailments from becoming life-threatening ones.

I've lived through a case of corporate illness myself. Many years ago I founded and served as CEO of an electronics manufacturing firm. The company struggled through several recessions and numerous changes in technology. It stayed alive despite key employee defections and interminable litigation with customers, vendors, and investors, as well as the other crises that invariably befall companies with unseasoned management.

I wouldn't have said I was unseasoned or inexperienced at the time, I might add. My educational background and work experience were considerable. It is hindsight that allows me to understand that I did not have the experience and skills required to manage that company successfully in that business environment.

The company pioneered some highly successful and unique products, enjoyed the services of many creative and dedicated employees, and successfully sold its products to blue chip companies around the world. I was proud that our products had a reputation for high quality, high reliability, and technical innovation.

Despite these significant achievements, the success and wealth I sought for my stockholders and myself eluded me. I was always confident, of course, that "next year" we would enjoy the fruits of our considerable labors.

The year of bounty never arrived. After 16 years of operation, I suddenly found myself at the head of a company careening toward bankruptcy. Although the company had been in and out of financial trouble a number of times, I had always been able to assemble the financial, creative, and emotional resources to lead the business back to recovery and on to new vitality.

Then luck turned its back on me. Over a relatively short time period, we suffered a major contract cancellation, our bank line of credit was terminated, we learned that our major investment in an engineering project would not be recovered, and an ex-employee conspired with certain customers to usurp a major product line. The timing couldn't have been worse, as the prime interest rate was then hovering around 20 percent.

Efforts to cope with what seemed to be insurmountable problems left us financially, physically, and emotionally exhausted. Liquidation of the company's assets under bankruptcy court protection to pay employees, taxes, and creditors appeared to offer the only feasible solution to the company's problems.

As the CEO and leader in defeat, the heavy burden of failure fell on me. As I accompanied the company through its death throes, lacking the necessary skills and resources to keep it alive, I struggled with anger, anxiety, and depression. It was a nightmare of despair and humiliation as customers deserted, friends turned their backs, employees betrayed the company, investors ridiculed us, and our creditors launched into a feeding frenzy on the carcass of our once-proud company.

The experience was an unrelieved trauma. I muddled through as best I could while the world as I knew it crumbled to ruins. If I had been able to get experienced consultant help to guide me through the process, I firmly believe it would not have been as agonizingly painful and that the results would have been far more beneficial for myself, my employees, and the company's investors.

Recovery was slow, but it came. I learned from the experience, rather like a student learning the answers to the test after flunking it. I started another business, a consulting firm dealing with troubled companies. I know now what I wish I had known then. Having guided over 50 companies through business distress, I am probably about 1000 times more prepared than I was when my own business collapsed.

The first key to getting out of trouble is to recognize you're there. Awareness is a difficult but necessary skill to develop for business survival. And often a business in trouble needs outside help—there must be a change agent to manage the crisis and help get things back on track. There is nothing wrong with needing help: the real mistake is needing help and not getting it.

I will share with you what a turnaround manager actually does to save the business and the processes and strategies to consider. Finally, the book provides some suggestions for you to increase your company's business fitness—whether you are just beginning a business for the first time, already running one, or recovering from a business disaster and thinking of starting all over again.

I should add that throughout this book, when I talk about the executive I am referring not only to chief executive officers of large corporations. The owner of any small business is also the executive in charge of its direction and success, because he or she is the major decision maker. For the sake of brevity in the book, I used the term "executive" to apply to business executives and business owners, in any size company.

Throughout this book every attempt is made to use nonsexist language. There are, however, certain areas where, for clarity's sake, the male gender is used. This is in no way meant to downplay the important role of women in today's business world.

This book does not offer five or ten easy steps to business success. There are no instant solutions, no magic cures. The purpose of this book is to provide information to heighten your awareness of the state of your business, to encourage you to learn from your own mistakes, and to give you the benefit of learning from the failures of others. Thinking and planning are your best defenses against business troubles. I hope this book will help you with both.

GARY GOLDSTICK

Bakersfield, California
August 1988

ACKNOWLEDGMENTS

When I made the commitment to write this book, I had as a major objective the creation of a work that was informative, interesting, provocative, and, despite the weightiness of the topic, enjoyable to read. Having spent many years writing dry, technical, and business papers, I decided to avoid the risk of abusing my prospective readers and sought the assistance of a professional writer. Fortuitous circumstances and a mutual friend brought Jenny Cashman to me. Her skill, ingenuity, and creativity in communicating the various facts and ideas that I had developed made this book both fun to write and (according to our reviewers) fun to read. Without her assistance in reviewing, revising, and editing, this book would not have emerged from the manuscript stage.

My secretaries Inger Summers and Norma Trout put in many long, bleary-eyed days in front of the word processor, churning out and revising the manuscript to schedules that were invariably unrealistic. Lauren Simmons and Heidi Ziolkowsky provided the research support, helping us find and evaluate the numerous references that we employed. Lauren also helped prepare the various figures. My daughter Gayle Goldstick assisted us in the area of literary and mythological references.

I was fortunate that so many capable and knowledgeable friends and business associates of Jenny and myself agreed to take time from their own busy schedules to review the manuscript and provide the comments and criticisms which proved so valuable during our rewrite efforts. I am deeply grateful to Dr. Edward Altman, Cathy Anthony, Jamie Bray, Mary Couture, Rachel Downing, Dr. Gary Emery, Larry Fox, Nancy Grant, Jeff Harbaugh, Dave Lampe, Lisa Mason, Jim Murphy, Philip Nelson, Wally Upton, and Kathleen White.

Finally, I would be remiss if I did not acknowledge the considerable contributions of my editor, Karl Weber, whose suggestions regarding the focus, organization, and length of the book proved invaluable.

G. G.

CONTENTS

1 | RISK AND REWARD: MORTALITY IN BUSINESS

You've got to know when to hold 'em
know when to fold 'em
know when to walk away
know when to run
you never count your money
when you're sittin' at the table
there'll be time enough for counting
when the dealing's done.

Every gambler knows that the secret to survival
is knowing what to throw away
knowing what to keep
'cause every hand's a winner
and every hand's a loser
and the best that you can hope for
is to die in your sleep.

FROM "THE GAMBLER," POPULAR SONG,
LYRICS AND MUSIC BY DON SCHLITZ
COPYRIGHT © 1978 BY WRITERS NIGHT MUSIC (ASCAP)

Business is a risky venture, and the cards don't always fall the way they should. The failure rate of American business is steadily increasing, with more and more businesses closing their doors. Table 1.1 shows failure trends since 1926 and indicates an alarming increase in the failure rate

TABLE 1.1.   AVERAGE FAILURE RATE OF BUSINESSES

Years	Average Number of Failures per 10,000 Businesses
1926–1930	108
1931–1935	102
1936–1940	58
1941–1945	25
1946–1950	21
1951–1955	35
1956–1960	53
1961–1965	57
1966–1970	44
1971–1975	39
1976–1980	31
1981–1985	96

Source: After *The Business Failure Record*. New York: Dun & Bradstreet Corp. (1987).

for business ventures. Business failure rates during the five-year period of 1981–1985 were the highest experienced in the United States since the Depression. Business bankruptcy filings over the past 10 years are also on the rise. In 1975 a total of 30,130 business bankruptcies were filed; in 1984 that figure was 62,170.

These are sobering statistics, yet people keep rushing to start new businesses, and few really understand the extent of risk they face. People tell themselves, "It won't happen to me." New incorporation figures indicate remarkable optimism that business is a good risk to take. In 1975 a total of 326,000 new businesses incorporated. In 1984 approximately twice as many new corporations started up (635,000). It is interesting to note that during the period of 1975–1984, corporate bankruptcy correlated with the new corporate start-ups.

Unfortunately, many of these businesses face hard times ahead. Dun & Bradstreet's carefully plotted *Business Failure Record* has shown that since 1952 an average of 53 to 60 percent of all businesses have failed within the first five years of operation. The odds are against a new business succeeding. Nor is a well-established business immune to failure. In 1985 an estimated 20 percent of business failures were of companies more than 10 years old. This means that more than 5700 firms with 10 years or more of experience couldn't keep their doors open.

Even if you predict a survival rate slightly better than Dun & Bradstreet, say 50 percent, there is a good chance that more than 300,000 of those 1984 new incorporations will be out of business by 1989.

Failure strikes at all levels of business. Highly visible and successful business executives have led their companies to disaster. Large corporations have ignored the warning signs and collapsed. Even the outstanding companies chronicled in Peters and Waterman's *In Search of Excellence* are not failure-free. A subsequent report in *Business Week* shows that of the 43 companies glowingly featured in the book, 14 were no longer performing with such brilliance a mere two years later.

Even more startling is the fate of the 10 most profitable U.S. companies selected by *Forbes* 15 years ago. In 1985 only three of them were still standing firm, while four had extremely poor returns on equity and three no longer existed as independent companies.

The enormous risk involved in a business venture cannot be overemphasized. Starting a business is not a safe bet, nor a sure route to independent wealth. Norman Augustine, an author and lawyer, provides a fascinating comparison of the life expectancy of a new business with the life expectancy of those engaging in a number of activities we consider to be highly dangerous—like parachuting out of airplanes and climbing Mt. Everest. The probability of fatality for these higher-risk activities is summarized in Table 1.2.

As Augustine notes: "There are many risks in this world, but few have a failure probability as intimidating as starting a new business."

Yet the lure of business is still strong, because the rewards of success are so great. Business offers the excitement of continuing challenges,

TABLE 1.2.   PROBABILITY OF FATALITY FOR HIGH-RISK ACTIVITIES

	Approximate Probability of Fatality (%)
Indianapolis 500 (10 races)	5
Sport parachuting (1000 jumps)	6
Astronaut (10 missions)	20
Ascending Mt. Everest (or dying in attempt)	30
Going over Niagara Falls in a barrel (1 time)	33
New business after 3 years	38

Source: N. R. Augustine, *Augustine's Laws*. New York: Viking Penguin (1986).

and provides both money and power. Even more important, it offers people the chance to take control over their own destiny.

CREATIVE DISASTER

Wile E. Coyote is waiting for the roadrunner. (You remember Wile E. Coyote, the popular cartoon character from Warner Bros. Pictures, Inc.) This is his 1347th attempt at capturing that elusive creature, but this time he knows he'll succeed. Knife and fork in hand, napkin around his neck, he stretches back the giant rubber band that will send him streaking after the speedy bird, and waits.

Everyone knows what's going to happen. With a taunting "beep beep," the roadrunner zooms past. Wile E. Coyote carefully releases— and is catapulted straight into the ground. Everyone also knows he will scrape himself off the desert floor and try again. Wile E. Coyote never gives up.

He would have made a great entrepreneur. Each ingenious scheme that falls flat gives rise to another. And another and another—there's no end to the creative energy that Wile E. Coyote expends in his perpetual chase. His persistence is applauded, and the audience cheers him on— to one more failure. Falling off cliffs, getting pounded by huge boulders, running head on into a mountain—it's all in a day's work. He brushes off, and schemes again.

The business person heading a distressed company may often resemble this Saturday morning cartoon character. Like Wile E. Coyote, he dreams up incredible schemes and launches into action. When he fails, he dusts off and forges full speed ahead, confident that the next time around he'll succeed. Friends and family tend to reward his persistence, and admire the fact that he never gives up.

Unfortunately, he may also have some of the blindnesses that Wile E. Coyote suffers in his single-minded pursuit of the roadrunner. The coyote is always forgetting where solid ground is, and looks down much too late, when he is already headed at full speed in another descent to the bottom of the chasm. He misjudges how sturdy or reliable something is that he is depending on for safety. He forgets to read the fine print.

He also repeats his mistakes, in countless variations. Even though the coyote has ended up, five times, on the wrong side of the boulder from a catapult he constructed, he's going to try that contraption one more time. Of course he gets smashed by it.

Occasionally it even occurs to Wile E. Coyote, as it occurs to the executive, that he is inviting unnecessary grief. Who can fail to relate to Wile E. Coyote's sudden flash of sanity as he is trying to dislodge a pile of rocks precariously balanced directly overhead, when he pauses and holds up a sign that reads: "In heaven's name, what am I doing?"

Deadly Duo: Perseverance and Denial

Unending yet unproductive activity is not uncommon in business. The executive becomes caught in a cycle of action, obsessed with the chase itself, and cannot stop. Activity is confused with progress, and the assumption is that as long as the company is doing something, it is moving forward. Risks are ignored or discounted, and schemes that Wile E. Coyote might scoff at are placed in motion.

In the business world, the quest may even have a certain sacred quality, akin to the search for the Holy Grail. An illusive, shining goal is vaguely defined. Many perils and constant tests of courage and commitment wait along the path. Sometimes the only thing the executive can be quite sure of is that the Holy Grail has not been found yet.

He sees himself as invincible, and his past business experience may have taught him, indeed, that he can triumph against incredible odds. He lives by maxims such as "nothing ventured, nothing gained." Business failure happens to other, less stalwart executives.

The outside world goes along with this attitude, until the business starts having problems. Then business schemes that were called "creative" are relabeled "foolhardy." The executive who clings to the self-image of invincibility and remains addicted to the chase is in danger of falling flat on his face. As other people begin to doubt his ability, he may try to prove his belief in himself by personally backing his business. What were his strengths may become his greatest weaknesses. The power of positive thinking, which helped prevail over problems in the past, may keep him from recognizing how much trouble he, and his business, actually face.

The company and the executive with a successful track record are especially vulnerable to missing or misinterpreting signs of business distress. Unfortunately, past successes are no guarantee of future profitability. There's no magic formula, no system that can always succeed. Any company can get into trouble—and even fail. Many smart executives have missed the warning signs of impending failure or made decisions that sealed the doom of the businesses they led. This will continue to happen, because business is a risk, a calculated gamble, and gambles don't always pay off.

LIFE AFTER DISASTER: TURNAROUND TRIUMPHS

Companies of any size get into trouble, and may seem doomed to failure. New actions taken in a mood of frantic desperation often only make things worse. There comes a point when everything has been tried, all last-ditch efforts only prolonged the agony, and the business, as well as the personal lives and fortunes of the executives, is in shambles. But this doesn't have to happen.

A business of any size, while inevitably facing the risk of failure, can also get out of trouble, or at least minimize the scope of the disaster. The secret to survival, however, is rarely found within the company walls. Executives who may be excellent at creating or running a company don't often have the skills or experience to fix a business in crisis. Even if they do have the expertise, what they lack is the objectivity to stand back from the trees and see the forest.

Enter the turnaround manager. By the time he or she walks through the company's front doors, the business often desperately needs drastic action to stay alive. The turnaround manager is a modern-day St. George with a scalpel, brought in to slay the dragons of the outside world— the creditors pounding at the door—and at the same time to perform delicate surgery to save the life of the business in distress.

When a company is losing money daily and the stakes keep rising, it's time for emergency treatment. The sooner help is called for, the more likely the business will survive. The company can no more effect its own salvation than a heart patient can do his own surgery. Imagine Wile E. Coyote standing in front of a mirror, with a book on "10 Steps to Heart Bypass Surgery" in one hand and a scalpel in the other. His failure would be understandable, because the situation is so ludicrous. So is expecting a company that is struggling for its life to heal from within.

What the turnaround manager brings to the business is a revitalizing force, a fresh perspective, and an ability to integrate a deluge of information. The turnaround manager can provide a new plan to deal with the old problems and has the energy and resources to follow through.

Megatrouble: Wickes Meets Sandy Sigaloff

One of the most widely known success stories of a turnaround is the tale of Sandy Sigaloff's rescue of Wickes, a chain of retail stores on the brink of disaster.

As reported in the *Los Angeles Times Magazine*, in 1982 Wickes was nearly $2 billion in debt and desperate for a savior. It found Sigaloff, who already had a reputation as a rescuer of troubled companies. He joined the company a month before Wickes filed for Chapter 11, and as chairman, chief executive, and president took decisive measures to bring the company back into control.

He sold the company's unprofitable outlets—17 stores were closed or sold—and worked to salvage the others. He made broad changes and many cuts in personnel, reduced the number of employees from 38,000 to 28,000, and made it clear that he expected top performance from those who remained.

The company more than survived. Wickes came out of the protection of the bankruptcy court in January 1985, after creditors had been paid in full by using a combination of cash and securities. Within six months, the company was able to pay $1 billion in cash to acquire a number of companies, and in 1986 Sigaloff has $1.4 billion, raised by selling a new debt issue, to continue in his plan for acquisitions and expansion.

The turnaround worked, even though the business was very, very ill.

The ads on television said: "We got the message, Mr. Sigaloff." But did we? The message is not just that Wickes is alive and doing well, not only that Sigaloff led a successful turnaround. A clear part of the message is that with proper help, provided in time, megatrouble can turn around into megabucks.

Smart Moves for a Small Company: The Story of Fifth Season Travel

What about the small, independent company that finds itself suddenly facing disaster? Thousands of companies on the verge of business failure cannot attract the interest of a big-corporation turnaround expert such as Sigaloff or Chrysler's Lee Iacocca. That doesn't mean they couldn't benefit from turnaround intervention.

In 1977 Fifth Season Travel was a small travel company in a lot of trouble according to an article in *Working Woman*. The business, started by four attorneys as a side business to handle vacation travel for friends as well as to provide some free travel for themselves, was $40,000 in the hole and facing impending bankruptcy.

The owners brought in a friend, accounting teacher Patti McVay, to see if she could help to make things better. She made things a great deal better, taking the company from its status in the red to become a $50 million business by 1985.

The turnaround was a phenomenal success, because McVay saw a market segment that was virtually untouched at that time—catering to and coordinating business travel. She structured the company's entire plan around going after that market, lined up clients to provide leverage for loans, and negotiated her way out of the mess the company was in. She became the majority owner and chief executive of a business that she led to be among the top 50 companies in the travel business.

BETTING ON SURVIVAL

No matter how big or small a business is, the basic reasons for business trouble and potential disaster remain the same. Big corporations and small companies alike are subject to the same economic risks, the same possible errors in judgment, or factors overlooked.

How do you figure your changes for success? What are the factors that make up the odds for trouble or profit? And why do some businesses seem to stay on the road to profitability so much more easily than others? These are some of the issues that will be discussed in the following chapters.

To keep from becoming a business failure statistic, you need more than a good idea and money in the bank. You need to know when to call for help, and how to realize when your business is in trouble. Remember, "You've got to know when to hold 'em, know when to fold 'em, know when to walk away and when to run." That's not just common sense: it's the secret to survival.

2 | HOW HEALTHY IS YOUR BUSINESS?

A wise man should consider that health is the greatest of human blessings, and learn how by his own thought to derive benefit from his illnesses.

HIPPOCRATES

Business is a constant test of the strengths and weaknesses of the company in relation to the economic and market environment in which it operates. A truly healthy business can survive many setbacks because it is properly prepared for difficulties and aware of the signs of business problems. A business that falls ill doesn't have the same adaptability to outside events or immunity to internal breakdowns. When a business is in trouble, even the most capable manager may find it difficult or impossible to create and implement solutions in time.

A clear understanding of the health of the business is important. It is especially vital to recognize business problems before they put the company into a situation where its life is in danger. If the business is already bleeding and in critical condition, the only way to save it is to get it into surgery and through intensive care.

It's sometimes difficult to assess whether the business is suffering from the minor aches and pains of a temporary setback or whether that financial fever is the symptom of something more serious than the business equivalent of a common cold. The proper prescription depends on an accurate diagnosis. You don't take two aspirin and go to bed when you're suffering from chest pains. If your business is suffering serious health problems, ignoring the symptoms can only lead to greater distress.

WHERE AND HOW MUCH DOES IT HURT?
A DIAGNOSTIC SELF-TEST FOR THE BUSINESS

The first thing a turnaround manager does in determining the potential for a workout situation is to evaluate the company's health. Like a corporate doctor, the turnaround manager takes the company's temperature, gives it a thorough "physical," and prescribes a treatment plan to turn the business around.

But how can you tell when your company needs a doctor, and when you can take care of the situation yourself?

Goldstick's Business Health Index (pages 11–19) is a tool that attempts to determine objectively the company's level of adversity, a self-test for you to diagnose the general health of your business. The questions cover a full range of factors that affect the well-being of your company, from plain dollars and cents to business relationships. The test does not require a calculator or a computer program to complete—it is a simple evaluation tool you can use without leaving your desk. Take a few minutes to evaluate your company's health.

The test is based upon my years of experience in working with troubled companies and the common symptoms that appear time after time when the business is in financial distress. Its main purpose is to encourage you to focus upon what is actually happening in your business, and to alert you to possible trouble zones.

You might have several members of the management team take the test. Answers should match, of course, and if they don't, someone is harboring misconceptions about the company's health. The "patient" cannot get well unless all of those responsible for its health and welfare understand the problems that exist.

GOLDSTICK'S BUSINESS HEALTH INDEX

The statements presented refer to conditions that exist within your company. Read each one, decide whether it is true or false, and circle the number in the appropriate column. Some statements may not apply to your business, depending on its size or organizational structure. In those cases circle N/A. Your score is determined by adding the numbers circled.

Financial

Dollar signs and other numbers: what's the bottom line?

Liquidity

		T	F
1.	Collection agencies have filed or threatened to file lawsuits against our firm.	3	0
*2.	Tax liens have been filed against our firm.	3	0
3.	We never use the "float" in our checking account in order to solve our cash flow problem.	0	1
4.	Our controller or bookkeeper does not spend any appreciable time (that is, more than two hours per week) talking to vendors who are requesting payments.	0	1
*5.	We are "current" in all of our withholding taxes and sales taxes.	0	3
6.	The average collection period for our accounts receivable is no more than 50 percent greater than the no-discount credit terms we offer.	0	2 N/A
7.	All of our accounts payable are being serviced in accordance with the agreed terms, that is, paid in a timely manner.	0	3
8.	Financial statements consisting of at least an income statement, a balance sheet, and accounts receivable and		

T   F

accounts payable agings are prepared monthly and reflect both the revenue and the expenses for the period.   0   2

*9. Inventory procedures are in effect which ensure that we have an accurate account of our usable inventory at the end of the month.   0   2
                                                                                N/A

*10. The accounts receivable balance appearing on our financial statement accurately reflects what our customers acknowledge they owe, and what they are capable of paying under the terms of our agreement with them.   0   3
                                                                                N/A

11. Our cash-in-bank account balance accurately reflects the actual funds in the bank after all the checks have been written and mailed.   0   3

12. The accounts payable balance reflected in our financial statement includes all invoices that have been presented to us for payment, including those that we may be disputing.   0   3

Growth and Profitability

13. Unit sales volume (number of units, hours, or tons of merchandise billed) is decreasing.   1   0

14. The company has reported a pretax profit (excluding extraordinary items) for the preceding two years and expects to report a profit this year.   0   1

15. Sales, general, and administrative expenses as a percentage of sales are increasing.   3   0

16. The gross profit margin for our core products has increased over last year's profit margin.   0   1

17. Major decisions about new business, new products, new markets, and acquisitions reflect a clear organizational strategy.   0   2

	T	F

18. The turnover rate of our inventory (number of turns per year) has improved over last year's results.   0 1 N/A

Control Systems

19. The company has a business plan that sets forth the company's strategic and operational objectives and programs for the ensuing year.   0 2

*20. The company operates in accordance with a budget and cash management system that is consistent with its objectives. Expenditures against the budget are recorded and monitored. Substantial deviations are analyzed periodically.   0 3

*21. The company's sales organization prepares sales forecasts, and its performance against the forecast is monitored. These forecasts are used to establish inventory and personnel levels.   0 3 N/A

22. The company has a program to quantitatively measure customer satisfaction.   0 2

23. Individual responsibilities for monitoring and achieving financial goals are clearly defined.   0 1

Management

Is it multiplying or dividing in your business equation?

The CEO's Leadership

24. Our company has a well-defined mission and set of goals, which are frequently communicated to our employees. The mission and goals are in writing and a copy is available.   0 2

25. The chief executive officer frequently interacts with employees at various levels of the company.   0 2

		T	F

26. Employees in our company are well informed as to how well or how poorly the company is meeting its stated objectives.   0   1

***27.** Our company lacks resources (money, equipment, space, personnel) to meet its short-range objectives and fulfill its contractual obligations.   3   0

28. Major decisions, such as organizational changes, capital appropriations, and new facilities, are guided by a formal well-defined approval process.   0   1

29. A single individual has ultimate responsibility for the company's day-to-day operating decisions.   0   3

Key Managers

30. All of the managers who report to me are qualified by education, experience, loyalty, motivation, and competence.   0   1

31. The turnover in management staff has been greater than 20 percent per year.   2   0

32. There are employees in the organization who are being carried because of family relationships, longevity of service, emotional ties, or other noneconomic reasons.   2   0

33. I do not believe that the performance of the firm could be improved by replacing any of the key managers.   0   1

The Management–Board Relationship

34. The members of the board of directors are independent-minded and intelligent businesspeople whose education and experience encompass the technical, financial, and marketing aspects of the industry in which the company operates.   0   2

N/A

	T	F

35. There is a lack of mutual rapport, trust, and respect between the chief executive and the members of the board of directors.

    3 0
N/A

36. All of the directors come to the board meeting prepared to discuss relevant issues and participate in a constructive manner.

    0 2
N/A

37. The owners or the major stockholders who are active in management work very well together. They communicate with each other and in groups, openly and frankly, and have mutual respect for each others' opinions.

    0 3

38. The board of directors or management meetings are productive, and the issues affecting the health and growth of the company are presented in a professional manner with adequate analytical data. The issues are discussed thoroughly, and rational, timely decisions are usually made.

    0 3

Overdiversification, Overleverage, and Overexpansion

39. The key managers of the company are able to carry out their responsibilities within the normal work week and rarely have to work evenings or weekends.

    0 1

40. The key areas of the company are adequately staffed with individuals who have the capability to handle their responsibilities in normal day-to-day manner.

    0 2

41. The ratio of the company's total debt to equity increased over the past year.

    2 0

42. Debt service (interest plus principal) as a percentage of gross profit has increased over last year's figure.

    2 0

External Factors

Business affairs: love at first sight, but at second glance?

T F

Banking Relationships

43. We frequently receive calls from our bank, advising us that our account is overdrawn.   3 0

*44. We are current in all of our interest payments to our bank and are in conformance with all of the provisions of our loan agreement.   0 3
N/A

45. Our banker is friendly, cordial, and cooperative, and is always eager to assist us in any way he can.   0 2

46. Our banker calls frequently to inquire about the status of the loan and asks very piercing and serious questions.   2 0
N/A

47. Our banker has inquired about our willingness to pledge additional collateral (company or personal) to secure our loans.   3 0
N/A

Legal Affairs

48. Except for collection efforts being pursued against delinquent accounts receivable, the company is not involved in any litigation.   0 1

*49. Assuming the company is presently involved in litigation where it is the defendant and the worst-case scenario should occur, the company would be able to pay the resulting judgment and still comfortably finance its continuing operations.   0 3
N/A

50. If the company is involved in a lawsuit where it is the plaintiff, the minimum expected recovery will exceed the maximum legal cost to be expended.   0 2
N/A

51. The chief executive officer of the company spends more than 10 percent of his time on the legal affairs of the corporation, including regulatory and litigation matters.   1 0

T F

Single Customer–Single Vendor Dependence

52. More than 35 percent of the company's receivables or inventory is associated with one customer.   3   0

*53. In the event the company should lose a major customer to a competitor, the company could be reorganized so that profitability was not affected.   0   3
N/A

54. In the event the company's major customer filed for bankruptcy, so that all the associated receivables and unique inventory had to be written off, the resulting write-down of assets would not jeopardize the requirements of the company's agreements with its bank.   0   3
N/A

55. If any one of the company's material or support service suppliers suddenly went out of business, the company could easily replace that supplier in a time frame that would not materially affect sales levels, contractual obligations, or profitability.   0   3

56. All of the company's existing suppliers are providing material and services on schedule and of the quality that is consistent with the company's obligations to its customers.   0   1

Changes in Market, Technology, and Environment

57. The market for the company's major products and services is quite soft, and we must cut prices frequently to preserve our market share.   3   0

58. Our company is among the top four firms (in terms of market share) in the major markets that we serve.   0   1

59. Our pricing policy is tied to the dominant firm in our industry, and our price increases and decreases frequently follow its lead.   1   0

T F

60. We have, in the ordinary course of business, been able
to replace products that competition and technology have
made obsolete.   0 2

Totals

	Your Score	Asterisked Questions Score
Financial (1 through 23)	. . . .	. . . .
Management (24 through 42)	. . . .	. . . .
External Factors (43 through 60)	. . . .	. . . .
Total Score	. . . .	. . . .

(Total Score = Financial + Management + External
Factors)

When you have totaled your test score, check your business health
against the levels listed below. Pay particular attention to your score on
the asterisked questions. These questions were designed to identify life-
threatening conditions within the company. Accumulating any points
for these questions indicates the business is experiencing very serious
problems.

Level One: You Passed the Physical (Scores 0 to 20 and no points on asterisked questions)

Your business is probably in top condition. If you scored in this range,
your company appears to be operating smoothly. The key elements
necessary to ensure survival and continuity, and to deal with future
uncertainties, are in place. This is not to say that you do not have any
areas of vulnerability—every business does—but most aspects of the
business seem to be under control.

Level Two: Your Business Is Running a Fever (Scores 20 to 50 or any points on asterisked questions)

No need to panic, but if you scored in this range, your company has
some serious problems that must be addressed immediately. Your firm

is vulnerable to any number of factors or events that could leave your company in a downward spiral. This score demonstrates that some serious issues are simply not being addressed. Your firm needs a plan to stop the deterioration and turn the company around. If you could deal with your problems internally, you probably would already have done so.

Level Three: Surgery Is Indicated (Scores 51 and above)

This is an emergency alert. If you scored in this range, your company is already in a tailspin and is a candidate for the bankruptcy court. The deterioration has advanced to the point where the very existence of the firm may be in doubt. The personal equity of owners and managers who have guaranteed bank loans is in jeopardy. In order to preserve the business and the assets of the firm, you must take immediate action to secure help.

HOW MUCH TROUBLE IS TOO MUCH TROUBLE? STAGES OF ADVERSITY

The test in the previous section provides the first step of an evaluation process for determining how much trouble the business is in. The next step is to look at how much time there is to set things right, which is a function of the stage of adversity in which the business is operating.

A company moving from a high degree of health toward terminal illness, and ultimately death if no treatment is applied, passes through stages of deterioration. Each stage reflects more adversity than the preceding one, with increasing financial pressures and burdens on both management and employees. As the situation worsens, profitability and cash availability change. Figure 2.1 profiles the stages of increasing adversity.

In addition, each stage reflects changes in the extent to which management has control over the timing and content of its responsive actions to the adversity. As the company moves through the stages, more and more people associated with the business become aware of the seriousness of the situation.

The stages of business adversity are:

Stage A: Both profit and cash are increasing and have been increasing for some period of time. Future projections show that this trend will continue. These are the signs of a very healthy company.

Stage B: Profit has started to fall off but cash continues to increase. The business is still quite healthy, generating profits and enjoying high cash reserves, but the decrease in profits may signal a downturn, indicating that things are not as healthy as they used to be.

Stage C: Both profits and cash are decreasing. The company has reached a stage of adversity that indicates the need for prompt attention to problems.

Stage D: Losses start to develop and cash balances are melting away. When the company is in this stage, its health is clearly in danger.

Stage E: There are no funds to pay for essential supplies and services, and payroll is met only after herculean efforts. In this stage the company might well have a feeling of impending doom. The chief financial officer of the business may be preparing to notify the chief executive

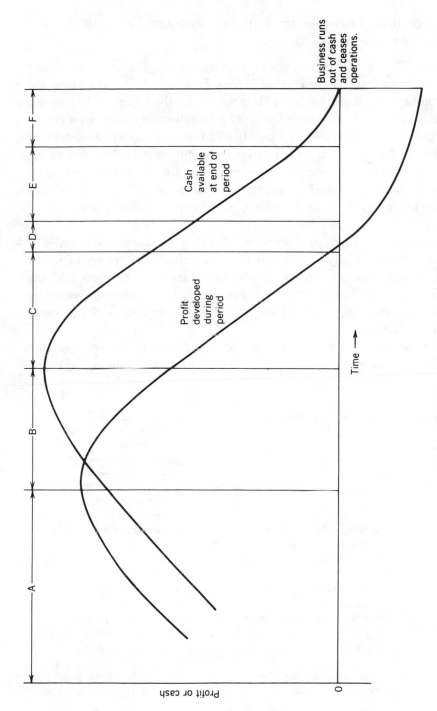

FIGURE 2.1. Stages of adversity.

21

officer that on a certain day in the not too distant future the business will be unable to pay its bills.

Stage F: Cash balances are nonexistent or negative. The company may have issued checks that cannot be covered. At this stage the company has failed, fizzled, or is otherwise finished. Repeat the scenario in stage E, only this time the chief financial officer acts out a classic "good news, bad news" scene. He tells the chief executive officer that they've finished doing the payroll, using the new checks, and all the bugs are out of the computer system, saving the company many hours of accounting time. He presents the checks for signature, then adds the bad news: there is no money in the bank to cover them.

As the business moves progressively through the stages, the knowledge of the company's adversity tends to move outside the sphere of senior management and the board of directors to include the bank and the investors, as well as middle management, key employees in sensitive positions, and ultimately all employees and competitors. In essence, everyone knows.

Similarly, as the business moves through the stages of adversity, the ability of management to control the content and the timing of its re-

TABLE 2.1. STAGES OF ADVERSITY IN THE BUSINESS

Stage	Description	Who Knows, Who Cares
A	Increasing profit—increasing cash	Senior management, the board, investors, the bank, professionals
B	Decreasing profit—increasing or stable cash	Same as stage A
C	Decreasing profit—decreasing cash	Same as stage A plus middle management
D	Continued and projected losses—decreasing cash	Same as stage C
E	Continued and projected losses—projected liquidity crisis (cash projected to equal zero)	Same as stage C plus certain employees in key positions, such as purchasing and accounting
F	Imminent liquidity crisis—no money to pay bills	Same as stage E plus trade creditors, competitors, and all employees

sponsive actions diminishes, until in stages E and F control is lost—except for choosing the undertaker, the time for the service, and the casket.

The advantage of early detection of business problems is identical to the advantage of early detection of cancer: the earlier the detection, the more options are available to effect the changes that can lead to a turnaround and the more time there is to implement these options. The longer a businessperson waits before making the hard choice to implement corrective action, the lower the probability that the business can be kept from failing.

If the process is not halted by appropriate intervention, the death of the business is inevitable. What happens in a turnaround is that intervention is made at some stage in the deterioration of the company's financial situation—an intervention that will cause the downward sloping lines to turn back up, in essence to turn around and head upward toward healthy profitability and adequate cash availability.

Unless a treatment program is set in place to heal the company's illness, the business will continue from one stage to the next toward ultimate failure.

Table 2.1 summarizes the stages in the drift and decline of a company and indicates the three variables that can be associated with the process:

Management's Control over Responsive Action	
Content	Timing
Total	Total
Total	Total
Total	Total
Somewhat limited	Somewhat limited
Very limited, depends on balance sheet	Very limited, depends on balance sheet
Extremely limited	None

1. Who has knowledge about the company's level of adversity and who cares?

2. To what extent does management have control over the actions it can take to deal with the adversity?

3. To what extent does management have control over the timing of the actions it can take to deal with the adversity?

ADDING IT ALL UP: PRESCRIPTIONS FOR ACTION

Once you have determined what level you scored and what stage of adversity the business is in, you can consider what must be done to get the business back on the road to financial health.

Table 2.2 shows the prescription for action, based on the Goldstick Business Health Index (GBHI) level and the stage of adversity of the business.

Prescription I: Look over the answers that contributed points to your score and discuss those areas with your management staff. Investigate what corrective measures are appropriate. Establish a priority list of items and work on that list diligently to keep your business in top form. If the situation continues to deteriorate, consider bringing in outside help.

Prescription II: Discuss the issues that have been raised by the test with your management team and get their suggestions for corrective action. Consider getting outside help to formulate and implement solutions in those areas where you may not be able to determine or take appropriate action yourself.

TABLE 2.2.   PRESCRIPTIONS FOR ACTION

GBHI Level	Stages of Adversity	Prescription
I	A,B,C,D	I
	E,F	III
II	A,B,C	II
	D,E,F	III
III	A,B,C,D,E,F	III

Prescription III: Your high score and stage of adversity indicate that your firm does not have the skills or the time to stop the tailspin and formulate and implement a turnaround program without expert help. Call in a turnaround specialist immediately.

OTHER METHODS FOR INDICATING THE LEVEL OF ADVERSITY

The self-test that was presented in the previous section provides a useful indication of a company's operational and financial difficulties. The executive who wishes to pursue this matter in greater detail can make use of a considerable amount of relevant research that has been done.

The most notable researcher in this field is Dr. Edward I. Altman, now a professor at New York University, who uses analytical tools to predict bankruptcy. His models combine financial ratios (such as current assets to current liabilities or total debt to total worth) in a linear equation to provide a measurement of solvency. Firms with a measurement that exceeds an upper threshold value are considered to have a low probability of becoming insolvent, while firms with a measurement that falls below a lower threshold are considered to be candidates for bankruptcy. A mathematical technique known as discriminate analysis is employed to calculate coefficients and threshold values so as to provide the maximum discrimination between bankrupt and nonbankrupt firms.

THE PATIENT IS IN SHOCK: DIFFICULTIES IN ACCEPTING THE DIAGNOSIS

No one likes bad news. Shock is a natural reaction if your business is not as healthy as you thought. Perhaps you secretly suspected that problems in the business were getting worse, yet you can't believe the company is in a tailspin.

To verify the results, have several people complete the Goldstick Business Health Index test (if you have not already done so). It is very important that the answers you give on the test reflect what is actually happening in the firm, not what you wish were happening or expect to be happening in the near future.

You might go back and take the test again, using answers that would have been true a month ago, or several months ago. Compare these "historical" scores against the present state of the company. If a downward trend exists, or if there has been no improvement, the comparison will confirm that the business is in the process of losing precious ground.

Many businesses in trouble suffer from an inability to accept a diagnosis that indicates a life-threatening illness. Pretending the business is not sick, however, will only complicate the process of returning to health. Why put your company on the critical list by delaying a hard look at the reality of the situation?

3 | A PLAGUE OF ERRORS: THE 13 CAUSES OF CORPORATE ILLNESS

It isn't that they can't see the solution. It is that they can't see the problem.

The good health and the vitality of a business are based on the proper balance of many complex variables. As in personal health, when one major symptom is ignored too long, a critical illness may result. Sickness may also result from the cumulative effect of many seemingly minor aches and pains, if the causes behind the symptoms are not treated.

A company does not usually get into serious trouble overnight. It's a gradual process, and many warning signs can indicate future problems. A common factor of all businesses in distress is that symptoms of business health problems either were not detected or were ignored until they could no longer be overlooked.

The risks of being in business are continuous, and there is no guarantee that what worked in the past will continue to work in the future. Being in business requires a present investment based on a future expectation, and there is no way to know the future result until the risk is taken.

A person opening a store, for example, does not really know until the store has been opened, how many people will actually walk through the front door and buy something, no matter how many marketing studies were done. Nor can the store owner know how many customers will be returning to buy items six months after the grand opening.

Business failure is often attributed to bad luck. Executives may say, "If only this hadn't happened, the company would have done fine." Strangely enough, bankers and other creditors take a dim view of the bad-luck theory. In reality—and reality is a key word here—the majority of businesses fall on hard times because of errors made by management. Donald B. Bibeault, a turnaround specialist, found in a survey of troubled businesses that only 9 percent of businesses fail due to sheer bad luck. The overwhelming majority suffer from errors of commission due to bad analysis or bad judgment.

It is no crime for an executive to make mistakes in running a business. Learning by doing is part of the territory. What is critically important, however, is to see mistakes for what they are, and not gloss over errors. It is not "looking for trouble" to take the time to examine and monitor symptoms which, if ignored, could lead to business failure. If management puts in place an early warning system, all of the causes of business failure discussed in this chapter can be anticipated, guarded against, or ameliorated. An early warning system does not have to be a complicated one. What is needed is a set of procedures to monitor critical business variables, such as inventory, market share, competitors' technology, pricing, manufacturing costs, and customer satisfaction.

Blaming external factors when a warning system could have saved the day—and the company—is a common defense of management who either failed to take action when the company needed it, or through its actions put the company in jeopardy. Proper monitoring for danger signals is as important to a business as tuning into the weather report and studying the charts are to the captain of a ship at sea. A management team that acts without appropriate information is likely to see its business end up on the rocks.

There are 13 major ways businesses commonly get into trouble, 13 "bad-luck" causes directly attributable to management or the lack of it.

Errors of Omission

1. Lack of planning to deal with an increase in the cost of debt

2. Change in the marketplace

3. Technological advances

4. Changes in the physical environment

5. Disruption of key relationships

Errors of Commission

6. Overexpansion

7. Overleverage

8. Overdiversification

9. Overdependence on a single customer

10. Inadequate control systems

11. Dissension in the management team

12. The "Peter Principle" as it applies to business growth

13. Inadequate leadership of the chief executive

Blaming the executive or the management team for the company's problems is not the purpose of the turnaround manager, nor the keystone of the workout process. Honest evaluation of why the business got into trouble is vital so that realistic solutions can be developed. This awareness may forestall repetition of some of the causes of business collapse, or even cure the problems that might lead to business distress.

Businesses can't avoid distress with automatic ease. The old saying, "What you don't know can't hurt you," has no place in the business world. What executives don't know or refuse to see *can* hurt them and may make their business a statistic in the business failure records. Every one of the errors discussed in this chapter may be a symptom of an illness that could create a life-threatening crisis for the business. If a business suffers from many of these symptoms, action is long overdue.

TOO MUCH OF NOTHING: ERRORS OF OMISSION

Sometimes businesses run into problems not because executives did something wrong, but because they failed to foresee difficulties and to establish contingency plans. These are risks that executives failed to take into account, often because they didn't seriously consider what might happen to the business if external factors changed drastically. The company gets into trouble by not being sensitive to, or planning for, changes in the business environment.

Any one of the five errors of omission can seriously affect the health of a business, force the executive into a difficult business situation, or put the company at the risk of total failure.

Error 1:   In for a Penny, in for a Pound: An Increase in the Cost of Debt

Debt is a fact of life in business ventures. When the cost of borrowing money becomes higher than anticipated, and there is an insufficient profit margin to pay the debts, a business is in trobule.

The rise in the cost of money may be totally outside the control of the business. If the prime rate rises sharply, as it did in 1981–1982— from 10 to 22 percent—it has a devastating effect on pretax profits. A business cannot afford to assume that such an increase will never happen, especially in the current economic climate. With the deficit situation and the present trade imbalance, the swings in the economic environment are becoming increasingly large, and the possibility that these factors will adversely affect business is very real.

How to service the debts already incurred becomes a major problem. If the profit margin is inadequate to service the increased cost of debt, the company must reduce its operating costs or borrow new money to pay for the old debt. If the profit margin is already small, the first option may not be feasible, and finding a bank to lend money to pay interest and other costs of debt is not likely if the company is considered marginal.

Symptoms

A business whose profit structure does not accommodate an increase in the cost of debt experiences an increasing inability to service its existing debt without a corresponding reduction in operating expenses. Cash flow problems often accompany this situation, as the business shifts its debt burden to trade creditors and the financial position of the business deteriorates.

Error 2:   Status Quo Only Works for Peter Pan: Changes in the Marketplace

Every business should be aware that the market for a product or service may change. There is no such thing as a stable and constant marketplace.

As in the first error of omission, events completely outside a company's control may trigger market changes.

Decontrol of an industry, for example, drastically alters the company's potential for success. Businesses involved in the trucking industry suffered from the backlash of decontrol in 1981 as prices dropped as much as 25 percent after government-set rates were no longer enforced.

In the roller-coaster oil industry, many companies took opportunities at the wrong time, seemingly unaware that market changes would seriously impact their business ventures. The activities of the domestic steel industry are a prime example of striking when the iron was far from hot. By 1980 the oil industry's demands for oil well casings, drill pipe, and tubing far exceeded the capacity of U.S. steel companies, even though the steel industry had seen signs that an oil and gas boom was coming.

The need for oil-related tubular goods rose sharply, and foreign producers stepped into the void, providing about 35 percent of the 6.6 million tons required in 1980. U.S. companies scrambled to grab part of the market, investing millions of dollars in expanding their production. The predictable happened: an oversupply of steel pipe started to build up. Armco, a large steel company in Ohio, was among those who realized that they had moved too late and finally abandoned a planned $671 million expansion.

Similar problems may result when an industry is so profitable and attractive that it draws too many new businesses without enough customers in the marketplace to keep everyone solvent. The computer industry was a recent victim of this kind of market problem. The rush to computerize corporations and smaller businesses in the early 1980s attracted to the computer industry many entrepreneurs who were eager to share in the profits. Computers were hailed as a technological necessity that no one could do without, and the business world spent a bundle to become part of the computerized future.

Business was indeed booming for the computer companies and computer-related firms at the start of the computer craze. In 1983 U.S. Department of Commerce statistics recorded a 25 percent growth in computer orders. In 1984 there was still a quite respectable 15 percent growth. In the first eight months of 1985, however, computer orders grew only 1.8 percent. The computer industry finally had to face the fact that it had lost its wind.

Many businesses who had bet their last dollar ended up seeing red. Even the huge IBM suffered from the industry slump, along with the smaller Apple Computer and Control Data corporations. For the smaller, newer companies in the market, the picture was even grimmer. The computer industry slump eroded the profits of many makers of mainframes, minicomputers, microcomputers, and semiconductors. The overenthusiastic entry of software and service companies into the marketplace created a deadly case of oversupply.

Symptoms

Warning signs that a business is failing to appreciate or adjust to market changes are a loss of market share, decline in sales, and lower customer loyalty.

Error 3:   The Burned-Out Light Bulb: Technological Advances

When Thomas Edison invented the light bulb, candlemakers should have been very nervous. One person's bright idea can completely change the business opportunities of an entire industry. Current technological advances are so frequent that it is hard for companies to even maintain an awareness of them, much less keep one step ahead of competitors. There is no way to predict what developments or discoveries could happen tomorrow, and the technological breakthrough of one company can be the death knell for its competitors.

Even a seemingly minor change in the technological sophistication of a product may leave a business holding the bag with the inventory it can never hope to sell at a profit. In 1982 the number of channels on CB radios was expanded from the standard 24 to a new 48. What customer wanted an old radio with only half the channel range? Radio distributors with huge inventories of 24-channel CBs, once a hot item, were left with no outlet for their outclassed stock, and many went out of business.

A newcomer to a business who dreams up a better mousetrap can put the fear of failure into established brand name companies. The oversized Prince tennis racket is a classic example of this kind of technological turnover. *Fortune* magazine reports that in two years, from 1979 to 1981, Prince expanded from a mere 8.5 percent of the market to capturing an astounding 30.7 percent. This caused AMF Head's market share to decline from 31.6 to 26.3 percent and the old standby, Wilson, to drop from 19.2 to 10.7 percent. With a patent that keeps a corner on the market until 1993, Prince continues to enjoy the profits of this radical departure in design, in spite of an overall decline in the tennis racket market.

Symptoms

The symptoms of a business losing ground because of changes in technology are similar to those due to marketplace changes: loss of market share, decline in sales, and diminished or total loss of customer loyalty. In many cases, the business may face a necessity for substantial price decreases, even below cost, to maintain any sales at all.

Error 4: There Goes the Neighborhood: Changes in Physical Environment

The physical environment in which a business operates is also subject to change without notice. One day a store may be in a thriving business district, and a few years later it may find itself in an unfrequented section of town.

This has happened to countless businesses in malls or downtown areas that were ideal locations when the business began, but deteriorated as new business centers developed. Sometimes the opposite occurs, and a brand-new business complex suddenly finds itself in direct competition with a revitalized downtown business district. In either case, it is usually gradual attrition, until one day the executive wakes up with a headache in the form of a long-term lease commitment in a physical environment that cannot possibly support the company.

Another form of environmental change is not dependent solely on the physical location of the business. A company operating in an industry that sells throughout the United States can suffer from an increase in local labor costs. It can't afford to compete unless it moves into a cheaper labor market.

A high-technology company in the Los Angeles region could, for example, face problems in the cost of hiring quality engineers. This geographical region is dominated by many aerospace and defense firms and by the military, so wage and salary schedules are determined by these industries. The private sector company must then compete against salaries offered by government-funded projects, which do not need to show the same margin of profit. The result is that the company is unable to attract the labor it needs at a price it can afford to pay.

Symptoms

Major signs that problems are developing due to environmental changes are a gradual decrease in sales, dwindling profitability, and diminished productivity. The slowness of the business deterioration makes it particularly difficult to identify this symptom—these are not rapid changes.

Error 5:   True Blue Isn't the Color of Business: Changes in Key Relationships

Every business has key relationships upon which its operations depend: important customers; key salespersons, suppliers, or employees; the company's attorneys, auditors, investment bankers, major investors, lenders, and members of the board of directors. When the business is running smoothly, these relationships are often taken for granted, and business decisions are based on their continued presence.

A relationship is not a constant. A disruption of any of these key relationships can cause a discontinuity in the company's operations, which may seriously impair the company's ability to continue earning the same profits or maintaining the same market share as in the past. Loss of a major customer to a competitor, for example, will affect the company's market share and probably its profitability. The company may then have to curtail its investment programs to maintain its profitability level; it may have to lay off certain personnel or revise its estimates of earnings.

A serious dispute with the company's auditors over methods of treating certain expenses or evaluating inventory to the extent that a financial statement cannot be agreed upon, could result in either the resignation of the auditors or their termination by the company. In either case, the effect will be to create concern and anxiety.

Since auditors are viewed by the general public as the "monitors" of the company's performance, resignation or dismissal of the auditors may cause the company's reports to be viewed with suspicion. They will not be seen as having the same credibility as in the past. That in itself may impair the company's ability to raise capital for an expansion program or even to maintain its viability.

Suppose the company's major secured lender decides that it no longer feels that the company's business is profitable and withdraws as a lender, providing relatively short notice. This situation will seriously affect the company's financial plan and force management to seek out alternate lenders, who may be reluctant to deal with a company that has just been dumped by the previous lender. If the initial lender withdrew because the company's collateral position had deteriorated, it is likely that the only funds the company will be able to find in the marketplace will be available at a substantially higher price than it paid to its previous lender.

A key sales manager who suddenly quits because he has decided that his potential with the company is not what he had thought it would be, also places the company in a difficult position. He may be leaving because of the deterioration in the company's market, conflict with the company's management, or his own disenchantment with his supervisor, or he simply may decide to exploit his closeness to the customers and the market by selling himself to a competitor.

The rule in business is that the individual who is closest to the customer controls the market. A key salesperson can, if he decides to, exert negative leverage on his present company and deliver a substantial portion of his present client base to a competitor. If a sales manager decides to sell out to the competition, the company often loses not only a key employee but also important customers. In an effort to try to retain those customers, the company might have to offer incentives in the form of price reductions or increased services, all of which will affect the company's profit.

Besides a direct sellout by a member of the company's sales force, a business may also lose a major customer who finds another source of supply that is cheaper or more convenient. A key vendor can inflate prices, putting a squeeze on the business and throwing planned expenses out the window. Labor union demands may also significantly alter the business relationship with employees.

Symptoms

Unhealthy changes in business relationships may take different forms. A major warning sign in client–customer relations is an important association that suddenly terminates or begins to deteriorate dramatically. A business knows its banking relationship has fallen on hard times when it starts having meetings at the bank instead of at its own offices.

NOW YOU'VE DONE IT: ERRORS OF COMMISSION

On the other side of the coin in troubled businesses, there are errors made by management who took action, but whose actions were less than helpful to business health. Management errors of commission are the result of faulty perceptions of the world, bad analysis of situations, or simply bad judgment calls.

Error 6:   The Castle Just Crossed the Moat:
Pitfalls of Overexpansion

A business that is growing rapidly can get caught up in the euphoria of successful sales figures and expand far beyond the company's resources. Arbitrary increases in sales volume are not synonymous with success. In cases of overexpansion, the business grows faster than the working capital required to sustain the expansion, and faster than the management and the control systems required to manage the growing company. Expansion must be slow enough for the business to protect itself from problems.

Working capital—current assets minus current liabilities—must grow along with sales. The unique way business is conducted in an industry gives rise to a different sales to working capital ratio required to maintain business health. Industry examples of the average sales volume that can be supported by a dollar of working capital are shown in Table 3.1.

Symptoms

If working capital fails to keep up with sales, cash flow problems result, which will show up in slow payment of bills, bank overdrafts, and COD purchases. In addition, the rapidly expanding company that fails to allow time for its management and control systems to keep pace will lack sufficient personnel to adequately manage, and errors will result. Creditor collection action is usually inevitable.

Error 7:   Robbing Peter to Pay Paul:
Problems of Overleverage

The company that overleverages debt is headed for a rude awakening. When a business assumes a downswing will not happen and gambles on the future by incurring debt, it is essentially structuring its debt in the hope that miracles will continue to occur.

Unfortunately the world cannot be relied upon to share the same optimistic attitude. A business that finds itself faced with a crippling level of new fixed-cost obligations, without a corresponding explosion in business profits, may lose its forward momentum altogether. When there is simply too much debt for the business to handle comfortably, the management will spend all of its time worrying how to pay the bank, rather than concentrating on the growth of the business.

TABLE 3.1. WORKING CAPITAL REQUIREMENTS FOR SELECTED INDUSTRIES

Industry	Ratio of Sales to Working Capital*
Manufacturing	
Bread and bakery products	12.2
Drugs and medicine	3.8
Fertilizers	6.4
Plastic materials, synthetic resins	6.8
Metal office furniture	4.5
Wholesalers	
Dairy products	16.9
Electronic parts and equipment	6.5
Fuel oil	22.9
Hardware and paints	5.4
Sporting goods and recreational goods and supplies	5.5
Retailers	
Books and stationery	5.7
Computers and software	9.3
Dairy products and milk dealers	17.8
Farm equipment	4.8
Men's and boys' clothing	4.2
Service organizations	
Accounting, auditing, and bookkeeping services	4.0
Computer programming and other software services	5.6
Farm product warehousing and storage	16.0
Employment agencies	10.6
Engineering, architectural, and surveying services	5.3

* Ratios are those of upper quartile companies within the industry.
Source: Robert Morris Associates, 1985 Annual Statement Studies.

How much debt is too much? The company needs a predebt service profit which comfortably covers the debt service on fixed-term and fixed-rate loans. The profit margin should also cover debt service on loans tied to the prime rate so that an increase in prime can be accommodated. This margin of safety fluctuates as the economic environment changes. When a business fails to keep this comfort margin, it may be placed in a very vulnerable position if there are changes in the business environment.

During a period of growth one thriving and highly respected service company decided to move to a much larger and more expensive office space. Inherent in the decision was the assumption that the business would continue to expand rapidly, with new clients more than justifying the expense. They signed a lease obligation that committed them to considerably higher fixed costs for running their business and invested heavily in leasehold improvements that were financed by their bank. Then the unthinkable happened. The business didn't expand to cover the debt obligation. The new office and its leasehold improvements became an albatross, and the business began to slip into a downward spiral toward financial disaster.

Symptoms

When the company has overleveraged debt, its fixed-cost expenses become comparable to or exceed its operating profit.

Error 8:   What You Don't Know Will Cost You: Perils of Overdiversification

Diversification is a business strategy of expanding into new products or new markets. The process of diversification may be accomplished by acquisitions or mergers, or by investing in a new business venture. As a method of increasing profits or spreading risk, diversification can be a wise practice in business ventures, but it sometimes is taken to extremes that jeopardize business health.

A common problem with diversification is that every time the business enters into a new area, it faces new markets, new problems, and new considerations, almost as though it were a brand-new business. The beginning efforts in a new direction take time, resources, and investment as the company builds a client base to capture part of the market share. There is a price for this "education," and many businesses cannot afford the learning process.

Simply put, if the entrepreneur or the executive has no previous experience in the business, he simply doesn't know what he needs to know to succeed.

Symptoms

Chaos in the business is a common symptom of the company that has overdiversified. The company is confronted with more challenges than it can manage. Management is overworked, constantly fighting fires, and continually surprised by circumstances it did not anticipate.

Error 9: All the Eggs in One Basket:
Overdependence on a Single Customer

A dependable customer whose orders are a steady and reliable source of income is a boon to any business. The more of them a business has, the better. Problems can arise, however, if that wonderful client becomes the central focus of all business activity. When most of the sales dollars are concentrated on a single customer, that customer is in a position of enormous power.

The business in this situation not only caters to the client, but is totally dependent on the customer's business for survival. The customer begins to control the business, and the company is in the position of being rather like a poor relation. It may have to beg the customer for payment to meet its payroll, to pay the rent, and to cover other operating expenses.

Even worse, the business can become the victim of the customer's problems. Its future is determined by the customer's future, and if this favored client goes into a business decline, it drags the company with it. Bankruptcy is a contagious disease, and more than one business has lost everything because it was held hostage to a failing customer's needs.

An architectural firm that had teamed with one developer for the majority of its business found itself in such a situation. The developer provided a large number of projects, such as shopping centers, financial centers, hotels, and condominiums. It seemed like the proverbial match made in heaven.

The architectural firm soon was depending on this developer for more than 70 percent of its work, and since there were so many projects, the architectural firm did not market its skills and capabilities to other developers. Then the problems started. When the developer had cash flow problems, the architectural firm was the last to get paid. In an atmosphere of supposed "teamwork," several projects were taken on from the developer without executing contracts. The amount of money actually owed became a matter of dispute. The architectural firm had gone into debt to be able to continue working on this developer's projects. Despite its long working relationship it found that it was unable to collect its receivables. The firm was forced to liquidate.

A similar scenario is frequently played in the electronics business when a small, struggling company lands a major contract with an aerospace

firm or a large computer company, and views the contract as a vehicle
that will propel it into the big leagues. Large companies tend to be very
demanding of their vendors, paying slowly and as little as they can
while demanding high degrees of responsiveness, performance, and
quality in services or products. They frequently want special enhancements
and unique features on the products they purchase so that the product
and the inventory that the small company develops are unique to the
major customer.

If the customer decides that either it doesn't want what it ordered or
its needs have changed, it can usually find a pretext for not taking
delivery of the products. If this action drives the small supplier out of
business, little recourse is available. Efforts at litigation are usually met
with frustration, since the large customer has legal resources unlikely
to be equaled by a small supplier, and the larger company has sufficient
economic clout to find alternative vendors to meet its needs.

These situations can occur in any industry, and usually develop gradually, as what seemed to be a sweet deal turns sour.

Symptoms

A limited customer base is a red flag for this symptom of business illness.
The company finds that most of its receivabies, or a substantial portion
of its sales, are concentrated in one client, or that a large portion of its
inventory is unique to one customer.

Error 10:   Broken Reins Won't Hold Runaway Horses: Inadequate Control Systems

It is very easy to overlook the importance of control systems when a
business seems to be doing well. Keeping track of all the resources and
process variables is a tedious side of business, but crucial to catching
business problems before they can become full-scale crises. Every key
resource, including money, inventory, and property, as well as every
process variable must be measured, monitored, and controlled.

For a control system to be effective, the company must have an accounting system that is relevant, accurate, and timely. Absence of an
adequate information system precludes the company from knowing what
it has done, what its present condition is, or what its future performance
is likely to be.

The accounting system is considered to be accurate if the information that is collected and reported reflects the physical realities of the business (that is, if the inventory amount on the books is $100,000 and there is $100,000 of physical inventory).

The accounting system is considered relevant if the information collected and reported is appropriate for the operation of the company. (For example, if the company is a manufacturing operation, the accounting system will collect costs on the various products and processes.) The accounting system is considered to be timely if the time lag between the creation of the data and their collection and reporting allows management to take effective action.

The control system should also provide the company with sufficient data and the opportunity for control consistent with the volatility inherent in the variables being measured and the resources being controlled; that is, it must "track" the swings. The control system at the New York Stock Exchange during the so-called Black Monday crisis of October 19, 1987, exemplified inadequate control. The demands on the system in terms of the number of transactions per minute were such that the computers and the communication systems could not keep up. As a consequence, the time lag that developed between a transaction occurring and the reflection of that transaction in the price of a stock, market index, and so on, was such that investors and traders did not have up-to-date, accurate information. In addition, the inability of investors to have their trades processed on a timely basis exacerbated the problem. As a result, the stock exchange system failed to maintain and report an "accurate" market.

In order to control any aspect of a business, it is necessary that the control system collect the input elements, monitor the processes, and measure the output elements. The person who reviews the information and evaluates the system's performance, the controller or decision maker, is part of the control system.

If the process to be controlled is a manufacturing process, for example, the input elements would be raw material, labor, and the services required for that manufacturing process. The output elements would be finished goods. One process requiring control would be the level of inventory. The dollar value of material, labor, and overhead for the process would be measured. The market value of the finished goods over a period of time would also be measured and compared against the cost of manufacturing the product. The controller or decision maker would then be able to determine whether modifications in the manufacturing process should be made. This might entail lowering the cost of material or reducing the cost through relocating the manufacturing plant.

Another example would be a control system for the collection of money. The input element would be the goods shipped, the input measurement the dollar value of the goods shipped on any given day; the output element would be the checks received, the output measurement the dollar value of the checks received on any given day.

In this case, the controller or decision maker would compare the value of shipments against the value of collections for specific periods of time. The results might indicate a need to change the company's policy on credit and could suggest providing early payment discounts or withdrawing such discounts.

An effective control system will measure the important attributes of elements to be controlled and make sure that the measurement process actually does measure what it purports to. Each measurement should have a dollar value translation to aid in decision making. The control system should also build in sufficient reporting time, which will allow appropriate changes to be made when necessary.

A company interested in future profits must invest in the present enough to build an adequate control system that can signal potential problem areas. Too often there are a lot of data but no information on which to base management decisions. Either reports don't exist or, if they do, they are not read or understood.

Symptoms

Important reports and analyses essential to making intelligent management decisions regarding the operation of the business are not available or are seriously outdated.

Error 11: Cats among the Pigeons: Dissension in the Management Team

Ben Franklin said it best when the colonies launched their venture for an independent nation in 1776: "We must all hang together or assuredly we shall all hang separately." A business is a team effort, and if infighting among managers and owners becomes bitter, the business itself will grind to a halt. When management dissension is unmanageable, the business becomes paralyzed and begins to deteriorate. The company cannot do business in a professional manner.

There are many relationships within a business that can suffer strain and conflict. Problems between two partners or between an owner and the CEO can have a profound effect on the healthy functioning of the company, even when all other aspects of the business seem to be going well. Chances are, however, that if there are problems within management, they will not remain there but will ultimately affect all levels of the business.

Symptoms

Animosity, backbiting, and a lack of respect and trust among owners and managers are all signals that the management is not united in running the business. Unproductive board meetings in which major problems go unresolved often result from dissension in the executive ranks.

Error 12: Silk Purses Aren't Made from Sows' Ears: Goldstick's Rule and the Peter Principle

"In a hierarchy, every employee tends to rise to his level of incompetence." With these words Lawrence Peter defined the Peter Principle and added to the permanent vocabulary of the corporate world. Some competent employees can end up in positions where incompetence is thrust upon them. Goldstick's Rule is a corollary to the Peter Principle: *as a company grows, certain employees tend to become incompetent for the positions they occupy.*

The growth of a company creates new problems for a business, and employees who were competent when the company was small may suddenly find themselves in positions where their skills are no longer sufficient to do the job. They are not incompetent in the true sense, but their jobs outgrew them. The demands of the position they are in are higher than the position for which they were hired. They are overwhelmed and ill-equipped for the new level of responsibilities thrust upon them.

A key systems engineer at a high-tech firm specializing in electro-optical equipment, for example, had been the creative genius behind many of the company's early products. He was the key resource who would design equipment, check it out, and deliver it. Over time the company grew, and his title changed from systems engineer to vice-president of engineering. However, he was still operating in exactly the same capacity he had at the beginning, when only two other engineers were in his charge. He did not really lead the engineering organization, and it operated in an atmosphere of benign neglect, as he continued to spend the majority of his time performing equipment checkout procedures. Upper-level management recognized his many years of service to the company and his strong stock position, and was reluctant to disturb the status quo.

His lack of leadership, however, resulted in an engineering department that was poorly directed and extremely inefficient. Several of the company's key hardware and software engineers resigned their positions because they could not get any direction or guidance from the vice-president of engineering.

A similar problem developed in an oil refinery where the person acting as treasurer/vice-president of finance had almost no training in accounting and virtually no understanding of finance. The bookkeeping skills for which this person was originally hired were good, but as the company grew its performance demands far exceeded the vice-president's training. Since there was no understanding of the importance of establishing financial controls for quick feedback on the status of the plant, data on the plant's operation were usually 15 to 30 days late. This time lag made it impossible to determine the extent of losses until a month had already elapsed. The company discovered, much too late, that it had lost almost a million dollars a month for several months because this key financial monitoring position was not filled by someone capable of performing the necessary tasks.

Symptoms

A company facing this problem will notice low morale and poor team spirit among employees who were previously very enthusiastic about the company. In addition, the company will suffer from a lack of supervision, a lack of leadership, and a failure to make prompt decisions.

Error 13:   Is There a Leader in the House?
Inadequate Leadership of the CEO

An even bigger problem than the employee whose position surpasses his or her skills is the chief executive officer who lacks the leadership abilities necessary for the healthy functioning of the business. There may be a temporary lapse in executive fitness, due to the stresses of business or personal problems, or it may be a problem the executive has had all along.

There are a number of tasks that fall to a leader in a company, and the chief executive officer must do these—and do them effectively—to lead the business.

The chief executive must clearly define why the business exists and where it is headed. This "mission statement" should address what business the company is in, what is the scope of the business, and what growth direction the company is pursuing. The chief executive must communicate this mission to employees, customers, and other persons involved in the organization, to provide both a corporate identity and an understanding of the purpose of the business.

For the company to prosper, the chief executive must also establish short-term and long-term objectives. In the financial realm, these would include goals for the level of sales, market share, level of profitability, return on investment, and other financial measures of success.

To maintain good employee relations, the company's head should also set goals and provide feedback so that employees know what is expected of them and how well they are doing. Communication should not be limited to annual performance reviews. Rewards, in the form of raises, free time, fringe benefits, or the opportunity to participate in major projects, are a crucial part of the feedback system. Frequent feedback on performance, paired with rewards, increases employee motivation and commitment to the overall objectives of the business.

Another task of the chief executive is to provide the resources and support—financial, emotional, and physical—to enable the company to accomplish its mission. This is doubly important when the company faces difficult times. If the business runs out of money, it is up to the leader to find new sources of capital. When the company is being harassed by creditors and unhappy customers, the chief executive should "rally the troops" and give them hope that the future will be better.

An effective leader not only fulfills these responsibilities, but accomplishes the tasks in a positive manner. It is not simply a matter of doing the right thing, but also of doing it in the right way. Good leaders have a vision for the company, communicate this vision to followers and the outside world, and have the ability to adhere to this vision through difficult times. They also have both a positive self-regard and a belief in the efficacy of their efforts.

Symptoms

If leadership is lacking, there exists a lack of communication, poor team spirit, an obscuring of the organizational purpose, lack of responsibility at various levels, inadequate supervision, institutionalization of nonproductive situations, and an inability to solve long-standing problems. A common explanation for a lack of solutions becomes: "It's always been that way," and management avoids confrontations that threaten sacred cows.

LESSONS FROM EXPERIENCE: WHAT RESEARCH SHOWS

One of the most careful examinations of the causes of business failure was done in a study by Philip B. Nelson of 13 corporations that ended up bankrupt. Nelson, an economist, approached his study from the perspective of the behavioral theory of the firm. The study provides a wealth of information and insight into a behavioral understanding of corporations in crisis.

The common causes Nelson found matched the experience that we had noted in our work with financially troubled companies—experience that led to the development of the 13 errors discussed earlier in this chapter. The four major causes of a company's financial problems, according to both our experience and Nelson's research, are: change in market, overexpansion, lack of control systems, and lack of leadership.

It also appears that companies get themselves into financial difficulties for a number of reasons, not one single error. Half of the companies we have worked with suffered from four to six of the 13 causes of business failure. The result is not surprising. After all, management that is not astute and aware, or is prone to errors of commission, will manifest this tendency in a number of ways.

The histogram in Figure 3.1 provides a graphic illustration of the percentage of companies exhibiting each of the 13 errors that lead to business disaster.

CORPORATE ILLNESS: GREATER THAN THE SUM OF ERRORS

The 13 causes of business illness outlined in this chapter represent the numerous ways a business may find itself at risk of serious distress.

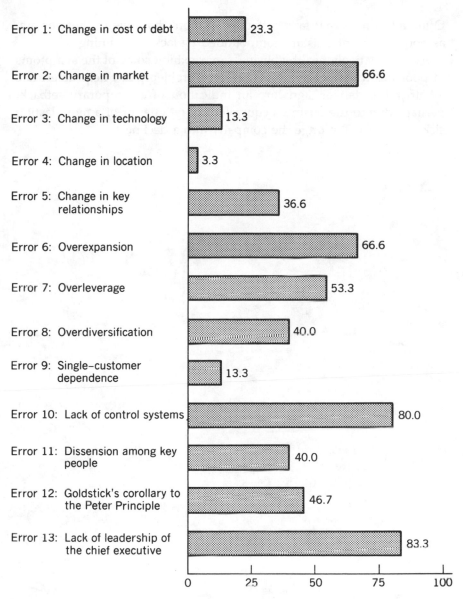

Error 1: Change in cost of debt — 23.3

Error 2: Change in market — 66.6

Error 3: Change in technology — 13.3

Error 4: Change in location — 3.3

Error 5: Change in key relationships — 36.6

Error 6: Overexpansion — 66.6

Error 7: Overleverage — 53.3

Error 8: Overdiversification — 40.0

Error 9: Single–customer dependence — 13.3

Error 10: Lack of control systems — 80.0

Error 11: Dissension among key people — 40.0

Error 12: Goldstick's corollary to the Peter Principle — 46.7

Error 13: Lack of leadership of the chief executive — 83.3

FIGURE 3.1. Percentage of companies suffering from each of the 13 causes.

Often a business that fails suffers from more than one of these errors, as poor judgment calls are compounded by lack of planning.

Even a relatively healthy business may exhibit some of the symptoms of poor health. Diagnosis of the central problems can help determine whether the danger signs are an indication of a temporary setback, perhaps due to the business equivalent of fatigue, or of a more lasting sickness that will plunge the company into a decline.

4 | "GIVE IT TO ME STRAIGHT": ESCAPING THE TRAP OF DENIAL

Faced with the choice between changing one's mind and proving there is no need to do so, almost everyone gets busy on the proof.

JOHN KENNETH GALBRAITH

Denial is a human response to an unpleasant reality. In the business setting, it is a common reaction to adversity. Unfortunately, when those running the business deny their trouble, they are unable to work on solutions that might allow the business to survive.

The executive who clings to the fantasy that everything will be better tomorrow, or that there is nothing to worry about to begin with, is setting the stage for disaster. Facing reality is even more difficult for him if others around him, both within the company and in the outside business community, support his fantasy. They spend all their time and energy in mutual reassurance when it would be more productive to seriously analyze the problems that besiege them.

In this chapter, we explore how denial operates and why it continues, and we discuss the fantasy "escape hatch" theories that executives often develop as a defense against reality.

THE EMPEROR'S CLOTHES: A TALE OF NAKED DENIAL

The story of the emperor's new clothes is a familiar one. It goes something like this:

Once there was an emperor who was very proud of his wealth and especially his wonderful clothes, which were a symbol of his power and magnificence. Two weavers came to town one day and offered to make him the most beautiful clothes he had ever seen. They would use a magical material: it would appear invisible to anyone who was unfit for the office he held, or anyone who was incredibly stupid.

These clothes would be magnificent. The emperor paid quite a price to the weavers, and while they prepared the clothes, he ordered a grand procession to show off his new and wonderful vestments to all of his people.

Now, the weavers couldn't really weave such magic cloth—they had just hit upon a masterful swindle. They set up a loom and pretended to work away at weaving thread into cloth, although in reality there was nothing there. The emperor's representatives sent to monitor the weavers' progress, his faithful chief minister and other worthy statesmen, did not want to admit that they could not see the clothes. Did they want the emperor to think they were unfit for the office they held, or that they were stupid? Of course not! When finally the emperor himself went to try on the clothes, he also pretended to see them, just as everyone else had. The weavers had counted on that, because they knew that the emperor's pride and self-esteem were at stake. His ministers risked not only their self-esteem but also their jobs, so they all pretended to see clothes that were not there.

The emperor held his grand procession. He walked out among his people, while chamberlains pretended to hold the ends of what was supposed to be a magnificent cape. All of the people made believe that they were awed by the sight he presented—each one of them thinking, "Am I incredibly stupid or unfit for the job I have?" Nobody wanted anyone else to think that, and so they said nothing. Then a little child called out, "But he has nothing on!" Soon everyone was saying, "The emperor has no clothes!" to the embarrassment of the emperor and all his ministers.

The Allure of Denial: Executive Protection against Reality

The emperor in this story became caught in a cycle of denial because he wanted to believe what the weavers told him. He needed to justify his initial decision to hire these weavers—in fact he had even given them the title Imperial Weavers. If that decision was the right one, then the cloth was indeed magical. And if the cloth was magical and appeared invisible to those who were stupid or incompetent, then he had to see it. He wanted other people to believe that he was incredibly smart and the best emperor of all time.

What he wanted to believe was more important than what was real about the situation—and the longer he pretended to see the clothes, the more investment he had in believing he could see them. The members of his court also had an investment in maintaining the fantasy. They all openly denied reality while secretly fearing that the cloth was invisible to them because they were stupid or incompetent.

What happens in a troubled business is often similar. The head of the company, the key executives, and the employees all pretend that nothing is wrong, even when they secretly fear that there are problems. Even those outside the business—creditors and the bank—may play into this pattern of denial.

Denial is a very natural human response to an unpleasant reality. Initial denial is not, by itself, a terrible mistake. However, the trouble deepens when the denial goes on for too long. Closing your eyes to problems doesn't make them go away. What happens all too often is that the executive—and others involved—readjust their perceptions to fit the fantasy that nothing is wrong, rather than accepting the reality of the situation. The fantasy makes them feel better, stronger, and more in control.

Unfortunately, denial doesn't change reality, and it doesn't leave any room for action that could remove the need for the illusion. The emperor didn't really have confidence in his own intelligence and competence. He wanted an external validation that would put his secret fears to rest. Commissioning this magnificent set of new clothes was a symptom of his need for public approval, and that need motivated him to deny that he couldn't see the "magic" cloth. He *knew* he couldn't see the clothes, and that frightened him into pretending. Denying reality made him *feel* better.

Flight into Fantasy

When executives deny the reality of business problems, they do so out of fear and a feeling of helplessness. If the problem isn't there, it doesn't have to be solved. In denial, the executive clings to the fantasy that the business is healthy—a fantasy that may have been reality at one point in time, but is no longer true. In some cases, the business never was a profitable operation, and time and circumstance have simply revealed its shortcomings. In any case, the reality that the business is in trouble may be rejected, at least for a while, because of the executive's need to believe otherwise.

Fantasies and fairy tales from our childhood reinforce the concept that good wins over evil, and that everything turns out all right in the end. Bruno Bettelheim, a noted child psychologist, explores the importance of fairy tales and suggests in his book *The Uses of Enchantment* that children find comfort in fairy tales because they offer the concept of benevolent powers being available in times of crisis. This fantasy provides security because it makes sense of the baffling and frightening world in terms that the children can understand—an understanding not based on facts, but on the child's own experience of the world. In fairy tales, the child is assured of a safe place with a certain ending—monsters vanquished, help in time of need, magical intervention, and rewards for being brave and daring.

What worked in childhood carries on into adulthood. If the executive is secure, he can more easily afford to seek rational explanations and take in real-world data. But insecurity, brought on or increased by stress and the fear of failure, may bring about an instinctive retreat to the safer thinking of the past. The more insecure he is, the more he may withdraw into himself. Within his own mind, he can then build a safe place, a refuge from the storm.

Fantasy can be an enormous comfort to the executive under stress and can become addictive. His problems seem overwhelming, and if he can convince himself that there are no problems, or that the problems can be solved by magical intervention, he doesn't have to do anything different.

He can't solve the business's problems, so he tells himself that there are no problems to solve. To keep that fantasy alive, he must shut down some of his thinking processes. He cannot allow input, or he must distort input that challenges his underlying belief—a desperate hope—that the business is not in trouble. An executive who is denying that his business is near collapse, for example, may be reluctant to take the self-test presented in Chapter 2. He avoids discussing possible problems with his colleagues, and tells himself he does so "to avoid unnecessary panic." He may even make it clear that he doesn't want to hear about problems, making others reluctant to bring critical information to his attention. The executive busily denying the company's distress does not want to hear or see anything that will confirm his fears.

ESCAPE HATCH THEORIES: THE EXECUTIVE'S MAGIC WAND

As much as an executive denies that there are major problems in the business, it is very likely that he or she secretly fears the business is in drastic trouble. So executives often develop a rescue fantasy—an escape hatch—to give them a way out if things "get really bad." They don't think they will have to use the escape hatch, but they have these secret solutions, just in case—things they tell themselves and others.

Optimism prevails and becomes a life raft to cling to in case the ship goes down. Escape hatch theories give the executive the illusion of problem solving and the false comfort of seeming to be in control.

The Center of the Universe Theory

Secret Solution: "They can't afford to let me fail." In this escape hatch the business executive tells himself or herself that the business is very important to the creditor or the banker pressuring for payment. The executive makes the assumption that no matter what happens, everyone else will continue to bend over backward to keep this business alive—as if the bank or the creditors were dependent on the success of this business for their own existence. They are not.

The Leprechaun Connection

Secret Solution: "I know a guy who knows a guy who has a line on money." The executive who depends on this escape hatch is counting on gold at the end of the rainbow. The infusion of money may very well help his business, but his source is questionable and very remote.

The Perry Mason Defense

Secret Solution: "We have a large claim against this guy, and once we win the settlement. . . ." Lawsuits often seem to offer very bright hopes for vast sums of money to bail out a business in distress. If a company has litigation pending, it is tempting to see this potential lump sum of money as the answer to all problems. When an executive holds this solution as his ace, he may forget that the prospects in a lawsuit and the amount of money expected are always much higher at the beginning of litigation than at the end.

The Mother Lode

Secret Solution: "We're about to be awarded a large contract, and this one will make all the difference." Executives who believe in this escape hatch could have been miners in the gold rush days. They are always hoping that the next project will be like striking a pure vein of gold. In the business context, they tell themselves that a big profitable contract—just around the corner—will make them rich beyond their wildest dreams.

The Talent Scout Just Spotted Me

Secret Solution: "We're being seriously looked at by a major company. . . ." This solution counts on the possibility that some other company with a great deal of money will recognize the worth of the failing business, appreciate the sterling quality of the executive running it, and therefore take over the liabilities, provide lucrative opportunities, and leave the management's power intact.

Just Another Round in the Game of Life

Secret Solution: "We've survived trials and tribulations before, and this is just another one. . . ." A company that has had ups and downs and survived rough times before is a prime candidate for this escape hatch. It seems as though the present situation were just one more round of difficulties, so the executive can reassure himself that this time is no different than before.

The Magic Spell

Secret Solution: "I will dazzle them with my footwork." In this escape hatch the executive doesn't have the slightest idea what to do, but he figures that if he can talk loud enough and long enough, a solution will appear. He counts on being able to charm his creditors and bank into helping him, regardless of the facts, as though he had cast a magic spell to get them on his side.

Reality Check: Will the Escape Hatch Open?

Some of the solutions listed as escape hatches could actually work to bail out the business in distress. However, they must be evaluated with the same scrutiny as any business plan, because the probability that they will save the business may be extremely low. The lower the probability of success, the less influence such an eventuality should have on any last-ditch effort to save the company.

Usually these escape hatch theories are vaguely stated and not carefully thought out. They are beliefs not solutions, and unfortunately, there is a very big difference between a hope and a plan. When put to the test, these life rafts may turn out to be full of holes.

There are some common flaws in escape hatch theories, which reveal them to be fantasies rather than actual solutions. When put to the test, an escape hatch not grounded in reality will turn out to be a dead end.

Any real escape hatch should be scrutinized using the following four questions.

1. *Is the plan detailed?* Most fantasy escape hatches are vaguely defined and full of "ifs." A real plan will have a detailed description of who is involved, how the contact will be made, and steps that must be completed to implement it. The details must be complete enough so that if the escape hatch were to be needed tomorrow, all that would be necessary would be to follow the plan.

2. *Is it certain that the plan could take place?* The probability of an escape hatch working is another major factor when considering its potential. If there are too many ifs in the plan, it cannot be relied upon as a solution. Each if decreases the overall probability of the plan's success.

3. *Is there a guarantee that it can be implemented quickly?* Timing is a crucial factor in any solution to business distress. An escape hatch that may work but is likely to get bogged down in time-consuming delays is not an escape hatch at all. One thing a distressed business can never rely on is time. A major creditor may refuse the shipment

of necessary materials tomorrow. The bank may call the loan. Time is compressed and a crisis needing a solution will not wait.

4. *If the plan is so great, why wait?* If your solution is a good one, why is it being held in reserve? If it isn't being put into place now, then when? If the executive is blocking feedback about how the business is doing, how will he know when to open the escape hatch? What will signal that things have deteriorated to the "really bad" level for which he was saving the escape hatch?

Most often, escape hatch theories are simply a formalized method of denial. Created to help maintain the illusion that the business is not really in trouble, they fuel the belief that no matter what happens, the executive can wave the magic wand, open the escape hatch, and solve the company's ills. The executive should be aware that the more he relies on an escape hatch, the less likely it is that the company will work on developing viable solutions to its problems.

THE EMPEROR REVISITED: THE WEAVERS TELL THEIR SIDE OF THE STORY

Let us return now to the tale of the emperor and his new clothes. Only this time let us consider the tale from the perspective of the weavers. Suppose we give them the benefit of the doubt, and assume that they didn't truly intend to fleece the king. Suppose, in fact, that the story went like this:

Once upon a time there were two weavers who were deeply in debt. They were months behind in their rent, and they owed the grocer, the butcher, and the poultry farmer. They had run out of credit with the silk merchant, the wool merchant, and the goldsmith who spun gold thread for them. They had borrowed heavily from the members of the emperor's court, and there was no one they could think of who would lend them another shilling.

They didn't know what to do. There they sat, in their empty, once prosperous shop, with their looms and needles gathering dust. What they really needed was a big order. If only they could make some marvelous clothes for someone who would tell everyone what wonderful weavers they were. *Then* business would pick up. But who would hire them?

Now this land was ruled by an emperor who was obsessed with clothes. He had huge closets to hold his clothes and he always wanted more—clothes more fine and fabulous than the ones he already had. Thinking about this, the two weavers came up with a plan. If they could get the emperor to commission a set of clothes, they knew they would be back in business again.

They drew up plans and sketches for clothes that would be the envy of the land, and they asked one of the members of the court to get them an audience with the emperor. The designs they proposed were really quite good, and the emperor was delighted. He called for the exchequer of the treasury to give the weavers a large sum of cash so they could get to work on making those marvelous clothes.

The two weavers went home in high spirits, visions of throngs of wealthy customers dancing in their heads. But when they got to their shop, they found the landlord placing a big padlock on the door. The landlord explained that he was locking up the place until he got payment. The weavers were dismayed. They could never weave the fine cloth for the emperor without their looms. They had to have their shop, so they paid the landlord with some of the money from the emperor. With so much money, surely they could spare some for the landlord.

The landlord, who was a close friend of the butcher, went to tell him that the two weavers had come into money. The butcher rushed to the weavers' shop, demanding the money they owed him. It was such a small sum, they figured they could pay him too.

The butcher, returning to his shop, ran into the grocer and told him that the two weavers had finally paid their debt to him. The grocer, a large man with a temper to match, marched over to the weavers' shop to get his money. They couldn't say no.

The money from the emperor was dwindling. Before anyone else could show up demanding repayment, the two weavers went to see the silk merchant and the goldsmith to order the materials they needed for the cloth they would weave.

However, the silk merchant pointed out that the two weavers owed him already for his last two shipments of silk and wanted full payment before another thread left his shop. They pleaded and cajoled and finally talked him into taking a portion of what was due, with promises to pay the rest later. He agreed to deliver the silk within the week.

The two weavers did the same thing at the goldsmith's shop, though he was even more reluctant than the silk merchant to part with his thread. They had to give him the very last of their money to get him to agree.

A week went by, and the silk and the gold thread still hadn't arrived. When the two weavers went to the silk merchant, he said he had changed his mind. He had found out how much money the goldsmith had gotten, and he felt he hadn't received his fair share. He decided that he didn't want to extend any more credit to the two weavers—he had already lost too much money on them. The goldsmith said the same thing: without full payment, he would deliver no thread.

The two weavers, flat broke, went home desperate. That's when they came up with their scheme. We'll say the cloth is magic, they thought, and that it is invisible to anyone who is stupid or incompetent. They figured, quite rightly, that no one would admit to not being able to see the cloth. This plan was only to work as a delaying tactic, to buy them more time. They fully expected that they wouldn't have to carry on with this magic-cloth routine for long. Soon, they were positive, they would be able to get the materials they needed to create a suit of clothes worthy of the leader of the land. So they pretended to weave. They set up their looms and moved the shuttles back and forth and hoped that no one would challenge them. It was, after all, only a bluff, and they were not sure it would work for one minute.

The emperor, anxious about how his grand new clothes were coming along, sent his chief minister to take a look. The chief minister, having heard about the cloth's magic properties—everyone in the land was aware of that by now—didn't want to confess that he couldn't see a thing. He reported to the emperor that the cloth was very fine, the pattern very intricate. The next honest statesman said the same.

Everyone who stopped by to see the weavers work also pretended to see the cloth that wasn't there and marveled at its quality and brilliance. Even those who suspected that it was a scam said nothing, because if the weavers pulled it off, they would be rich and could pay all their debts. A lot of people wanted this to happen, so they could get back the money the two weavers owed them.

When the emperor himself came for a fitting of the clothes, he didn't want anyone to think he was stupid or unfit to be the emperor, so he too commended the weavers on their work.

The emperor planned a procession to show off his clothes and his importance. On the day of the parade, he carefully pretended to put on the invisible coat, trousers, and mantle. The chamberlains pretended to pick up the ends of the train, and together they proceeded through the streets.

The crowds roared their approval and amazement. What marvelous, stupendous clothes, they all said. That is, until a little boy—to whom the weavers didn't owe any money and who didn't care whether people thought he was stupid—cried out that the emperor had no clothes on at all. Soon everyone agreed that the emperor had no clothes.

And so it ended. The moral of the story is this: *there is always someone who has no investment in maintaining a fantasy.*

DANGERS OF DENIAL

The mind's ability to reshape reality to fit beliefs is a phenomenal talent. What people tell themselves—no matter how distorted the perception—can be powerful enough to override all evidence to the contrary. So it was with the emperor, and so it is with many executives of troubled businesses. The perceived distortion is compounded by the fact that people act on their faulty perceptions.

People clinging to denial are often only one step away from depression. If they were to let reality sink in, they wouldn't know what to do with the flood of information, and that sense of helplessness is a key element of depression. Denial, in that light, can be viewed as a self-protective mechanism. It is the best coping mechanism they can come up with.

Denial effectively disrupts the entire world view of the executive, and so reality becomes very threatening. It is hard to let go of the only thing that seems to provide comfort. In a troubled business, however, denial only delays the inevitable. The moment of truth will arrive, welcome or not, and hanging onto denial until the company becomes another business failure statistic is a high price to pay.

THE EYE OF THE BEHOLDER: THE OUTSIDE WORLD'S VIEW OF THE BUSINESS

When a company begins to get into serious trouble, lenders and investors climb into their life jackets, lower the dinghies, and sail away from the sinking ship. Suppliers put the company on cash only, customers begin to hear rumors about the trouble and cancel shipments, and employees start to freshen up their resumes.

DAVID A. SILVER

Remember, in *The Wizard of Oz*, when Dorothy and her traveling companions finally reached the Emerald City and pulled aside the curtain to discover that the Wizard of Oz was a fraud? They had clung to their belief in the Wizard through many perils, and then, in that one swift moment, their faith in the Wizard was destroyed. They were shocked and dismayed, then angry that they had been tricked.

This is what happens when a business continues to experience difficulties in meeting its obligations. The cumulative effect of small failures in making payments or delivering products will result in a change in attitude toward the business, which the executive cannot understand.

In this chapter, the perspective of the most important members of the executive's outside world is examined and explained. Business distress alters the company's relationships because the outside world begins to perceive the company in a different light.

BEHIND THE CURTAIN WITH THE WIZARD OF OZ: THE OUTSIDE WORLD'S DISILLUSIONMENT

Even if the executive maintains a strong level of denial regarding the company's problems, there is usually an undercurrent of uneasiness that pulses strong and steady. The outside world may recognize the warning flags before the executive does, and if the onlookers begin to worry about the company's soundness, the way they treat the executive and the company will be affected on both the business and the personal levels. When a business is in trouble, the same people who expressed confidence in the executive and were eager for a business relationship may well become distrustful and critical. Ultimately they may move to disassociate themselves from the business.

Tightening the Purse Strings: The Banker's Perspective

The bank that has acted as the major lender to a business venture has a great deal at stake when the company gets into trouble. The relationship between the banker and the business can be seen as a sort of ill-fated financial marriage.

In the beginning the two were introduced and mutual interest was kindled. During the courtship phase, the banker is eager to learn more about the company, and the more he sees, the more he wants to be involved with the business. Affable meetings take place in the company's office, and the company's chief executive is treated with courtesy and respect. The loan is proposed and granted; the financial marriage takes place, and a rosy future seems guaranteed. The relationship flourishes in a honeymoon atmosphere, and the bank wants to help the company in any way it can.

Then the honeymoon is over and troubles begin to surface. Additional information about the company comes to light; the nature of the market changes; the bank didn't understand some of the critical features of the business. Concern rises, and the bank begins a period of close monitoring of the company's operations. Reports and meetings increase in frequency. Meetings are far from friendly; they are tough-minded and serious and take place in the bank's offices.

Disenchantment is strengthened daily. This isn't the attractive alliance the bank had in mind. The bank sees declining bank balances, a lack of timely financial statements, and notices of liens. It wishes it had never committed to the relationship. Divorce is imminent, and the bank encourages the company to terminate the relationship and find another lender. When the banker finally snaps out of denial, anger results. The valued customer is now treated as a troublesome debtor.

Halting the Supply Train: Trade Creditors Pull the Plug

A business relies on a network of trade creditors who can provide the goods and materials needed to make the company run. In turn, trade creditors count on the business to pay for what it buys. When the company is doing well, this is not a problem.

When a healthy business becomes an ailing one, the major vendors move from a position of trying to sell merchandise to one of concern about the open account. Then the late payments begin. The first time it happens, it is not a pattern; the tenth time it is no longer considered an isolated incident.

The trade creditor stops shipping on credit and demands COD payment. If that action fails to provide the security the creditor wants—the COD checks start to bounce—the next time only a certified check is accepted. When that strategy doesn't prove effective, the creditor then works to eliminate what is essentially involuntary credit. No shipments are sent without cash in advance.

Dealing with the Tax Man: Government Creditors

The government is a creditor with a great deal of power. Government agencies that assess or collect taxes include the Internal Revenue Service, which assesses and collects social security taxes, withholding taxes, and income taxes; the state Employment Development Department, which collects unemployment taxes; the state Board of Equalization, which collects sales tax and use taxes; and others.

These agencies have certain common characteristics: they look to the company to calculate and report taxes that are due and to pay the reported amounts. In the event that the company does not file the appropriate returns, pays late, or fails to pay its taxes, penalties are assessed.

Government agencies differ substantially from trade creditors in their power and their relative interest in the distressed company's troubles. People who work for government agencies rarely care whether a particular company remains in business or fails. There is no one working for the government agency that has a vested interest in a company's continued health.

The collection agents of the government are similar to collection agencies that take on accounts for various trade bureaus. In some cases there are personal contact and cooperation, but this cannot be predicted and varies from individual to individual.

The government differs from trade creditors in that it has the power to have the company's bank account levied without notice, without court order, and using its own discretion and timetable. Government obligations also differ from general trade obligations in that certain types of obligations cannot be discharged through bankruptcy proceedings.

Squeezing the Turnip: The Power of Customers

Customers keep the company in business. If there were no customers or clients, the company would not exist. Most companies have a few customers with whom they conduct a significant part of their business— even if their overall customer base is broad—and these customers have a great deal of power when the business is in distress.

Major customers can be a source of stability for a company, providing long-term predictability and profitability, or they can be the troublesome cause of recurring cash flow and production problems. The quality of the company's customers affects its ability to control prices and profit margins, the leverage it can exercise on its customers in terms of shipping dates and payment terms, and the strength of the ties between the company and its customers.

A company's large or steady customer often enjoys a special relationship, receiving low prices, fast delivery, and sometimes a unique inventory that meets the needs of that customer alone.

When a business begins to experience problems, the customer may start looking for another source of products or services. Customer loyalty is based on short-term memory, and the prevailing attitude is, "What have you done for me lately?" If service performance or quality declines, the customer may begin to look for reasons to avoid payments, and receivables may be placed in question. A contract that exists between the company and a major customer might become the basis of costly and bitter litigation.

Adding Up the Problems: The Company's Auditors

The company's CPA is in a delicate position—an outside person with an inside track. In a professional capacity, the CPA prepares financial statements on which other "outside world" people base their decisions about the business. These financial statements reflect the professional opinion of the CPA that the reports are in accordance with generally accepted accounting principles, and that they display the financial position of the company.

Financial reports are only as accurate as the information received. The CPA relies on the company's management to provide the necessary information, and if this information is incomplete or misleading, the financial reports will not reflect the true health of the business. Auditors will not audit what they do not see, and they cannot audit what they do not understand.

In a troubled business, the CPA may suspect, or even know, that he or she is not getting the whole story. This can undermine the relationship between auditor and executive. Trust falters and the CPA becomes concerned. The CPA worries about getting paid and about keeping the company as a client.

Often the CPA will continue to work and, hoping things get better, is reluctant to suggest—much less insist—that the company get outside help to manage the crisis. In fact, the CPA's investment in the company's success may cloud his or her judgment about the state of the company's finances. The CPA may well become part of the cycle of denial and accept—even promote—the myth that all is well.

Defending the Castle: The Company's Attorneys

Like the CPA, the attorney frequently serves as a counselor to the business client. The attorney is usually made aware of the company's problems when the client arrives at a hastily convened meeting with a summons and a complaint from a supplier. The client tells the whole story, emphasizing the facts that justify why the client hasn't paid the creditor.

The client usually wants the attorney to use his skills to beat back the uncooperative creditor and, ever the optimistic entrepreneur, will stress the uniqueness of this particular situation.

The attorney, who generally has a snail's eye view of the company's situation, will usually follow the client's instructions and go forth to do battle with the ungrateful creditor, ignoring the fact that the lawsuit may be a symptom of more serious financial problems.

Waves from Circling Sharks: Competitors in the Same Seas

Even the most friendly of the company's competitors cannot be expected to be saddened by information that the business is experiencing difficulties. If the business flounders, it means that customers will be looking for a new place to buy products and services. Competitors are always attempting to expand their share of the market. When a business becomes shaky, competitors often view it as a golden opportunity to expand their own business interests.

All too often competitors may actually work to help speed the distressed company's downfall. They do this through interaction with the company's customers, suppliers, and employees, as well as with other competitors.

A competitor may advertise the company's problems by spreading rumors, exaggerating difficulties, and distorting the situation so that customers become anxious about the troubled company's ability to provide the product or service they have been buying. If a customer drops the troubled company, the competitors gain.

Employees become another target as competitors attempt to hire away key employees with the intent to weaken the failing company's ability to perform. The competitor maintains pressure on selected employees, hoping to offer an opportunity they cannot refuse. As the company's situation worsens, the employees may decide they can no longer afford to pass up the competitor's offer.

Competitors may also spread the word to the company's suppliers that the business is failing. Since the supplier's sales representative may already be taking heat for the credit extended, this may panic him into placing the troubled business on a COD or cash basis, thus exacerbating an already bad situation in the distressed company's production facilities.

Finally, competitors often bring up a company's woes at trade shows and trade meetings—crucibles for manufacturing and exchanging gossip—and take great glee in recounting every detail of the company's misfortunes.

The Country Club's Doors Are Closing: The Social Community's Response to Business Distress

The executive's personal life and status in the community are also affected by business distress. Business associates may be personal friends and, at least, are members of the same social circles. The desire to maintain a certain standard of living and appearance of success may result in settling bills that sustain the image rather than those that should be paid for business reasons. The tab at the country club or the gardener's wages may get top ranking in the executive's shrinking budget.

Embarrassment and social disgrace are feared by some executives to an extraordinary extent, and the lack of cash flow in personal accounts has a far greater impact than the fact that the company itself is sufferng severe financial distress. In the small entrepreneurial or family-run business this can easily become a problem, as company assets are used to settle personal debts.

The stigma of business failure is not entirely the figment of an executive's imagination. The social community often reacts negatively to business trouble, and business failure is the kind of crisis that tests which members of the social circle are indeed friends.

The image of the successful executive is sometimes more emotionally important to a businessperson than taking the necessary steps to curb spending. Ultimately, attempts to maintain this image are doomed to fail. As bills go unpaid and local personal creditors experience the executive's inability to meet commitments, the community at large will become aware of the financial problems of the company.

EVERY PERSON FOR HIMSELF: DYNAMICS OF THE OUTSIDE WORLD'S RETRENCHMENT

The Accommodation Phase: Pleas, Promises, and Second Chances

A business usually gets into trouble slowly. As the first round of setbacks hits the company's cash box, the company finds bills difficult to pay. However, this rarely alarms either the executive or various stakeholders. This is especially true if the company has a long-standing relationship with the people to whom it owes money. It may be relatively easy to convince creditors and others that minor cash flow difficulties are the only problem and that they will soon be solved.

In the accommodation stage, the outside world accepts the company's requests at face value. Verbal justifications and explanations are often all that is necessary at this juncture. The bank is patient and understanding. Trade creditors ship materials on a credit basis. Customers accept the delay in deliveries, though if the quality of the product or service is less than normal, there may be complaints or demands for replacements.

How long the accommodation phase continues is based largely on the solvency and business health of the various players. If a trade creditor is himself suffering from cash flow problems or other symptoms of financial distress, he cannot afford to accommodate another's business problems for very long. The bank holding the major loan may have many such "problem" loans on the books, and the company's inability to meet payments could be seriously affecting the bank's overall financial situation. This can result in the bank calling the loan—without warning—even during the first stages of the company's business distress.

The Compromise Phase: Self-Protection and the Executive's Slipping Halo

When an executive continues to ask others to accommodate the payment problems of the business, relationships become strained. The willingness of the outside world to support the company's requests begins to fade. Promises move to a new level. A compromise agreement is worked out to keep some activity going on both sides. The company may negotiate to pay all new bills as they are presented as well as some percentage of the outstanding debt.

In this phase, stakeholders in the outside world move to protect themselves and their investment in the business. Their confidence in the company's ability to make good on promises is waning. They begin to lose faith in the executive's competence. The outside world works to eliminate the credit extended to the company.

Up to this point, even those pressuring the company for payment may still believe in the executive's underlying capability in running the company. They just want their money—it's nothing personal. They may still view the company as unlucky, but not at fault. This often doesn't last.

If the company remains in trouble, the outside world's confidence erodes, and the business relationship suffers a serious blow: a loss of faith. The executive's credibility and competence are questioned. The creditors no longer believe he can do what he says. There have been too many promises broken.

The Conflict Phase: Disassociation, Criticism, and Blame

There comes a point when members of the outside world are no longer interested in compromise. They want—and may desperately need—their investment back, and they will do anything to get it. It may seem to these stakeholders that litigation is their only recourse.

The relationship with the executive, already strained, enters a phase of bitter accusation. The outside world holds the executive to blame. Creditors wish they had never developed a business relationship with the troubled company. In this acute phase of self-protection, creditors are often looking for a scapegoat. They conveniently forget that they chose to associate with the business in the first place, and rather than accept responsibility for the decisions that drew them into the relationship, they tend to point the finger of blame at the executive for "suckering" them into business dealings.

HOW CAN THEY DO THIS TO ME?: REACTIONS OF THE EXECUTIVE

The executive of a troubled company typically is frustrated and angry when the outside world will not continue to accommodate the company's needs. He or she is shocked, surprised, and feels betrayed, wondering how everyone could turn against the company when it just needs "a little time" to straighten things out.

It is all a matter of perspective. Just as it is easier for the outside world to blame the executive for failed commitments, it is more comforting for the executive to blame others for the company's problems. He feels as ill-used and betrayed as his creditors do, if not more so.

Blame, unfortunately, does not change the reality that the business is in trouble. If the executive clings to the belief that outside forces are responsible for his woes, it only deepens the company's distress. As long as he is using blame as self-defense, he is still caught in the cycle of denial. No solutions are possible while denial is in full force. Shifting responsibility to others leaves him and the company in the powerless role of victims of fate. Taking responsibility is the only way to take charge and regain the power to act.

Blaming the Messengers of Ill Tidings: Lessons from Oedipus

It is unfortunate that Freud had to use the tale of Oedipus to illustrate his theory of the supposed sexual desire of a boy for his mother—what he called the Oedipus complex. Unfortunate because, setting sexual connotations aside, the tragic story of Oedipus provides so many insights into human behavior in times of crisis.

Just to set the record straight, when Oedipus married Jocasta, the widowed wife of King Laius—whom Oedipus had inadvertently killed—he had no idea that she was his mother. He had not the slightest inkling that Laius had been his father, or that by killing him he was fulfilling a prophecy that Laius would die by his son's hand.

As the story begins, Oedipus is king of Thebes, which is suffering from widespread famine. In those days, the oracle at Delphi took the place of the management consultant, and people tended to take really severe problems to the oracle for guidance. The oracle provided Oedipus with the cryptic answer that Thebes had to cast out the slayer of Laius, and then all would be well.

Oedipus was all for this, and immediately started questioning people about the circumstances surrounding Laius's death. He was eager to get to the bottom of it, identify the killer, cast him out, and end the famine.

But it didn't work out quite the way he expected. Tiresias, a seer of some note, was brought before the king to assist in this problem. When Tiresias told Oedipus that he—Oedipus the king—was the problem facing Thebes, how did Oedipus react? Did he thank Tiresias for clearing up the mystery, ending the search? Was he grateful for the knowledge that he himself was the problem?

Hardly. Oedipus insulted Tiresias's ability as a seer, and threatened him with dire consequences for telling such a lie. He raged and asked Tiresias who put him up to lying. Finally Oedipus decided that Creon, his wife's brother, had instigated the whole thing to force him off the throne.

Oedipus remained steadfast in this belief, yet he had a nagging fear that he didn't have all the facts of the story before him. After much seeking, he located a herdsman who it was said held the key to the truth. The herdsman, a shepherd who had been in the service of Laius, reluctantly revealed that he had been given a young boy and instructed to kill him. The child was the son of Laius and Jocasta, and prophecy said he would grow up to kill his father. Out of pity, the shepherd didn't kill the child, but instead gave him to a king in another land.

Thus were Oedipus's worst fears confirmed, and he finally admitted the truth to himself. He was in fact the son of Laius, had killed his own father, and married, unwittingly, his own mother—thereby fulfilling another prophecy, which he had been trying to avoid in the first place.

As in all good Greek tragedies, this story has a predictable additional tragedy: Jocasta committed suicide. Oedipus blinded himself with her brooch and wandered as an outcast for years.

This fate is not in store for the executive who fails to recognize that the problems of the company may very well rest at his or her doorstep. But the reaction of Oedipus to the news that he was the center of the problem is similar to the reaction of many executives who head businesses moving full speed toward disaster. The story of Oedipus should make them think twice about rejecting the possibility that the financial distress of the company may be the result of actions taken, in good faith, by the executives themselves.

For the executive facing hard times, it may seem easier, or even justifiable, to accuse others of causing the business's problems. Blaming the outside world is a short-sighted perspective.

6 | INTERNAL BLEEDING: WHAT'S HAPPENING INSIDE THE COMPANY

Half a league, half a league
Half a league onward,
All in the valley of death
Rode the six hundred . . .

Theirs not to make reply,
Theirs not to reason why,
Theirs but to do and die . . .

ALFRED, LORD TENNYSON

UNDER SIEGE: ALL IS NOT WELL ON THE HOME FRONT

At the same time that the outside world is reacting to the ill fortunes of a company in distress, the situation within the company is usually far from calm. If the chief executive and other management are busy denying that problems exist, they may overlook or underrate the symptoms of the company's internal distress. What they are most immediately aware of is that the company is battling a largely unsympathetic—and unfair in their view—outside world. They expect their employees to rally around the company in its hour of need.

In facing the external demands, management may be turning its back on very serious in-house problems. It is relatively easy for the beleaguered executive to ignore the symptoms of declining employee morale and reduced production, especially if the changes have been gradual or if control systems aren't in place to flag potential danger signs quickly.

Even if management has been tracking certain problem areas, there may be a desensitization toward symptoms of poor health as they continue over long periods of time. Operational problems that have been going on for some time begin to seem normal. What might have worried the executive six months ago becomes accepted as "the ways things work." The chronic and familiar problems become part of the new definition of the company's state of health.

The company's overall health status is determined by the tasks it performs and by the functioning of its personnel. A business that is suffering severe financial difficulties grinds slowly to a halt—or a very reduced level of operation—in both areas.

A Picture of Health: Profile of a Smoothly Operating Company

Before examining more closely the internal workings and dysfunction of a troubled company, it is important to step back and review what a healthy company looks like. As in a person's own physical health, knowing what ideal health is can help the person work toward achieving that picture of health.

The healthy company has sufficient liquidity—the life blood of the company's ongoing operation—to keep all the parts in motion. Accounts payable are paid on time, the controller/bookkeeper doesn't have to waste time talking to vendors requesting payments, and inventory procedures keep accurate track of usable inventory at the end of the month. Financial statements come out on time, and the status of accounts receivable and cash in bank is clearly known. There's no need to resort to using float, and the company is current on withholding and sales taxes. The business is not threatened by tax liens or lawsuits from collection agencies.

A smoothly running business also has a clearly outlined business plan with strategic and operational objectives for the coming year. A budget and cash management system is in place and sales forecasts match those goals. Monitoring systems make sure the company is on target. Profits are up, and the turnover rate of the inventory is improving.

When it comes to people, high employee satisfaction goes hand in hand with a well-coordinated management team and good communication between the two. The members of the board of directors and the chief executive enjoy a relationship of mutual rapport, trust, and respect, and all work together toward accomplishing the goals of the company.

The foregoing is the basis of a healthy company's successful operation. A company that is lacking in one or more of these areas may seem to be operating well in spite of certain problems. In reality, it is a company riding on luck rather than a systematic method of ensuring proper functioning, and if major stress is added, the weak links will break. The illusion of success will go out the window and "suddenly" the business is on the edge of failure.

Perpetual Motion: Elements of the Business

The picture of the healthy company as outlined gives an overview of the climate and operation of the business. In terms of the tasks performed by a smoothly operating company, an easy way to look at the production process is to consider the company's tasks as being part of a feedback loop. In a healthy company this loop is a continuous flow of raw materials and skills producing an end product. In a company suffering some phase of illness, the flow is interrupted, and blockages prevent it from running properly.

The different stages of the manufacturing loop illustrate this process. At the beginning of the loop are the professional skills, drawings, or plans—the information needed to create the product—as well as raw materials, supplies, labor, and machines. These elements enter the loop and are melded together to create the final product.

The product is then evaluated in the measurement loop to allow corrections to be made, as needed, to keep the process functioning.

In a manufacturing plant it is easy to see that an inability to provide any of the elements required at the start of the loop will result in delays or actual shutdowns of the plant. One missing part can force a plant operating at full speed to shut down completely. The factory has to start and stop—losing the critical inertia of the smoothly running plant—and costs go up while efficiency, quality, and delivery speed go down. When the continuous process of the business is interrupted by repeated shutdowns, the pattern will tend toward higher swings and instabilities.

Once the cycle of depletion and despair is in full swing, the product deteriorates, orders decrease, and the company's fragile production loop is further threatened. The inability of the company to gather together the means of production results in failure to make the system operate.

WHEN BAD THINGS HAPPEN TO GOOD COMPANIES: DYSFUNCTION IN THE LOOP

When a business is having problems, this does not remain a secret for long. As the normal day-to-day flow of the business is threatened, middle management is often among the first to know that there are serious problems. This is the level where difficulties with the production schedule are handled. Lack of payment often results in needed supplies or parts not being shipped in time to keep the continuous flow operating. The purchasing agent and the front-line manager will take their problems to a middle manager, who will try to work out an agreement, some sort of accommodation with the controller and the vendor, so that the line can start up again.

Sales managers and representatives, pressing for orders, soon discover that the representatives are not getting paid. Accommodation only works so many times, and then orders begin to dry up. Declining orders threaten the already disturbed production loop. Facilities managers have increasing problems with machines that they can't fix or refurbish; equipment begins to show signs of wear.

Once the production loop is sufficiently disrupted that it comes to even a temporary halt, the company's fragile financial health may move into a crisis phase.

WHOSE OX IS BEING GORED?: MANAGEMENT AND EMPLOYEE CONCERNS

Each member of the troubled company, from the board of directors to the front-line employee, has a different stake in the company's continued operation. There are common concerns to each level of management and employment, based on each group's position with the company and what that means to the employees' lives and livelihoods.

Board members, who serve in an advisory role, may fear that they will be tainted by association with a loser, and will worry about the investment they have made in the company. The company's performance reflects on their capability to direct a business venture, to choose executive talent, and to plan appropriately for the future. Their competence may be called to question—or so they fear—if they have been involved with a company that was troubled.

Senior management also worries about reputation and hopes that being involved with a failing company will not adversely affect future careers. Long-term vision makes senior managers wonder how it will look to prospective new companies who may consider hiring them. They too fear that their competence will be questioned in the atmosphere of "guilt by association."

Middle management focuses on the potential impact on present jobs rather than on future ones. Middle managers are more likely to fear loss of job security than do senior managers. For them it is not so much a question of how their competence or skills were employed, but whether there are jobs out there, at equivalent levels of pay and responsibility, should the company fail.

Other employees are most concerned with losing their jobs and wonder where they will find new ones. They do not share in the responsibility for the company's decisions, and so are less likely to fear that the problems of the business reflect on their competence or job worthiness.

ACTIONS SPEAK LOUDER THAN WORDS: EMPLOYEE BEHAVIOR PATTERNS

Employees in a troubled company may react in a variety of ways, depending on each individual's coping patterns and attachment to the company. Common responses to the company's distress range from total, unthinking acceptance to active betrayal of the business. This is true not only in the difficult times before a turnaround is attempted, but also during the turnaround itself. A company under stress will invariably see the effects on its employees.

> Employees will be going through the motions dully. Speculation, gossip, rumors, small meetings at the water cooler or in the hall; passing the buck, tardiness and absenteeism will be the symptoms of the prevailing malaise. Employees, customers and vendors alike are waiting for the other shoe to drop. Where are we going, and who's making the trip?
>
> John W. Whitney

The chief executive often seems to expect that all the members of his or her staff and management team will stand by the company no matter what happens. Nothing could be further from the truth. In fact, patterns of behavior in even the most trusted employees may change under the stress of the company's troubles. The executive who fails to realize this may be placing the company in increased jeopardy.

Blind Acceptance: This reaction is almost a form of denial that something is wrong. Employees who respond with blind acceptance will keep turning up for work every day, without questioning what is going on, and will hope that the business will continue to employ them.

Total Loyalty: Employees who are totally loyal are a godsend to the troubled company, because they maintain faith that the company will prevail. They usually work hard and long to help it through its time of need. These people are often emotionally tied to the company and continue to see the executive as competent and in control.

Conditional Loyalty: Conditional loyalty is the response of employees who don't have quite as strong ties to the firm but are willing to stay—for a while or under certain conditions—to see whether the company can pull through. They may make it clear that they cannot accept a pay cut, or that if things get worse they will go, but they are usually up front and straightforward in their dealings.

Leveraging the Boss: Employees may take advantage of the company's precarious circumstances and leverage their position—depending on how much the company needs their skills—to increase their pay or status within the company. They usually make demands that can be met—and perhaps must be met in the time of crisis to keep things from getting worse.

Desertion: Some employees will simply jump ship when the trouble begins. They pull out their résumés and look for an opportunity to leave as soon as possible. They don't want to have anything to do with the hard times ahead.

Betrayal: Employees who feel betrayed by the company, may use this time of vulnerability for the business to actively betray the company. They may provide information or trade secrets to competitors, or they may quit their jobs to join competitors, taking part of the client base with them. They may actively talk down the company throughout the business world, sabotaging its attempts to stay afloat.

Criminal Behavior: Some employees take betrayal to a real low and steal from the company, like a looter at a disaster site. They may abscond with money, equipment, supplies, products, or anything else they can. This could happen systematically because the business is too busy looking at other problems to keep a close watch over operations.

STORM WARNINGS: WHAT CAN BE LEARNED FROM A CLIMATE SURVEY

How do you know what your employees are thinking and feeling about the company? It is hard to invite—and, sometimes, even harder to get—direct feedback from employees about how they perceive and understand the company.

A survey of employee attitudes and expectations was developed by the McBer Company, based on research started in 1968 at Harvard Business School. This Organizational Climate Survey Questionnaire can be used to gauge the internal temperature of the organization.

The organizational climate describes properties of the work environment that are experienced directly or indirectly by its members—properties that are measurable, can be described in specific terms, and can be changed, including properties of the work environment that influence its members' motivation and behavior.

One series of questions in the survey explores the employee's attitude about the company as it presently exists. The employee is given a statement about the company environment such as: "There is not enough reward and recognition given in this organization for doing good work," and is asked to rate the extent of his or her agreement with that statement (definitely disagree, inclined to disagree, inclined to agree, or definitely agree). A second series of questions measures how employees would like to see the organization develop, such as: "There is no need for more reward and recognition to be given in this organization for doing good work."

The surveys are typically administered and scored by an independent consultant. Employees are encouraged to be candid and are assured that their responses will be held in strict confidence.

The *total climate* score is an overall measurement of employee attitude toward the organization, that is, the perceived positive climate. The equation for determining the organizational climate is

$$\text{Total climate} = \text{responsibility} + \text{standards} + \text{rewards}$$
$$+ \text{ clarity} + \text{ team spirit} - \text{ conformity}$$

The variables examined in this survey are defined as follows.

Conformity: The feeling employees have about constraints in the work organization; the degree to which they feel that there are too many rules, procedures, policies, and practices to which they have to conform, rather than being able to do their work as they see fit

Responsibility: The feeling that employees have a lot of responsibility delegated to them; the degree to which they can run their jobs on their own without having to check constantly with the boss

Standards: The emphasis that employees feel management puts on doing a good job; the degree to which people feel that challenging goals are set

Rewards: The degree to which employees feel that they are being recognized and rewarded for good work, rather than being criticized and punished when something goes wrong

Clarity: The feeling that things are well organized rather than being disorderly, confused, and chaotic; the feeling that the lines of authority are clearly understood

Team Spirit: The feeling that good relationships prevail in the work environment, that management and fellow employees are warm and trusting, and that the organization is one to which people are proud to belong

A number of studies have shown that there is a statistically significant relationship between a company's financial performance, such as growth in sales, growth in earnings, and similar factors, and high total climate. A high total climate and high scores for the variables of responsibility, standards, rewards, clarity, and team spirit are associated with companies exhibiting good financial performance; a low total climate and a high score for conformity are associated with companies exhibiting poor financial performance.

The data accumulated by the survey can be analyzed to determine the following.

1. How the company compares with others; for example, with a profitable entrepreneurial company

2. Whether there is a significant difference between the values of the variables that the employees, as a group, presently perceive and the values they would prefer to perceive

3. How the various employees perceive the organizational climate and the extent to which they would like it to change

4. How the various individual employees perceive the organizational climate and the extent to which their perceptions deviate from the mean

5. How the various individual employees would like to change the organizational climate and the extent to which their desire deviates from the mean

The results of the analysis for one troubled company are illustrated in Figure 6.1, which compares the perceived and desired profiles for the organization as a whole with the profile of an ideal entrepreneurial organization. As the figure shows, there was a substantial difference between the climate that employees experienced and the entrepreneurial climate. This is important, because the strategy that had been espoused by management required an entrepreneurial climate as opposed to the climate that actually existed.

Using this example, the report analyzing these results concluded that employees of this company would like to see an improvement in the company climate. All variables, with the exception of standards, were viewed as falling substantially short of the desired values.

In substance, the employees reported that it was hard to get new ideas accepted, and that unnecessary rules and hierarchy got in the way of accomplishing the job. They felt that they were not given sufficient responsibility and that there were inadequate recognition and rewards for their accomplishments. They also reported that frequently there was a lack of direction, and lines of authority were often not clearly drawn. Obviously there was room for improvement in how the employees felt about the organization.

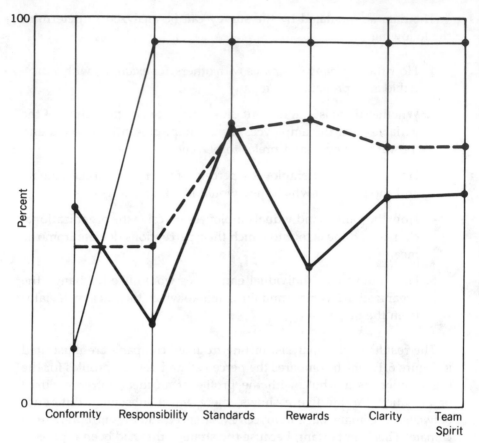

FIGURE 6.1. *Organizational analysis profile, perceived and desired climate.*
——— *ideal climate;* – – – *desired climate;* ▬▬▬ *actual climate.*

NEUROTIC ORGANIZATIONS: MIRRORS OF NEUROTIC LEADERS

A very interesting approach to understanding organizational behavior, developed by Manfred F. R. Kets de Vries and Danny Miller, suggests that organizations may actually take on the characteristics of their leaders. In their book *The Neurotic Organization* they hypothesize that the neurotic behavior of key organization members, such as the chief executive officer, permeates all aspects and functions of their organizations, colors the organizational culture, and establishes a dominant organizational adaptive style.

This style will influence decisions about strategy and structure, and will become the invisible hand that drives, directs, and selects the behavior of employees and managers within the organization.

Neurotic Behavior: An Overview

Personality styles are patterns of behavior through which individuals relate external reality to their own internal dispositions. These clusters of behavior remain relatively stable over an individual's lifetime. They develop as a child matures and interacts with the world, and reflect those strategies that the child devises to achieve objectives and avoid failures.

As the child becomes an adult, some of these behaviors become integrated into his behavior pattens. The extent to which an individual invokes these behaviors when they are inappropriate (do not facilitate meeting his objectives) or counterproductive (actually prevent him from achieving his objectives) determines whether we refer to these behaviors as "neurotic."

Most individuals have certain mildly dysfunctional neurotic traits. These might include a propensity toward temper tantrums, shyness, anxious behavior, withdrawal, and depression. Occasionally people will exhibit a number of behavior patterns that manifest a certain "neurotic style." They may display such characteristics so frequently that these behaviors become rigid and inappropriate. Although these individuals function in the day-to-day world and do not need psychiatric treatment, their inflexible and frequently inappropriate behavior limits their effectiveness as individuals and as managers. Their neurotic thinking and behavior will distort their perceptions, evaluations, decision making, and goal setting. As a consequence they will not be in a position to deal effectively with the problems that confront them.

FIVE STYLES OF NEUROTIC ORGANIZATIONS

The work of Kets de Vries and Miller proposes that neurotic organizations reflect five common neurotic styles of behavior that are well researched in psychiatric and psychological literature: paranoid, compulsive, dramatic, depressive, and schizoid. In the course of their practice and research as management consultants, they discovered that many organizations exhibit neurotic behaviors matching these individual neurotic categories, and it appears that such behavior stems from the neurotic style of the dominant players in the organization.

Their experiences with poorly performing organizations that are run by a dominant chief executive officer indicate that the personal style of the manager has a strong input on the strategy, structure, and environment of the company. Any elements of neurotic pathology in the executive's personal style are likely to be manifested in the way the firm is run.

They found that healthy firms, on the other hand, typically manifest too broad a variety of executive personality styles for any one of them to determine exclusively the characteristics of the firm. While not all failing organizations are run by neurotic executives, those that are tend to be the most centralized and those in which the strategies seem particularly extreme or inappropriate. One indicator that the personality of the CEO may be the source of the failing firm's problems is that the symptoms of the firm's behavior are related and collectively form a pattern that is a direct manifestation of one particular neurotic style.

Figure 6.2(*b*), (*c*), and (*d*) illustrates how the organizational profile of each neurotic type compares to the profile of a healthy entrepreneurial firm, as depicted in Fig. 6.2(*a*).

Paranoid Organization

The paranoid organization [Fig. 6.2(*b*)] places primary emphasis on organizational intelligence and controls. An extensive monitoring system measures and reports on every aspect of the organization so that the entire organization can be carefully controlled. Suspicions of persons, both inside and outside the organization, tend to become institutionalized. Power is centralized in the hands of a few top executives. The management is likely to be overconcerned with hidden messages and special meanings.

The organizational profile of a paranoid organization is illustrated in Fig. 6.2(*b*). A paranoid organization will exhibit high conformity, standards, and clarity, but it will provide limited opportunity for responsibility and rewards. Moreover, the extensive systems of monitoring and control of employee behavior, and the environment of distrust which is all-pervasive, will depress team spirit. The paranoid firm exhibits a lack of a consistent

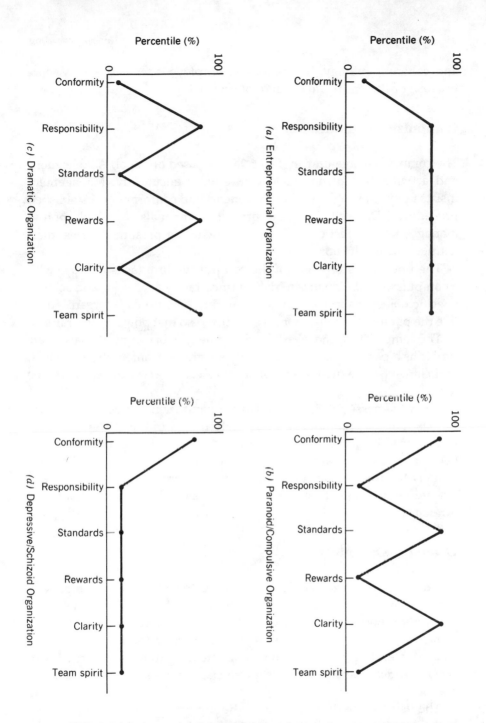

FIGURE 6.2. Organizational climate of neurotic organizations.

and coherent strategy. Managers and employees tend to feel insecure because of the entire atmosphere of distrust.

Compulsive Organization

The compulsive organization [Fig. 6.2(*b*)] is based on ritual. All operations and activities are planned and controlled meticulously. Management insists upon thoroughness, completeness, and conformity to established procedures. Detailed policy and procedure manuals are relied upon to manage every aspect of the business, including personnel, sales, marketing, and production.

The underlying objective of the compulsive firm (as is the case with a compulsive individual) is to reduce uncertainty at all costs and achieve specific objectives in a prescribed manner. A compulsive organization, like the paranoid organization, is structured so that power is centralized.

The compulsive firm will exhibit the same type of organizational climate profile as a paranoid firm, as Fig. 6.2(*b*) illustrates. Conformity, standards, and clarity will be high; responsibility, rewards, and team spirit will be low.

The weaknesses of the compulsive organization can be traced to traditions that are embraced so completely that both the strategy and the structure of the firm tend to become anachronistic. Bureaucratic thinking becomes dominant, and the organization is unable to respond appropriately to either threats or opportunities. There is usually widespread discontent among managers because of their lack of responsibility and influence.

Dramatic Organization

The dramatic organization [Fig. 6.2(*c*)] tends to be hyperactive, impulsive, dramatically venturesome, and dangerously uninhibited. Decision making is neither reflective nor analytic, and is usually based on "gut feelings," hunches, or impressions. The attention span of the executive in the company tends to be short, and management is prone to address a broad array of widely disparate projects, products, and markets in a very shallow manner.

The flair for the dramatic causes the top echelon to centralize power and to reserve for itself the prerogative to initiate bold ventures independently. Boldness, risk taking, diversification, overexpansion, over-leverage, and so forth are the dominant strategic themes, and the chief executive frequently attempts to create his own environment, independent of the reality in which he must operate. There is a tendency of the management to "bet the firm" on one venture after another. Usually a pervasive atmosphere of crisis prevails. Meetings tend to be highly emotional, and the chief executive enjoys being at the center of the stage. He rarely consults subordinates or staff experts in making key decisions. Participative decision making and consultation are alien to the dramatic organization.

The dramatic organization typically lacks an effective information system. Controls are lax, standards are flexible, and management and employees are usually fuzzy as to what their specific jobs and responsibilities entail.

The organizational profile of a typical dramatic organization is shown in Fig. 6.2(c). A dramatic organization tends to demand little conformity from its employees, allows them to assume considerable responsibility, and frequently rewards them generously with both monetary and psychic income. Standards and clarity are usually low, but team spirit is frequently quite high—it's a fun place to work with all the action.

The weaknesses of the dramatic organization stem from inconsistent strategies that have a high element of risk and cause resources to be squandered needlessly. Since the organization lacks standards and controls, it is virtually impossible to manage operational activities in a profitable manner. Second-tier managers are usually treated as gofers and used as mere instruments of senior management's whims.

Depressive Organization

The depressive organization [Fig. 6.2(d)] is characterized by inactivity, lack of confidence, and bureaucratic thinking. There is an atmosphere of extreme passivity, purposelessness, and hopelessness. What little is accomplished tends to be programmed and ritualized.

Depressive firms are found in protected environments in which there are a stable technology, customer base, and marketing preference. They tend to be highly bureaucratic, and leadership is virtually nonexistent. Control and coordination that do occur are accomplished through formalized programs rather than management initiative. There is usually a prevailing feeling among management and employees that they are not capable of either devising or implementing an effective strategy that can change the course of events for the firm. Such a firm drifts aimlessly without direction, goals, or a discernible strategy. The general attitude is one of extreme pessimism.

The organizational climate profile of a depressed firm is shown in Fig. 6.2(*d*). All variables exhibit low values, with a possible exception of conformity. The profile of the depressive organization is the exact opposite of that of the entrepreneurial firm.

The weaknesses of the depressed firm result from its apathetic and inactive management, lack of leadership, and lack of strategy. It cannot and will not respond appropriately to opportunities or threats.

Schizoid Organization

The schizoid organization [Fig. 6.2(*d*)] like the depressive one, is characterized by a leadership vacuum. The chief executive stays uninvolved in the business, avoids confrontation, and finds interaction with the management team both frustrating and unsatisfying. He frequently leaves the identification and resolution of problems to his subordinates. In the absence of clear direction from the chief executive, the schizoid management environment often becomes a political battlefield, where warring managers attempt to promote their own personal interests using the resources of the company.

A schizoid organization frequently lacks a well thought out product or marketing strategy. The chief executive usually fails to support any single program, switching his favor from one subordinate to another, depending upon who has influenced him most recently.

The environment of a schizoid organization is frequently similar to a sixteenth-century Italian court: deception, intrigue, and political infighting are pervasive. The political environment is a fertile breeding ground for the opportunist who is adept at currying the favor of the chief executive. The senior managers rarely collaborate, and the structure of the company will deteriorate to competitive and independent fiefdoms, each of which is jealously guarded by its manager. Information flow is restricted, and there is considerable suspicion among both management and employees.

The organizational climate profile of a schizoid organization [Fig. 6.2(*d*)] is similar to that of a depressive organization, since a lack of leadership, political infighting, the absence of clear strategy, and a pervasive atmosphere of distrust tend to depress all of the organizational climate variables.

The weaknesses of the schizoid organization result from its inconsistent and vacillating strategy, a politically charged atmosphere, lack of leadership, and climate of suspicion and distrust, which prevent openness, collaboration, and participative management.

The Critical Role of the Executive

The theory of neurotic organizational behavior makes it clear that the mental health and behavior of executives in power will have a profound impact on the actual operation of the business. The role the chief executive plays in determining the organizational climate, and hence effectiveness, in meeting the challenges of business is critically important.

What is happening inside the executive's mind and how he reacts and behaves under stress are important to understand. In the next chapter we explore what happens to executives in a distressed business.

7 OUT OF THEIR MINDS: EXECUTIVE EXPERIENCE IN BUSINESS DISTRESS

*Man can will nothing unless he has first understood
that he must count on no one but himself; that he is
alone, abandoned on earth in the midst of his infinite
responsibilities without help, with no other aim than
the one he sets himself, with no other destiny than the
one he forges for himself on this earth.*

JEAN-PAUL SARTRE

THE EFFECTS OF BUSINESS ILLNESS ON THE CEO: OVERSTRESS AND GRIEF

Business failure is a devastating experience. It is rarely just a commercial failure, because it affects the personal lives of all the people who have a stake in the business. The executive or owner who heads the company often has the greatest emotional and financial investment in the business, and is highly vulnerable to a sense of having personally failed when the company is in distress. If he or she sees the success of the business as a reflection of individual success, the pressure to keep the business alive—and deny its problems—is enormous.

Clear thinking and rational actions go out the window when the executive is under that level of stress. It may even be perceived, and hence experienced, as life-threatening. He can't afford to fail, and yet

91

the business is in trouble. The unthinkable is happening, and the fear of impending doom is immobilizing.

When the chief executive becomes unable to handle the increasing problems of the company, a cycle of incompetence often develops that cannot be broken from within. The cycle feeds on itself. Those connected to the business—even the banker holding a major loan—may also lose their perspective in the situation. They, too, have risked too much, invested too much in the gamble, to see clearly. Their money or careers are riding on the draw of the cards. Failure is inconceivable, even when it is inevitable. They keep counting on the executive who was leading them toward success to come through. It was his or her vision, brains, and creative force for the future of the company that got them all involved. Surely he, like Wile E. Coyote, can come up with one more scheme.

The problem is that when a business is on the brink of disaster, the creative brains that dreamed it into being are usually no longer fully functional. Continued stress takes a toll on executive competence. He or she can't think of new solutions, and if the way out were clear, it would already have been taken.

STRESS: THE ULTIMATE TRIGGER AND GREAT AMPLIFIER

Stress receives a lot of attention in today's fast-paced world. There are many demands placed on executives making decisions that affect the success of a business and its future.

Stress in itself, however, is a relative matter. It results from a person's perceptions and reactions to events. What is stressful for some people is an irrelevant event for others. Reactions to potentially stress-producing incidents can range from indifference in one person to anger, anxiety, depression, and even physical illness in another.

However, a number of events that may happen in a person's life are commonly stressful. The Social Readjustment Rating Scale, presented in Table 7.1, is a scale of stressful life-change events, an inventory of common stressful situations that studies have shown to have a potentially negative effect on a person's health.

This inventory of life-change events, developed by Drs. Holmes and Rahe of the University of Washington Medical School, has proven to be an accurate predictor of imminent illness or disability. The "stress score" is the sum of the scores of all the events that happened in the past year

TABLE 7.1. SOCIAL READJUSTMENT RATING SCALE

Rank	Life Event	LCU Value
1	Death of spouse	100
2	Divorce	73
3	Marital separation	65
4	Jail term	63
5	Death of close family member	63
6	Personal injury or illness	53
7	Marriage	50
8	Fired from job	47
9	Marital reconciliation	45
10	Retirement	45
11	Change in health of family member	44
12	Pregnancy	40
13	Sex difficulties	39
14	Gain of new family member	39
15	Business readjustment	39
16	Change in financial state	38
17	Death of close friend	37
18	Change to different line of work	36
19	Change in number of arguments with spouse	35
20	Mortgage over $10,000	31
21	Foreclosure of mortgage or loan	30
22	Change in responsibilities at work	29
23	Son or daughter leaving home	29
24	Trouble with in-laws	29
25	Outstanding personal achievement	28
26	Wife begins or stops work	26
27	Begin or end school	26
28	Change in living conditions	25
29	Revision of personal habits	24
30	Trouble with boss	23
31	Change in work hours or conditions	20
32	Change in residence	20
33	Change in schools	20
34	Change in recreation	19
35	Change in church activities	19
36	Change in social activities	18
37	Mortgage or loan less than $10,000	17
38	Change in sleeping habits	16
39	Change in number of family get-togethers	15
40	Change in eating habits	15
41	Vacation	13
42	Christmas	12
43	Minor violations of the law	11

Source: *Journal of Psychosomatic Research,* **2**, pp. 213–218 (1967). Copyright 1967, Pergamon Press.

of the individual's life. Research indicates that a person scoring less than 150 has a 37 percent probability of becoming ill within the next two years, while a score between 150 and 299 indicates a 51 percent chance of illness. For those scoring 300 or more there is an 80 percent chance they will succumb to illness within the following two years.

Executives heading distressed companies are likely to have scores close to or above 300, especially if they are anxious or depressed about the fate of the business. This places them in a high-risk category for a medical trauma to add to their troubles.

Studies have also shown that while a little bit of stress may be a good thing and induce an increase in performance, too much stress has negative effects on judgment and thinking ability. Performance improves gradually with stress, levels off at an optimum level, and then diminishes rapidly as stress increases beyond productive levels. With high amounts of stress, performance can grind to a halt. Since the executive in a distressed business is in a state of constant bombardment, without relief, it is all too common for his performance to suffer when the business needs him at his best.

Dr. Jekyll and Mr. Hyde: The Executive's Behavior under Stress

When an executive is under extreme stress, his or her behavior may well undergo radical changes. The once reasonable, easygoing executive may fly into rages, slam doors, jump on employees for minor errors, and get upset over minor details. The transformation is as drastic as the change from Dr. Jekyll into Mr. Hyde, and it is bewildering to business associates and employees of the firm.

It is also frightening for the executive, who at some level knows he is losing control. He can't cope. He can't keep from exploding at events that trigger him into behavior he may be secretly ashamed of.

Why is he acting so strangely? It is the result of an enormous overdose of stress, which he has been unable to diffuse. Everyone has a certain amount of stress every day—both positive and negative—and has a way of coping with it. In the troubled business, stress is increased substantially. Normal coping methods for handling stress—maybe a game of tennis or jogging in the morning—are not enough to counteract the stress of the situation.

IT'S ALL IN YOUR MIND: ROADBLOCKS AND DETOURS IN THINKING

In facing the daily crises of running a business that is experiencing financial difficulties, the executive's level of competence, and his ability to perceive accurately what is happening, often undergo radical changes. Stress is the major culprit, and it can cause increasing distortions in the executive's perception of the world around him.

In our experience as many as 55 percent of executives heading troubled businesses are unable to cope effectively with the problems and the environment of their failing businesses. This is explained by three factors.

1. Some simply lack the managerial or technical expertise to manage the business in its current economic environment. Their skills were adequate previously, but no longer are.

2. Some are good managers, but do not have the knowledge, skill, or leadership ability to make the adjustments in the company to effect a turnaround. Worse yet, they don't know that they don't.

3. Some are unable to cope with the excessive stress they are experiencing. The executive's usual ability to accurately perceive reality, gather data, perform analyses, make decisions, and take effective action often undergoes radical changes in the failing company.

The overstressed executive may exhibit one or more of the following psychological problems: (1) distortions in perception and reasoning, (2) anxiety, and (3) depression. We now discuss these three problems and how they can adversely affect executive competence and performance.

OUR WORLD VIEW: ITS PROCESS OF PERCEPTION AND REASONING AND THEIR DISTORTIONS

Everything that happens around us provides information for us to develop a "world view" within which we operate. We take in and evaluate this information, assigning meaning to it. This is a constant process of perception and interpretation.

On the basis of our perception and reasoning, we make decisions and then take action to implement these decisions. If the perception and reasoning processes are distorted, those decisions will be flawed, and the actions taken, counterproductive. An executive's ability to achieve correct, consistent, rational, and realistic decisions is dependent on his ability to perceive his environment accurately and to reason effectively.

Under stress the filtering and evaluative thought systems become overloaded, and information received is interpreted within the context of extreme peril. The emotional state of executives in troubled businesses alters how they perceive the world and how they think and act on those perceptions. Observations being made may also be distorted and reflect the person's biases, past experiences that do not necessarily relate to the present situation, or a disturbed or abnormal emotional state.

Remember the Indian tale of the six blind men and the elephant? Each blind man was holding a different part of the elephant and made an assumption of what the creature was like, based entirely on the one piece of information he had.

The man who touched the side of the elephant said an elephant is like a wall; the one who touched the trunk decided an elephant was like a snake; the man feeling the tusk concluded it was like a spear; another who touched the leg said the creature was like a tree; one who felt the ear said it was like a fan; and the man touching the tail said it was like a rope. Not one of them could "see" the big picture, and so their perceptions of the elephant could not be accurate.

There is an old joke about two men out for a walk. One of the men kept stamping his feet every few minutes, to the puzzlement of his friend. Finally his friend asked, "Why are you stamping your feet?" The man replied, "To keep away tigers." His friend said, "But there aren't any tigers!" To which the man replied, "See, it's working!"

This man's actions were based on faulty logic: if I stamp my feet, then the tigers will stay clear. In a business setting, an executive may keep repeating an action because he thinks that what he does keeps his business out of trouble. In reality, there is no relationship between his action and the end result. He is operating with a faulty understanding of cause and effect.

WOLF AT THE DOOR: ANXIETY IS KNOCKING

The phenomenon of anxiety represents one of the ways in which we deal with threats. As we experience the world around us, our cognitive processes are constantly reviewing data from the environment and assessing threats and our resources for dealing with them. We make a determination of the probability that damage will result (physical or psychological) and the likely degree of damage.

When anxiety is working properly, it acts as an attention getter. Its unpleasant feelings (tension and nervousness) and physiological symptoms (heart palpitations and nausea) make us aware that something is wrong, and induce us to change our behavior. The experience is unpleasant enough that we want to lessen it.

We may make a change in behavior, such as closing our windows and locking the car doors while driving through an unsafe urban area. By alerting us that we are in danger and by initiating defensive behavior, anxiety induces us not to be reckless.

In the business setting, an executive suffering from a high level of anxiety may react in any of the primal responses to stress: fight (become angry), flight (leave the scene), freeze (become immobile and helpless), or faint (become overwhelmed, shut down).

Unfortunately this is particularly ineffective as a coping response in the heavy demand situation in which an executive may be operating. Anxiety in the executive will undermine any chance the business has for recovery.

Anxiety can be activated by a number of situations that confront the beleaguered businessperson, such as unending disapproval from significant others (spouse, banker, major investor); extended stress on certain vulnerabilities, such as feelings of incompetence; overload of decision-making ability; or dwelling on the thought of an impending catastrophe (such as bankruptcy) that will subject the executive to public disgrace.

Although a person is well skilled and experienced in a particular activity, the anticipation of possible ineptitude and the subsequent damage may block that skill. In the world of sports it is referred to as "choking on the big play."

The core of anxiety is the executive's assessment of his vulnerability. Vulnerability is a person's perception of himself as subject to danger over which his control is lacking or is insufficient to provide a sense of security. The combination of an executive's perception of his skill in coping with a threat he anticipates, and his assessment of the damage that will result if he fails, establishes his sense of vulnerability in that particular situation.

If a person is in a situation in which he is vulnerable, the anxiety behaviors that were designed for his self-protection during the primitive stages of evolution may become mobilized and interfere with his efforts to cope. The same processes apply to physical threats, social threats, and psychological threats. If a businessperson is in a situation where he believes his vital interests are at stake and his competence is a key to achieving his objective, he might feel that he will not perform adequately. This will cause him to experience anxiety.

THE BLACK HOLE: DEPRESSION

Depression has been referred to as the common cold of psychiatric disorders. *Newsweek* reports that 30–40 million Americans will experience depression at least once, and that 30–40 percent of these will have several bouts with depression. At any given time, 6 percent of the adult population may be in the grip of this disorder.

Unlike the common cold, however, depression is an illness that can kill. Approximately 60 percent of those who commit suicide are severely depressed—and depression can hit people in every walk of life. Able, dedicated, and successful business executives, such as Alvin Feldman, CEO of Continental Airlines, and Eli Black, chairman of United Brands, have committed suicide during a depression brought on by business failure.

Those who are depressed are paradoxical in behavior: beset with problems, they stop trying to solve them. The depressed executive who requires expert help to save the business instead solicits advice from amateurs and shuns the experts. He has to arise early to interview for a job to replace the one just lost, and yet can't get out of bed. He doesn't exert himself but constantly feels tired.

The Cognitive Model Applied to Depression

The cognitive theory of depression explains this paradoxical phenomenon. This theory, developed through the work of Dr. Aaron T. Beck and his colleagues, describe the phenomenon of depression using the concept of the cognitive triad. The cognitive triad consists of three major patterns of thought that induce a depressed person to regard himself, his future, and his ongoing experiences in a unique and idiosyncratic manner.

Component 1:   The depressed person has a negative view of himself: he sees himself as defective, inadequate, a loser, and he attributes his unpleasant experiences to psychological, physical, mental, educational, or other defects in himself. He frequently acts as a prosecuting attorney arguing against himself and criticizing himself for these perceived shortcomings in his makeup. Finally, he believes he lacks the skills, contacts, luck, drive, or other attributes necessary to attain happiness and "success."

Component 2:   The depressed person exhibits a tendency to interpret his ongoing experiences in a negative way. He views the world as a battleground, constantly making demands on him with which he is unable to cope. He misinterprets his experiences so that he sees defeat and loss in every result, and he discounts explanations or positive evaluations that are equally plausible.

Component 3:   The depressed person has a negative view of the future. In the words of Beck et al.:

As a depressed person makes long-range projections, he anticipates that his current difficulties or suffering will continue indefinitely. He expects unremitting hardship, frustration and deprivations. When he considers undertaking a specific task in the immediate future, he expects to fail.

Depression is not simply a case of the blues, and it may not go away in the morning. The business executive heading a troubled company is likely to suffer bouts of anxiety and depression for extended periods of time.

When someone is in the midst of severe depression, or overcome with extreme anxiety, decision making is risky at best. Often bad decisions are made simply because the executive feels that he or she has to do *something*—inactivity increases the sense of helplessness and failure. Those bad decisions lead the company further into trouble and the executive, who has failed one more time, deeper into depression.

THE PIT AND THE PENDULUM: HORRORS OF ANXIETY AND DEPRESSION IN THE WORKPLACE

Once the full weight of reality finally hits the executive, it is a crushing revelation. The whole world, as he or she knows it, has changed from success to failure. While the business did not get into trouble overnight, sometimes the executive's change in perception may happen that fast. Denial no longer works: the fantasy is exposed. The executive is suddenly at risk for the very worst crisis in the leadership of the company.

Anxiety and depression are companion distress modes that may hit the executive who is overstressed, overwhelmed, and has no answers to increasing business problems, while admitting that there are serious problems that need to be solved. Seeing that there are problems brings the executive one step closer to dealing realistically with the company's critical illness.

If the swing away from denial could just stop at reality-oriented evaluation, the company could move ahead with actions that make good business sense. But more often than not, once the executive lets go of the "everything is wonderful" fantasy, the reaction is to shift into an "everything is terrible and I am a failure" style of thinking.

The chief executive's personalization of the company's troubles can plummet him or her into a depression that affects his or her behavior and decision-making ability to the detriment of the company, and with drastic implications for the executive's own life. While it seems that now, finally, the executive is looking at reality, the world seen through the eyes of a depressed and anxious person is a catastrophic disaster—and this is not reality. It may seem simplistic to say that business failure involves only money, but this is in fact true.

A highly depressed or anxious executive is operating with thought processes gone haywire. Distorted perceptions and thinking errors are compounded by the continued high level of stress the executive experiences.

As we discussed earlier, it is not the actual severity of the situation, but what the executive thinks and tells himself. What one executive may consider total disaster and worthy of suicidal desperation, another executive could view as just a tough problem to solve.

Either depression or anxiety—or, as is common, the two emotional states fluctuating between one another—can be considered the Achilles heel of the business in distress. These two relatively common emotional disorders are brought on by severe stress, and when present, they undermine the very skills the executive needs to cope with the problems of the financially troubled company.

WHO'S MINDING THE STORE?: EXECUTIVE TYPES

The psychological state of the executive is a major factor in determining how easily the business owner or executive—and the company—will be able to move from financial distress back into business health. The other component of successful intervention is the actual competence of the executive in charge.

Taking a look at these two aspects, executives can be classified into one of four categories:

1. Out of control and incapable

2. In control but incapable

3. Out of control but capable

4. In control and capable

Table 7.2 shows a matrix of these executive types, and Table 7.3 gives the percentages of business owners and heads of companies who fall into each category, based on our experience.

TABLE 7.2. CLASSIFICATION OF EXECUTIVES

| | | Psychological Condition | |
		Out of Control	In Control
Competence	Incapable	1. Executive is highly anxious or deeply depressed and has little or no competence as a managing executive	2. Executive is psychologically stable and is realistic about the company's situation; however, he does not have any skills as a managing executive
	Capable	3. Executive is highly anxious or deeply depressed; however, he has and does display skills and energy of a competent managing executive	4. Executive is psychologically stable, is also realistic about the company's situation, and has the skills and energy of a competent managing executive

TABLE 7.3.   PSYCHOLOGICAL STATE OF EXECUTIVES
(PERCENT IN EACH CATEGORY)

	Out of Control	In Control	Total
Incapable	42 percent	16 percent	58 percent
Capable	13 percent	29 percent	42 percent
Total	55 percent	45 percent	

Category 1: Out of Control and Incapable

The executive who has little or no management or leadership skills in addition to a poor psychological condition is way out of his depth when the business experiences difficulties. He cannot formulate and execute tasks and is unable to influence people in order to accomplish his goals. In addition, this type of executive is either in a perpetual state of high anxiety or in a deep depression. As a result, the executive is incapable of addressing a problem rationally, carrying out an assignment, or negotiating the resolution of a dispute.

Often the only way to help this type of executive effectively is to relieve him of all responsibilities for managing his business and to place someone else in the management role. If he cannot accept that only by giving up control of the business can he hope to preserve any assets of the company, it will be impossible to help this type of executive. In essence, the executive must, for his own good, "give up the keys to the store and get out of town."

Category 2: In Control but Incapable

Like the executive type just discussed, this executive has little or no management or leadership skills. However, his psychological state is good in that he has a grasp of reality and can comprehend his personal and business financial situation. As a result, he can recognize that he will need considerable professional help to turn the business around, and he is much more likely to ask for and accept it. He is therefore able to be a part of the turnaround situation since he will take direction and not inhibit or interfere with the rehabilitation process. His role will be to perform specific tasks that are not of an executive nature, while all of the executive functions of the business are handled by others.

Category 3: Out of Control but Capable

The executive in this category is highly anxious or depressed, but does have the necessary skills and energy of a competent managing executive. Because of his apparent competence at some times and his past performance as a capable leader, this executive may appear rational, in control of his environment, and exhibit fairly good people skills.

He will express total understanding of his financial situation and his own capability in its development. Creativity, intelligence, and eagerness to learn are earmarks of his personality. He will appear to have insight and understanding as to all of the factors that created the problems he now faces. He will express guilt and shame for his errors in judgment, for the money borrowed which cannot be paid back, for the employees who have been disappointed, and for the investors whose money he has lost. Indicating that he is ready to learn how to run the business effectively, he will seem eager to show that he can be successful.

Unfortunately the poor psychological state of this type of executive, often concealed by his competence, will prove to be the Achilles heel that virtually guarantees his failure.

He is usually very smart—in fact, so smart that he is confident that he can second-guess everyone and any situation. Often in the grip of a high level of anxiety, he has a strong compulsion to act, even in the absence of facts or in the face of facts indicating that a course of no action might well be the most productive response to the situation. His anxiety is usually so high that it can only be relieved by some kind of action.

That combination of high competence and poor psychological state makes it difficult for this type of executive to ask for or use any kind of assistance.

Category 4: In Control and Capable

The best of all possible worlds is the executive who is both in control emotionally and a capable leader and manager. This type of executive is aware of the errors which brought about his company's financial crisis, and while he may have suffered depression and felt guilty, sad, or ashamed, he moved past those states into acceptance of the new reality. He wants to embark on a new course. He is genuinely eager to solve his problems and is willing to rely upon assistance. For this reason, he and his business are likely to face a much quicker path to recovery.

Our experience suggests that the majority of executives at the helm of distressed businesses either are operating from an unstable psychological state (55 percent) or simply lack competence (58 percent) to perform their duties; 42 percent are both out of control emotionally and not capable as managers.

WHEN SUPERMAN'S CAPE IS MADE OF KRYPTONITE: THE VULNERABLE EXECUTIVE

What makes the executive who used to relish challenges and thrive on overcoming obstacles succumb to a cycle of increasing despair? What causes the vital and creative entrepreneur to suffer bouts of anxiety and depression? The key to understanding this phenomenon is to examine what is emotionally at risk for the executive in any business venture.

When a business fails, that failure threatens a vulnerable executive's own self-concept. Failure attacks self-esteem. Business failure may challenge the very meaning and purpose of the executive's life, especially if the success of the business has formed a large part of the executive's sense of self-worth.

Some executives whose lives are marked with outstanding successes have never experienced real failure. Their history is a chronicle of obstacles bypassed, setbacks conquered, and a high level of public recognition for their excellence. Defeat is not in their vocabulary, and failure is something that only happens to others.

When they are confronted with the imminent collapse of their business, they are not prepared for the devastating effect this has upon them. They don't have coping skills for failure because they have never needed to develop them. These are executives for whom business failure is often a time of intense personal crisis.

8 | WHERE'S THE FAIRY GODMOTHER? CHANGE AGENTS AND PROCESSES

The way out is through the door. Why is it that no one will use this exit?

CONFUCIUS

Problems have solutions. Life is not static, and no matter how immobilized an executive at the head of a troubled business may feel, no matter how frozen in time the company's problems seem to be, the clock ticks on. Something will happen.

In the first seven chapters of this book we explored the causes of business failure, the reactions of many of the participants and bystanders to this failure, and the effects of stress produced by business distress.

When a business falls into financial distress or plummets into failure, it often takes with it the fortunes and self-respect of those most closely associated with it. Business disaster is a blow to people's lives that sends them reeling. It can shake the confidence of the most competent and brilliant executives; it can tear apart families and destroy lives.

But it doesn't have to. Acceptance of problems is the first step toward solving those problems. It may seem that the gap between acceptance of the problem and creation of a solution is as wide a chasm as the Grand Canyon. But there are ways to bridge that gap. It is possible to get to the other side and be in the midst of solutions, instead of in a crowd of problems. First, however, effective change must take place.

Those in the midst of business distress or struggling in the aftermath of the disaster ask themselves why and how it happened. The less they understand the answers to those questions, the more they suffer from the fear that it will happen again.

Why it happened is always important. Understanding the cause provides valuable information to prevent it from happening again, and to develop realistic plans for the future. But while the business is collapsing, the why is less important than figuring out what to do next, and how to cope with the situation.

Consider the dilemma of a race car driver whose brakes fail while he is heading into a turn at 100 miles per hour. He doesn't stop to analyze why the brakes didn't work. His first goal is to survive the curve. Afterward he will talk with the mechanic and the pit crew to determine why it happened so that he can make sure it doesn't happen again. In the moment of crisis, the most important thing for him is to decide what to do.

REPETITION IS NOT CHANGE

Sisyphus, a legendary character from Greek mythology, is a classic example of unrewarded toil, and a very bad testimonial for the work ethic. He spends all of his time rolling a huge boulder up a hill. As soon as he has reached the top of the hill, the boulder rolls down to the bottom, and he has to start again. He is condemned to do this eternally. He works very, very hard, but he doesn't get anywhere.

In a similar fashion, the "Uncle George theory" of hard work and long hours is explained by Robert Ringer in his book *Winning through Intimidation*. Ringer suggests that "if you keep your nose to the grindstone and work hard, long hours, you are guaranteed to get only one thing in return, and that is *old* (and perhaps a ground down nose)." His theory is based on the example of his Uncle George, who owned a grocery store and worked 10 to 15 hours a day for many, many years in an attempt to get rich. He did not get rich, but he did get old.

Executives who operate under the Uncle George model feel it isn't fair that diligent and consistent work doesn't automatically bring rewards. That is true. Life isn't fair, and operating a business unfortunately falls under the rules of life. Persistence does not necessarily win the day. Nor will saving paper clips, recycling pie tins, not taking vacations, or reading trade magazines guarantee success. Doing the wrong thing, no matter how efficiently, may, and surprisingly often will, guarantee failure.

Peter Drucker, the noted management consultant, makes an important distinction between working effectively and working efficiently. Working effectively is doing those things that will make a difference and help you achieve your goals. Working efficiently means doing a task in a timely manner, at the quality level, and within the time constraints demanded by the situation. For example, producing a product at higher quality and at lower cost than your largest competitor would be working efficiently. However, continuing to invest in that product, despite information indicating a major decline in the market demand, would not be working effectively.

Persisting in a course of action regardless of whether it was proven ineffective may, some feel, illustrate good work habits or a stable character. There is the old maxim, "If at first you don't succeed, try, try again." But persistence can also be sheer folly, illustrating stubbornness, lack of creativity, and management paralysis. Remember Wile E. Coyote? A more persistent character was never created, but he would hardly be a good role model for effective progress.

MAGICAL INTERVENTION: THE TALE OF CINDERELLA

In the realm of the mind, where fantasy can hold its own or even win over reality, the process of change is often imagined as both quick and painless. Anyone who is overwhelmed with problems may well wish he had a magic wand to change everything in a flash. In fairy tales, the fairy godmother of someone else with magical powers—a good witch or a magician—shows up in the nick of time to save the person in distress. In these situations, the fairy godmother and her counterparts are acting as agents of change.

Cinderella was a young woman who had fallen on hard times. In the good old days, she had lived with her loving mother and father a nice, secure life. Then everything went wrong. Her mother died and her father remarried a horrible woman with two nasty daughters. The wicked stepmother and the terrible stepsisters did everything they could to make Cinderella miserable. She had to scrub, clean, and cook and to cater to all the wishes of these tyrants. She was reduced to wearing rags and sleeping on the hearth amidst the cinders—hence her name.

Cinderella tried to change the situation, to win the love of her step-relatives by working harder and harder, doing everything asked of her. But no matter how hard she worked, it didn't seem to make any difference.

Then came the day of the great ball, and Cinderella got her break. Along came a fairy godmother, who decked her out in beautiful clothes and sent her off to the ball. The prince fell in love with her, and everyone knows the happy ending.

Now let's look at the story in terms of the process of change that occurred. We will use the framework of the change process developed by Paul Watzlawick, in which he defines first- and second-order changes. A first-order change is "more of the same," the same behavior or action repeated again and again. This is what Sisyphus and Uncle George do, and it gets them nowhere. At the beginning of the tale of Cinderella, she too is engaged in first-order change, working very hard and getting nowhere. Then along comes a change agent, who applies second-order change. She changes the reality of Cinderella's situation and puts her in an entirely different framework—the royal ball—where her good qualities shine through.

We discuss these concepts of first- and second-order change in more detail later in the chapter. First let's look at examples of change in the business setting.

Any business in trouble would like the trouble to go away, whether the problems seriously threaten the company's health or simply its current profitability. It would be great to wake up in the morning and find all the problems solved. If the executive has accepted, on some level, that the business is in a lot of trouble, he'd like nothing better than to be able to wave a magic wand and change everything.

Every chief executive who finds himself at the helm of a business that is losing money knows that if he is ever to achieve profitability, he will have to do something. If he does nothing (zero-order change), no return to profitability is likely unless events outside of his control conspire in a benevolent fashion.

FIRST-ORDER CHANGE

Frequently an executive will opt for making "adjustments" in the way he does business. He will reduce costs where possible, such as overhead labor expense (secretaries, administrators, janitors, executive salaries, car allowances, health insurance) and expenses (travel, entertainment, office supplies, free coffee service). At the same time, he will increase prices slightly, while still remaining competitive, and continue to run the business in more or less the same way. These changes are first-order changes. There is nothing radically different in the way the business is run; it is more and more of the same. These changes may be sufficient to bring the company to a level of profitability that is satisfactory to the ownership.

An excellent example of the failure of the "more of the same" philosophy is offered by a litigation involving implacable and litigious adversaries, each of which has hired a competent and aggressive attorney. At the initiation of the litigation, each of the adversaries presumably is attempting to "solve" a problem and achieve a resolution in an economic and timely fashion.

But as the litigation proceeds, the attorneys proceed to create a mountain of paperwork; they haul each other, and their clients, to endless court hearings. As a result, the enmity between the litigants escalates. Each becomes increasingly committed to achieving "justice" and "equity" and to being "vindicated in a court of law." As a result, the "solution" to the problem of the dispute, which was the lawsuit that was filed, becomes the problem, precluding settlement, notwithstanding the substantial legal expenses that have been incurred by the parties.

Another common example is what happens when two shareholder groups who together have voting control of a corporation do not trust each other. In order to protect their interests, they decide to remain involved in the company's affairs, but since they have different objectives, business philosophies, attitudes, and resources, they can never agree on any plan. Their interaction paralyzes the company. Despite endless board meetings and the involvement of lawyers, consultants, and accountants, nothing is ever resolved to allow the company to move forward.

The principle that underlies all of these examples is that the unyielding, unquestioning retention of solutions that at one time may have been successful is bound to create new problems. All situations change over the course of time. Although a solution may have made sense at one time, the adherence to the pattern of behavior despite evidence that it is not working creates a foundation for new problems. The inability to discard assumptions that may be anachronistic precludes discovering other feasible, and perhaps better, solutions to the original problem.

The blind adherence to an accepted though ineffective solution has a double effect. First, it makes the chosen solution more and more useless and the overall situation thus increasingly hopeless. Second, it promotes the unshakable belief that there is only one solution, and this leads to the conclusion that one must do more of the same.

First-order changes are more likely to work with a company that is not in serious trouble. A business in distress has usually already tried all of the normal "fix-it" solutions, without effective change taking place. When these first-order changes do not accomplish management's objectives, something different has to be done.

SECOND-ORDER CHANGE

Second-order changes are "something different," and sometimes quite a radical departure from anything that had been tried before. For example, the company might merge with a competitor, a supplier, or a customer. Management might determine that one strategic unit is a millstone on the entire enterprise and sell off or liquidate that unit. The company might determine that it could substantially increase its market share of one product area and make heavy capital investments in both assets and marketing to promote that area. The result of any of these actions is a second-order change. The manner in which the business operates or serves its customer base will be altered dramatically.

Second-order change is quite different from first-order change. It is applied to what in the first-order change perspective appears to be a solution, because in the second-order change perspective this "solution" reveals itself as the keystone of the problem. For example, a supplier attempts to "solve" his accounts receivable problem by not shipping unless the debtor pays the old balance due. His "solution" only drives the debtor out of business, which results in the supplier never getting paid.

Second-order change should be applied to the new problem, namely, attempting to prevent the potential failure of the debtor and maximizing the net positive cash flow that the supplier realizes before the debtor fails.

It's Not Logical, but It Works

Second-order change usually appears unexpected, unpredictable, and illogical; first-order change always appears to be logical and based on common sense. One of the classical examples of this aspect of second-order change is illustrated by a common treatment for insomnia. A person suffering from insomnia may try many of the conventional home remedies, such as drinking hot milk, trying to keep his mind blank, and trying "not to think." These efforts will usually be in vain. Many people suffering from insomnia can be helped by a seemingly absurd, paradoxical injunction: "Lie in bed and do not close your eyes until you are fast asleep."

In the Here and Now

Second-order change techniques deal with the "here and now" of a problem; with *what* is wrong and *how* to fix it, not why the situation exists. In this regard, second-order change has more in common with behavior modification techniques, which attempt to change nonproductive behavior without completely understanding how that behavior developed, than with psychoanalysis, which hopes to change neurotic behavior by having a patient understand its origin.

Reframing the Problem

Second-order change techniques frequently rely on a process called "reframing," which changes the conceptual and emotional setting of a situation and places it in another framework. The new frame of reference fits the "facts" of the situation equally well or even better, but the shift in perspective alters its entire meaning. As a result, the meaning attributed to the situation is changed.

Tom Sawyer was an expert at using this technique. One Saturday morning, on a summer day when all the other boys were headed off to play, poor Tom was faced with the unpleasant chore of whitewashing 30 yards of board fence—a dismal prospect. But then Tom had a bright idea. When his friend Ben came along, Tom pretended he would rather whitewash than do anything else—that it was a unique experience that not everyone could do. He reframed the task from a chore to a privilege. In fact, he did such a good job of reframing that Ben begged to be allowed to whitewash in his place, and even gave Tom his apple to clinch the deal. Ben was followed by other willing boys, and Tom didn't have to do any work at all.

A CASE STUDY: APPLYING SECOND-ORDER CHANGE

A family company that had been in business for approximately 50 years, controlled by two shareholder groups, had been very successful for most of its existence. Its success was largely due to its manufacturing operations—its core business. In an attempt to diversify and shelter its manufacturing income, the company acquired real property in order to engage in land development. The land development activity required considerable investments of capital and resulted in large operating losses. Although the land development venture generated cash losses, the profitability of the manufacturing activity was sufficient to offset the losses and still yield an acceptable profit for the corporation.

The recession in the real estate industry during the early 1980s resulted in a dramatic reduction in the income from the land development venture. Suddenly the land development losses were no longer offset. But the company continued to follow the same practices, and for five years generated net operating losses to the extent that virtually all of its net worth was eliminated.

Over the years the shareholders and their representatives who participated in the operating management developed a number of business practices that were inconsistent with the best interests of the corporation and resulted in the shareholder groups losing trust and confidence in each other. These practices were:

1. The creation of separate businesses that provided services to the corporation on a noncompetitive basis, causing the corporation to either lose or forgo profits in favor of the participants in that particular business.

2. Each shareholder group "managed" a specific part of the business without any substantial input or interference from the others. They essentially divided the corporation into two fiefdoms and each

group nominated their own "baron" to rule the fiefdom; one baron ran operations and the other ran finance and marketing.

3. Perks and fringe benefits were allocated in an inconsistent and haphazard manner without any apparent reason.

4. The company had become a welfare department for the various relatives, associates, and friends of members of the two shareholder groups. Jobs and fringe benefits were dispensed without the company deriving any perceptible benefit.

5. Conventional management practices necessary to ensure operational and financial control were scarce; there were virtually no policies and procedures on expense reports, purchase requisitions, or department budgets, nor standards of performance for any of the sales or operating personnel.

6. The company had no marketing plan nor a concept of how one should be formulated. The company had been so successful in its core business for so long that the customers had literally built a path to its door. Thus when the business declined, the company had no clue as to how to stimulate or expand its customer base.

7. As the company fortune deteriorated, the company borrowed heavily to sustain the lifestyle of its shareholders and management, using its property and business assets as collateral. The heavy borrowing created a debt service requirement that the company was not able to satisfy without further borrowing. The company borrowed to the extent that no further credit would be extended by the financial institutions.

Strains on the company developed when the industry in which the company's core business participated entered a period of decline and the profits that had supported these practices dried up. One of the shareholder groups decided that the other was responsible for the demise of the company and managed to oust them from their management positions and, in the process, to terminate their incomes and fringe benefits.

The company was in adversity stage E (about to fail) when we became involved. In addition, the enmity between the two shareholder groups was high, preventing any type of coordinated effort to deal with the problems. The shareholder group that had been ousted from management was desperately trying to regain its position in order that its members might derive an income; the shareholder group that had done the ousting was just as determined that the ousted group would not be returned to any position of authority or responsibility in the corporation.

The following second-order change principles were applied to the situation to create the necessary conditions for the company's survival.

In order to resolve the issue of enmity and lack of trust that paralyzed the two shareholder groups (which was a consequence of previous "more of the same" behavior), independent professional management that reported to a board of directors was recruited and installed. This board of directors consisted of three members: one from each of the shareholder groups and an independent, prominent businessman, who was known and respected by the other two directors and the new chief executive.

To resolve the insider transactions that were detrimental to the profitability of the corporation, it was insisted that they be competitive with outside services that the company could purchase. No attempt was made to justify or criticize their creation from a historical perspective. Their existence was accepted and dealt with on a "here and now" basis.

Efforts were made to sell the company's development projects in order to terminate the negative cash flow from these operations. When these efforts proved unsuccessful, because the secured lender would not accept the terms that the proposed buyer had offered, the property was abandoned. This action was viewed by the lender and certain parties in interest as "illogical and certainly unexpected." However, it succeeded in capping the company's total potential loss, terminating cash drain and allowing management to focus all of its energies on growing its core business.

In order to ensure that the shareholders would not interfere with newly hired professional management, it was agreed that no shareholders would be directly employed by the corporation in either a management or a nonmanagement position. Their involvement was restricted to that of independent consultants. Their participation in the earnings of the corporation was "reframed" from salary and fringe benefits to consulting fees and dividends.

In addition to these actions, a new marketing program was devised and implemented, which substantially improved both the market size and the company's market share. The company also implemented the operating and financial controls that had been ignored.

As a result of these actions, the company soon became profitable, and the yearly loss of several hundred thousand dollars was converted to a substantial yearly profit. In this particular situation, the turnaround was accomplished in less than a year. Such is the power of second-order change.

THE RIGHT PLACE AT THE RIGHT TIME: BUSINESS TYPES

Businesses that have been profitable in the past and project profits into the future are successful because they have done two things very well. First, they have developed products and services that can be delivered to their market under terms and conditions that are consistent with the industry, environment, and economy in which the firm and its customer base operate. Second, they maintain a culture that fosters innovation, entrepreneurship, and market orientation, so that the products and services they develop anticipate and accommodate changes in the industry, environment, and economy. Peters and Waterman's *In Search of Excellence* and Clifford and Cavanaugh's *The Winning Performance* describe the characteristics of such firms and how they have achieved profitable growth.

Firms that are not able to report successful performance consistently exhibit a mismatch with the present environment, the future environment, or both. The situation is illustrated in Figure 8.1, which shows four types of companies categorized by their fit with both the present and the future environments. Figure 8.2 shows generalized historical and projected profit performance for the four cases defined in Figure 8.1.

Case I: Harmony and Continuity

The firm's strategy is adjusted to its present environment, which accounts for its sound economic performance. The future is an evolutionary and predictable manifestation of the present, which the firm will achieve in a gradual manner. A company's harmonious fit to both the present and the future environments is most easily achieved during periods of economic growth, stable technology, and relative tranquility in the marketplace.

A case I company achieves its future by extrapolation. It is apparent that the company has been successful in the past, and its profit plan indicates that it will be successful in the future. The case I company ensures its future through first-order changes—more of the same—and

How firm fits to existing environment

		Good	Bad
		CASE I	CASE II
How firm fits to projected future environment	Good	Strategy: Harmony & Continuity	Strategy: Adjustment
	Bad	CASE III Strategy: Transformation & Reorientation	CASE IV Strategy: Turnaround or Liquidation

FIGURE 8.1. Classification of companies according to how well their strategy fits with the environment.

this is one situation in which first-order change works. It involves very limited risk, and the results are predictable. Many of the companies discussed in *In Search of Excellence* and *The Winning Performance* are case I companies.

Case II: Temporary Misfit

The firm is not well adjusted to its present market situation, which results in its immediate unsatisfactory performance. However, it is anticipated that the future will be different from the present situation, and the firm is prepared, ready, and expected to achieve rich awards when this happens.

The company has been losing money, but it is projected to be profitable at some time in the future. Such a situation is typical for a new business. During the start-up phase of the business sales are low, expenses are high, and the firm is investing significantly in creating market awareness, building a customer base, and learning how to "do business." Losses are substantial but expected.

However, the firm has a business plan that predicts breaking even at some future point in time and ultimately being profitable. Another situation typical of case II is when a firm makes a substantial investment in the present (causing cash drain and high interest expense) so that its products and services will be available to meet an anticipated future market. This

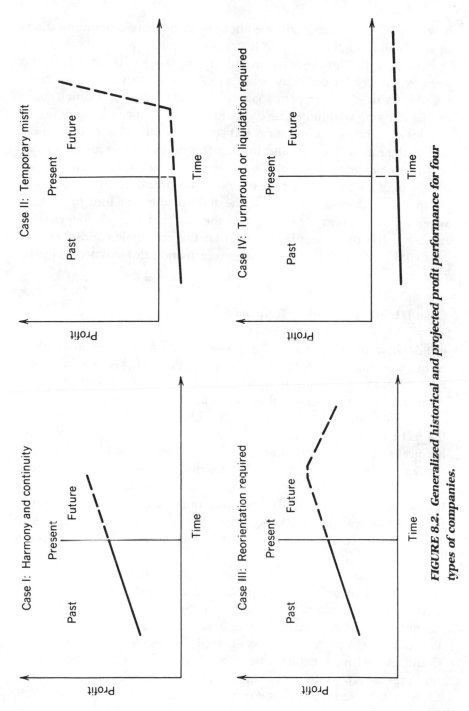

FIGURE 8.2. Generalized historical and projected profit performance for four types of companies.

117

is what MCI did when it invested in long-distance telecommunications in anticipation of changes in industry regulation.

Predicting the future is hazardous. There is a saying that "he who lives by the crystal ball must learn to eat glass," to which businesses should pay heed. A company that places itself in case II condition could be just thinking wishfully. The company could be experiencing difficulty and losses because the products and services it offers have come to the end of their growth cycle, and the falloff in demand has resulted in an extremely competitive market environment. During the past several years a number of go-go markets have fizzled quite abruptly, namely, personal computers and video games. At the time of the first hint of decline, when the companies were accepting the fact that they no longer were in case I, the prevailing belief was that the economic conditions that created the initial market would soon return and sales and profits would return.

Case III: Reorientation Required

In this situation the firm is well adjusted to its present environment and turns in profitable performance. However, the management foresees a hostile future resulting from technological, regulatory, demographic, or competitive changes that will preclude its continued profitability.

The company's history has been good, but management is aware of the fact that either technological or market changes are going to cause its profits to erode. A typical case III candidate would be a company that has enjoyed a dominant market position for many years and is faced with the anticipated entry of a major, well-financed company into its traditional market. A case III company must reorient its activities and resources to create products and services that will fare better in the future than those presently being marketed; if they do not, they will have no future.

Reorientation is a common business practice. Many organizations have reoriented or are in the process of reorienting their operations. General Electric shifted from traditional electric products to high technology, such as computer services and factory automation. Sears and Roebuck and American Express entered the financial services market. Gould moved from battery operations, which were the foundation of the corporation, to the production and selling of electronic equipment. Cincinnati Milacron reoriented from metal vendor to supplier of robotic technology.

These companies have obviously concluded that the environments in which they operated did not provide a future with sufficient prospects for growth and profitability. Therefore they decided to reallocate their assets and pursue products and markets that appeared to be more profitable. Obviously, a discontinuity will occur between the present and future states of such a firm, and that discontinuity presents a challenge to the company's management.

Case IV: Turnaround or Liquidation Required

The firm in this case is misaligned with its present environment; its performance can range from mediocre to poor. What is more, the firm cannot project that anything will change in the future to pull it out of the morass in which it is stuck. The travails of large firms that have plunged to this level of dispair are usually reported extensively in the nation's business press. In the period from 1980 through 1987 the dramatic efforts to attempt to salvage Chrysler, International Harvester, AM International, Wickes, Western Union, and others were well chronicled.

In case IV, the company has been unprofitable in the past and is expected to be unprofitable in the future. A case IV company is qualitatively different from a case II company; both companies must make some adjustments to continue to survive in their present. However, the case II company, while incurring losses, is still financially healthy (that is, in the early stage of adversity) and appears to have a future, which is a crucial asset when you have to talk to bankers, investment bankers, and venture capitalists about money. Many a company that was reporting huge current losses has been able to raise substantial debt and equity financing based on a plan that showed that the company had a very bright future.

Although both case II and case IV companies must make changes if they are to have a future, the case II company can point with pride at a successful past and present, which will substantially enhance the stature and credibility of the management as it seeks the funds and support to carry out its plan. A case IV company, on the other hand, has experienced such large losses that its very survival may be at stake if improvements in its operations are not made swiftly. A case IV company is operating in the later stages of adversity where a liquidity crisis and failure are no longer remote possibilities.

Case II, III, and IV companies must all deal with the same issue: how to convert themselves to a case I company in the future. It is clear that if they do nothing (zero-order change) or more of the same (first-order change), then a metamorphosis to a case I company will probably not occur. Clearly, each type of firm wants to transform itself into a firm that will exhibit predictable and stable growth in sales and earnings and command a high price for its equity. Such a conversion can only occur through second-order change.

THE CATCH-22 PROBLEM OF THE CEO

You may remember the movie "Catch-22," based on the book of the same name. It was, quite simply, the story of men in a bomber squadron at war, and particularly the story of Yossarian, a captain in the squadron and bombardier. It is this character from Joseph Heller's book who introduces the concepts of the Catch-22.

> There was only one catch and that was Catch-22, which specified that a concern for one's own safety in the face of dangers that were real and immediate was the process of a rational mind. Orr was crazy and could be grounded. All he had to do was ask; and as soon as he did, he would no longer be crazy and would have to fly more missions . . . If he flew them he was crazy and didn't have to; but if he didn't want to he was sane and had to.

The term "Catch-22" has become a popular representation of the double-bind, the "damned if you do, damned if you don't" dilemma which seems to be so much a part of life.

The chief executive of the troubled company is much like Yossarian in Heller's book. If he is out of touch with reality (that is, crazy) he will not realize that he needs help, and he will not ask for it. On the other hand, suppose he got through denial, he recognizes that his business is in trouble, and he is in touch with reality. The enormity of his problems may overwhelm him to the extent that he becomes depressed and anxious, and as a result of the depression and anxiety, he may be too immobilized to seek help. Thus the Catch-22.

As we discussed in previous chapters, the chief executive of the distressed company will likely be suffering from either anxiety or depression. The anxiety will arise from the threats that he perceives and from his belief that he will not be able to cope successfully with these new and dangerous situations. The depression will arise from his overwhelming feeling that he has lost, or is losing, something of great value, that he is responsible for the loss, and that he is helpless to do anything about it.

An anxious or depressed executive is hardly in the proper frame of mind to deal with the situations that a distressed business demands. A business that runs smoothly requires competent executive talent; a troubled company requires a superbusinessperson to keep it afloat, irrespective of its size, product, and market. Unfortunately the anxious and depressed executive is anything but a superbusinessperson. He will be hardpressed to cope with the myriad of demands that are being placed upon him. He has to learn a whole new set of skills: how to deal with creditors, how to husband cash, how to placate his bankers, what to say to disgruntled employees who are about to bolt the business. These are skills which he may never have used, and he must learn and perform them at a time when he is psychologically a shadow of the competent executive he once was.

Unfortunately his options in times of crisis are limited. The time frame in which business problems must be addressed and properly solved is measured in days, weeks, and months, while the time it may take an anxious and depressed executive to achieve a psychological condition in which he can function competently and cope with the demands of the business is measured in months and years.

As we discuss later, the management skills associated with insolvency and turnaround are unique and take years to develop. A typical experienced turnaround manager will have worked with as many as 25 companies at a minimum, and may have worked with as many as 100—in different industries, locations, and so forth. Not even the best and the brightest superbusinessperson is going to develop those skills in the pressure cooker of his own company's demise. In addition, a failing company does not permit learning through trial and error. You make a decision and there is no turning back. A wrong decision may mean not only the ball game, but the team. The chief executive who tries to learn the turnaround business using his own company as a "test case" courts disaster.

Simple solutions are appealing, and the executive heading a distressed business would love to think he can still be the savior of his company—all on his own. The flurry of books and articles outlining 10 easy steps to turn around your own company support that myth and perpetuate the problem—and the executive's sense of failure. If he could have, he would have done so already. There is a time when the best thing he can do for his company is to get outside help.

So there you have it: another catch-22 dilemma for the chief executive. He knows that changes must be made, but he doesn't know what to do. He doesn't have the time to learn what to do; and he doesn't have the mental and, perhaps, physical ability to cope. If he is fully aware of reality, he realizes that when it comes to digging his company out of its morass he "doesn't know what he doesn't know." Unfortunately he alone is in the position of power to make the decisions that will either save or bury his company. Jean-Paul Sartre's comments about man being in a perpetual state of anxiety, desperation, and loneliness become very meaningful to the chief executive of a failing company. As bleak as the situation is, and as frustrating as the catch-22 dilemma may appear, there is a way for the chief executive to effectively deal with his problem. How this is accomplished is discussed in the next section of this chapter.

CREATING THE CLIMATE FOR CHANGE

There are many lessons from the psychological sciences that can be valuable in the business world, especially in coping with business problems. In the book *Own Your Own Life*, Gary Emery deals with the methods that an individual can use to become independent. He introduces the three-step formula ACT, which is an acronym for

1. Accept reality

2. Choose to be independent

3. Take action

The formula is used repeatedly in the book to show how an individual, no matter how anxious, depressed, rich, poor, happy, or unhappy, can effect changes in his life and move from a situation of being highly dependent on others toward being independent, in charge of his own life.

We will modify this formula somewhat to create a climate in which the chief executive can resolve his catch-22 conflict and help bring about the changes his company desperately needs. Our ACT formula will stand for the following:

1. Accept reality

2. Choose to effect a second-order change

3. Take action to retain a change agent

Acceptance

Acceptance is not merely knowing something in a passive way: "I know my company is in trouble." It is rather a complete insight and understanding of the gestalt of a situation. Usually it is the final stage of an understanding reached by proceeding through the stages of grief. These stages are nonawareness, denial, anger, depression, anxiety, and finally acceptance. The typical reaction of a chief executive as he moves through the stages of acceptance is shown in Table 8.1. Psychologists have found that individuals exhibit considerable differences in the speed in which they move through the stages, or get stuck at any one stage. The length of stay in any one stage is a function of the extent to which the individual will distort reality; the greater the distortion, the longer the stay.

Achieving acceptance is the first step in being able to take effective action that will result in a change. As Gary Emery says, "You have to accept the fact that you have a flat tire before you can fix it."

We discussed the various stages of nonacceptance earlier in this book. Now we'll focus on some common manifestations of these stages that

---

TABLE 8.1. REACTIONS DURING STAGES OF ACCEPTANCE

Stage 1: Nonawareness
"We don't have a problem."
Stage 2: Denial
"We are merely suffering from a temporary cash flow problem."
Stage 3: Anger
"We could get out of this mess if only the bank would be reasonable."
Stage 4: Depression
"I don't see any way out of our cash bind; I really screwed up."
Stage 5: Anxiety
"What will we do if the vendors start to cut back on our credit, or if the bank won't renew our line of credit?"
Stage 6: Acceptance
"It is clear that what we've been doing hasn't worked and we need help."

prevent many chief executives from achieving acceptance, namely, rationalizing and explaining, blaming, guilt, and shame.

Moving Past Blame and Guilt to Action

When we blame others for causing a situation that we do not like, we attempt to shift the responsibility for that event from ourselves to them. Our entire legal system is concerned with the assessment of blame and the determination of monetary damages that should be associated with the blame.

Blaming someone or something for causing an event may be a natural human reaction, but in the case of companies suffering from financial distress, it is about as productive as Captain Queeg's search for the "strawberry thief" in *The Caine Mutiny*.

The key issue facing a business in trouble is *what can be done now*, not who caused the problem. The only thing that blaming accomplishes is to let off steam and vent frustration. Once the finger pointing and the tirade of anger are over, bad feelings and adversaries invariably remain where cooperative effort and allies are needed.

In any case of business distress or failure, the state of crisis is the result of a number of contributing factors. All of the members of the company's world—from creditors to employees—have been a part of what has brought the company to its deathbed. It can even be argued that everyone who denied the company's problem actually participated in its present distress.

This is not a comfortable thought. For example, a bank, holding a bad loan, may be quick to accuse the business of failing to meet its obligations, but that bank may also have contributed to the level of liability the business now faces by loaning money without adequate tracking. Did the bank require adequate financial statements, or did the bank join the cycle of denial and incompetence by pretending that there was nothing wrong? The process of posing and attempting to answer these questions does not contribute to the survival of the business. Rather it distracts everyone involved from focusing on the real issue: how to keep the business alive and turn it around.

A business on the verge of collapse must have support and assistance to survive. A failed business is an unnecessary trauma for all involved.

A dead business pays no bills, employs no people, and produces no contribution to the community.

A chief executive who finds himself engulfed in a vicious cycle of accusation and blame should recognize that he has two choices. He can keep his resentments, angers, vindictiveness, blame, and so forth functioning; or he can choose to be forgiving of all those who might have played a part in the company's demise. To the extent that he can be forgiving, he hastens his progress from nonacceptance to acceptance, and he is then able to work seriously on the survival of his business.

Rationalization and explanation are typical reactions of executives who find themselves in a financial morass. These behaviors can be viewed as defense mechanisms, invoked to help the individual deal with painful realizations and feelings of guilt and shame. Why did this happen? How could this have happened? Look at everything we did to prevent this from happening!

Understanding what has been tried and hasn't worked is far more important than attempting to understand why. The pursuit of why is itself a frustrating effort. There is usually no complete and satisfying explanation for everything that goes wrong in a business or program. Hypotheses can be posed and explored, and at best, after a long investigation, it might be possible to offer a plausible explanation. To the extent that valuable management effort is expended in wallowing in past failures, that effort and time are not available to deal with the issue of the present—namely, What do we do now?

The chief executive of the distressed company must realize that he simply does not have time to enter psychoanalysis either with or without a therapist. He must recognize that the endless rumination and mental reconstruction of all of the events that brought him to this stage merely keep him from acceptance and a new beginning. Understanding, recognizing, and frankly admitting mistakes in judgment and execution is valuable from the standpoint of a learning experience and becoming a better manager, but it will not change anything in the here and now. Change can only start to occur after the executive achieves acceptance of his present situation. Explaining and rationalizing the past is a block to that acceptance.

It is common for a chief executive of a distressed company to be overcome with feelings of guilt. I did it! How could I have done it? I can't live with this knowledge.

The essence of guilt, whether major or minor, is moral self-reproach. I did wrong when it was possible for me to do otherwise. Guilt always carries the implication of choice and responsibility, whether or not we are consciously aware of it.

                                                        Nathaniel Branden

Another feeling that frequently accompanies guilt is shame. Whereas we feel guilty when we believe we have broken our own moral code, we feel ashamed when we believe others are judging us as weak, childish, foolish, irresponsible, or because of something we've done. In many ways, guilt and shame are two sides of the same coin.

Businesspersons who are experiencing a financial crisis frequently experience shame over their inability to pay their bills or to live up to their contractual commitments. The feeling of shame occurs when you think others judge you to be immature, weak, inferior, immoral, irrational, and so forth because of your present financial situation. In fact, some people whom you value will indeed judge you in such a manner; a percentage will be empathetic and judge you in a benevolent manner; and the largest percentage frankly won't judge you one way or another, they will simply not invest any emotional or intellectual energy into your situation.

In order to overcome feelings of shame, psychologists recommend adopting an "anti-shame philosophy" and openly acknowledge (rather than conceal) that you are in a financial mess, and that you have some culpability for having created it. Pursuing this "full disclosure" policy will ultimately diminish the tendency to feel counterproductive shame.

Feelings of guilt and shame are both pitfalls on the way to acceptance and creating a climate for change. If the company is to go forward, it is critical that the chief executive avoid these pitfalls or at least minimize the amount of time he spends in them.

Branden, Emery, Beck, and Burns have written about the problems of guilt and how to overcome them. Some of their suggestions are summarized here.

1. Examine your thinking about the matter and ask yourself, "Am I totally responsible for the things that happened?" Try realistically to assess your portion of the responsibility for the situation—is it 100 percent or a smaller amount? (Gary Emery recommends using

a pie chart to depict how the responsibility for an event should be divided.) But whatever percentage of responsibility is appropriate to your action, accept it, acknowledge it, and be fully aware of it.

2. Do what you can to mitigate the damage or make amends to those who have suffered because of your failure. You may assign yourself a good slice of the responsibility for what happened; but is there anything you can do *now* to improve the situation? If so, do it.

3. Recognize that you have two options: you can accept the fact that you are an imperfect human being and therefore there will be times you will make inappropriate decisions because you do not have all the facts or do not possess the capability to properly evaluate the facts, or you can hate yourself every time you do something "wrong." Sometimes we do dumb things because we do not know what we need to know to do the smart things. There are times that we will fail because we do not have, or cannot get, the resources we need to succeed. A perfectionist outlook implies that we can be all-knowing, all-powerful, and are capable of following rigid rules of behavior.

4. Accept the fact that if you actually have done something that is inconsistent with your image of yourself, feeling guilty will not change anything or reverse the blunder in any magical way. Feeling guilty merely diverts your focus and energy from doing what is necessary to improve your situation from this point forward.

Choose to Make a Change

Step 2 of the ACT formula is: choose to effect a second-order change. The saying goes, "You can't control the cards you're dealt, but you can decide how to play them." The reality of your present situation is "the cards you've been dealt." You cannot change the cards; they are what they are. But you do have a choice in how you play them. In fact, you have three choices that can be made.

Choice 1: Do nothing, effect a zero-order change. Let the "chips fall where they may." Stop every night at the church, temple, or mosque of your choice and offer up a prayer to the appropriate diety. Turn the problem over to God.

Choice 2:   Try to solve the problem by doing better than you've been doing. Try cutting expenses by firing a secretary or two, cut back on the maintenance schedule, eliminate free coffee, divide the tablets in half, break the pencils in two and sharpen both ends, recycle the adding machine tape, monitor all long-distance telephone calls. Ask for new ideas from your staff; ask your bank, customers, vendors, IRS agent, and so forth for more concessions. Plead with your employees to work harder and faster, to take fewer breaks, to hold their paychecks over the weekend. In short, rearrange the deck chairs on your Titanic.

Choice 3:   Decide that what you have been doing doesn't work, and recognize that it is extremely unlikely that the skill, knowledge, and experience required to save your business resides in the closed system of yourself, your employees, and your professional advisor. The only rational course of action is to recruit a change agent from outside your present sphere of stakeholders.

This list of alternatives may not seem very attractive. In fact, it may cause you anxiety, and that is understandable. But having read this book as far as you have, you are in a far better position to make such a choice than most other chief executives of distressed businesses. At least you have some appreciation for how you got into this predicament and why you have not been able to extricate yourself to date.

Life is a series of choices. Sometimes we make good choices and we win the brass ring; sometimes we make bad or no choices and we go down to ignominious defeat and heartache. As chief executive you cannot escape the fact that you are responsible for making the key choices in the business, and you will be held accountable for the results. This realization may frighten you; however, your fear may begin to fade once you make your decision and begin to act.

THE NEED FOR A CHANGE AGENT

Everything takes time. To change thinking processes which have been thrown askew by stress is no easy, quick task. It takes time—an atmosphere of reduced stress is needed for the mind to get back on track.

In a troubled business, time is the rarest commodity of all—it is even more valuable than money. There isn't time for the executive to recover from the effects of overstress that have reduced his ability to manage effectively. Crises keep coming at him from every direction. Decisions need to be made. He may have neither the support of business colleagues nor that of friends. There is no safe path back to reality.

Even if the troubled business is not yet on the brink of disaster, it is still often a closed system from which it does not seem possible to form new solutions. The business keeps doing the same thing, over and over, which got it into trouble in the first place. As a result, no change takes place.

For the business to get past this impasse, there must be a change agent who can create a new way of operating for the company—someone who does not have the same mental framework as the executive managing the business. This is the role of the turnaround manager in a troubled business. What the business needs is someone in control who can make decisions—new decisions, not variations of past decisions. The turnaround manager, as the change agent, can apply second-order change to get the company back on the road to health.

The third step in the ACT formula is to recruit a change agent. To finish creating the climate for change you have to put your acceptance of the situation and your choice to effect a second-order change into practice. You have to find the person or persons that can function as change agents.

To use a medical analogy, if, after a series of diagnoses, you accepted the fact that you were suffering from a serious and potentially terminal disease, and you had made the choice to seek treatment, you would still have to find an experienced and competent doctor to treat you, and you would need to follow the treatment plan prescribed. To do otherwise would put your health—and perhaps your life—at risk. Similarly, failing to recruit a change agent will put the health of your business—and perhaps its very existence—at risk.

9 | HELP IS NOT A FOUR-LETTER WORD: HIRING A TURNAROUND CONSULTANT

A leader is best
When people barely know that he exists,
Not so good when people obey and acclaim him,
Worst when they despise him.
Fail to honor people,
They fail to honor you;
But of a good leader, who talks little,
When his work is done, his aim fulfilled,
They will all say, "We did this ourselves."

LAO-TZU

A business in distress is a business in the midst of a crisis. Once the decision is made that the company needs outside help, there still remains the problem of how to find that help. This is an emergency, and there is no time to lose.

Now a turnaround manager can be of lifesaving assistance to the business. A turnaround manager is a specialist whose skills and experience provide the resources to effect change. Like an emergency room physician, he or she must quickly assess the damage, prioritize the necessary actions, stop the bleeding, and stabilize the "patient." For a business in the grip of a life-threatening illness there is no ambulance to call, no emergency room prepared and waiting. At the point when the passage of each day may mean losses that can make the difference between continued life or imminent death of the company, it is important to know what to look for in a turnaround manager.

In this and the following chapters, we frequently use the terms "turnaround managers" and "turnaround consultants." While these terms are often used interchangeably, our intent is to distinguish them as follows. A turnaround manager is an executive who assumes the responsibility and is accountable for both directing and leading a turnaround effort. A turnaround consultant is a management consultant who specializes in the area of turnarounds; turnaround managers are, of course, frequently recruited from the ranks of turnaround consultants.

The purpose of this chapter is to provide some guidelines to assist the business in finding the help it so badly needs. We will suggest ways to evaluate whether the help is right for the business, and offer some insight into what makes a turnaround consultant different from other management consultants.

Before we discuss the unique qualities of the turnaround consultant, however, we take a look at the fears people have about consultants, and we provide an overview of the management consultant field in general.

A MULTITUDE OF FEARS: WHY PEOPLE AVOID HIRING CONSULTANTS

Before we look specifically at the tasks and talents of the turnaround consultant, it is important to understand the common fears that many people harbor toward hiring any kind of management consultant.

Many businesses are reluctant to seek help, even when it is obvious that the right help would improve things. Part of this reluctance may be due to a lack of confidence in finding the "right" help, and a fear that in hiring someone to help they may only end up with another liability.

A survey conducted by Krentzman and Samaras among 700 managers of small companies located across the country offers some insight into the common fears about hiring consultants. The survey inquired about the managers' experiences with consultants and probed their apprehensions as to the usefulness of outside help. Their analysis classified the concerns of business people into seven categories: fears relating to fees, failure, hiring the wrong person, disclosure, wasting time, lack of specific experience of the consultant, and fear of consultants in general.

Although the survey on which these results are based was conducted a number of years ago, it is as timely now as it was then. We hear expressions of the same fears from prospective and ongoing clients. Interestingly in spite of the fears about hiring consultant help, the survey showed that when the respondents had used consultants, they reported being satisfied with the results in 81 percent of the cases. Where respondents indicated that they would like to use consultants, they reported that they were not sure where to find one, how to evaluate one, how to use one, and what yardstick to hold to a consultant's performance.

MANAGEMENT CONSULTING: AN OVERVIEW OF THE FIELD

Part of the reluctance to hire management consultants stems from the considerable confusion that exists about what management consultants are and what they do. The title management consultant has come to be used as an umbrella term, covering almost any range of consultant services offered to a business.

> Management consulting is an advisory service contracted for and provided to organizations by specially trained and qualified persons who assist, in an objective and independent manner, the client organization to identify management problems, analyze such problems, recommend solutions to these problems, and help, when requested, in the implementation of solutions.
>
> L. E. Greiner and R. O. Metzger

ROLES AND TASKS OF THE MANAGEMENT CONSULTANT

The principal reasons for hiring consultants, given by clients who frequently use management consultants, fall into five broad categories:

1. Reduce uncertainty

2. Provide independent and unbiased judgment

3. Present new, creative ideas and a fresh approach to problems

4. Facilitate the process of diagnosing and solving problems

5. Act as a resource for information and perform tasks of a nature for which the organization does not have the capability

Everything Is Under Control: Reducing Uncertainty

One of the most valuable things a professional service firm has to offer its clients, whether it be a legal firm, an accounting firm, or a management consulting firm, is the minimization of uncertainty. The potential client is seeking peace of mind, confidence, and a reduced level of anxiety. The professional service organization, in addition to the actual services offered, holds the promise of producing more certainty in an area where the client feels uncertain and anxious.

A client's uncertainty has three sources. First, there is the basic uncertainty of not knowing with whom to deal, and on whom to rely. The client who desires to obtain professional assistance in diagnosing a business problem is faced with the problem of where to get it. Second, there is the uncertainty as to whether the anticipated cost of the consulting advice is justified by the value of that advice. Finally, there is the uncertainty associated with the problem itself: does the problem arise from marketing, financial, engineering, strategic, or personnel aspects?

A professional management consulting firm should be able to quickly determine whether it has personnel with the experience and skills to address the client's problem, estimate the size of the fees, and suggest several possible approaches to the problem.

The Outside Vantage Point: Providing Independent, Objective, and Unbiased Judgment

Management consultants who have no prior relationship with the principals, being unbiased and unprejudiced by the way things have been done in the past, can bring to the company the benefit of outside objectivity. Management consulting is, by its nature, an independent service. A professional consultant makes his own assessment of any situation and recommends, frankly and objectively, the proposed actions for the client and his organization, without any regard as to how these recommendations might affect the consultant's own interest. The detachment of the consultant is vital to his effectiveness. It is this detachment and independence that makes the consultant so uniquely valuable to the client, since the consultant is the one person to whom the client can talk and from whom the client can obtain competent and unbiased advice.

For a consultant to be effective, he must be independent in all of the following aspects of the business:

1. He must be financially independent in that he has no pecuniary interest in the action taken by the client.

2. He must be administratively independent in that he is not subordinate to the client, and cannot be affected by the client's administrative decisions.

3. He must be politically independent so that neither the client's management nor employees can influence him informally through social club memberships, political organizations, and so forth.

4. He must be emotionally independent in that he preserves his detachment irrespective of friendship with the client, and of other ties that may exist at the beginning or develop during the course of an assignment.

As a direct consequence of this independence, the management consultant is free to challenge sacred cows that other members of the organization have left unmolested. Many times the mere questioning of a previously sacrosanct subject has opened it to careful analysis and scrutiny, and sometimes even change. Frequently the open, direct, and piercing analysis by a consultant will challenge a chief executive to face up to problems or decisions that were considered too sensitive and emotion-laden to discuss.

The Creative Touch: Presenting New Ideas

Consultants are frequently the source of new ideas for the business because of the unique position they occupy in the business world.

> An individual becomes a management consultant by assimilating, through study and practical experience, considerable knowledge of varying management situations and by acquiring skills needed for problem solving and sharing experience with others: for identifying problems, finding relevant information, analysing and synthesising, developing proposals for improvement, communicating with people, planning changes, overcoming resistance to change, helping clients to learn from experience, transferring management techniques between countries, and so on.
>
> Milan Kubr

Over the years, as management consultants pass through many organizations in different industries and different locations, they learn how to use experience from previous assignments to help their clients deal with new situations. Consultants are exposed to varying circumstances and learn how to integrate their specific experiences into general trends and common causes of problems. They keep abreast of the management literature, of developments in management concepts, systems, procedures, and policies, and they apply their new-found knowledge to the business situations that they encounter.

Compare their experience to that of most corporate executives whose careers may have been limited to very few businesses, in one industry—and in some cases only one company. Their understanding of business is obviously limited by their own restricted experience. In addition, it is a rare executive who even attempts to stay abreast of developments in management theory and practice, much less to apply a new concept to his particular business situation. Executives have other concerns of a higher priority in the day-to-day operation of the business.

The Catalyst: Facilitating the Process of Diagnosing and Solving Problems

Consultants are frequently retained to facilitate the process of solving a problem, rather than just to solve the problem by themselves. Situations in which consultants are retained to facilitate problem solving are those where the size and scope of the problem cannot be defined, when the problem is unique and does not fall within the experience of the company or the consultant, or when the company and the problem involve as yet unidentified unknowns.

The consultant as an agent of change acts as a sort of business therapist, making the organization aware of its problems and soliciting its ideas for dealing with these problems. He employs intervention techniques and uses group dynamics to raise consciousness, stimulate thinking, and create consensus and commitment among the personnel. In addition, the consultant attempts to teach clients how to diagnose and solve similar problems in the future. The consultant's goal is to achieve a permanent improvement in the organization's effectiveness.

In the process role, the consultant refrains from promoting or imposing his own solutions. He is more concerned with passing on his approach, methods, and values so that the client organization has a substantial participation in the diagnosis and remedy of its problems. The behavior on the part of the process consultant is nondirective, since he acts on the basic assumption that far greater knowledge of the problem and its solution resides within the client than within himself, and that it is impractical for an outsider to attempt to absorb, analyze, and solve complex organization problems on restricted time schedules. Hence, the client must assume the major responsibility for problem identification, problem analysis, and solution formulation.

The First and Last Word: Acting as an Expert Resource

Greiner and Metzger have referred to the resource consultant as the General George Patton of the consulting profession, to distinguish him from the process consultants, who might be said to represent the Freudian side of consulting. The resource consultant provides technical expertise, and takes action for and on behalf of the client. He is highly directive and initiates specific actions to understand the client's problems. The resource consultant performs analyses, makes specific recommendations, and then undertakes to assist the client to implement these recommendations. He uses his technical and managerial expertise to supply information, perform studies, train staff, and design new systems, procedures, and policies.

The resource consultant, as a result of his education, breadth of experience, training, depth of knowledge, skill, and objectivity, is better able to diagnose and resolve problems than the client. The client is more skilled in running the business and producing a profit, but the consultant is substantially more competent to "fix" the organization so that the client can run it effectively.

THE SPECIAL ROLE OF THE TURNAROUND MANAGER

In the case of the business in distress, the tasks facing the turnaround manager are specific to the situation. We have discussed these steps in a descriptive sense in previous chapters. Now we look at the specific skills, qualities, and experiences that the turnaround consultant will need to carry out a program effectively.

The turnaround consultant is a specialist whose expertise allows him to intervene in the highly charged atmosphere of a business in distress and effect resolution in a timely fashion. What distinguishes the turnaround consultant from a traditional management consultant is the environment in which each works. A turnaround is usually performed in a high-stress crisis environment, which demands quick assessment and decisive action. Resources are low, tempers are high, and the clock is always ticking. There is no time or room for trial and error. This is no battleground for the inexperienced or unprepared.

> A traditional kind of professional manager is geared to grow something within a reasonably healthy environment, with adequate resources to get the job done. He is not used to negative forces working against him in an environment of shortages—shortages of money, shortages of products, shortages of cooperation, shortages of everything. That is an environment that most people really don't understand. They've never been there before.
>
> Donald B. Bibeault,
> interview with Frank Gristanti

There is a substantial difference in the qualities needed to be an effective turnaround manager. A good custodial manager builds his company by using a strategy of actions that are "more of the same." There is a progression and continuity to the future based upon what has been done in the past. People, strategies, tactics, policies, and procedures are changed incrementally under the direction of the custodial manager.

The turnaround manager, in contrast, must take the best aspects of the existing situation and be prepared to take drastic action to achieve the required objectives. The necessary changes will rarely be incremental. Small, progressive changes do not convert case II, III, and IV companies into a case I company.

In our discussion of the characteristics that you should look for in a turnaround consultant, we focus on those that you should be able to observe and discover, or verify through checking references. The "ideal" turnaround consultant is typified in various writings as a tough-minded, objective, self-confident, and self-aware individual. Some turnaround consultants fit the stereotype; others, who are just as competent and successful, do not. The right turnaround consultant for one company may not be the best choice for another.

With this in mind, we will turn our attention to three aspects of the turnaround consultant that are of critical importance: personality, skills, and experience.

The Personality of the Turnaround Leader

> They have learned how to identify sore spots. They aren't people-oriented; they're people users. They don't have a lot of friends, they are not social successes, they are just known as blood-and-guts guys. They are the George Pattons of the business world. Usually there is a lot of loner in them, too. They like to make decisions by themselves. They usually are very decisive—very, very decisive. This comes from a natural feel and lots of experience. I think there is less science to it and just a willingness to achieve results. They are very achievement-oriented people.
>
> Donald B. Bibeault,
> interview with Robert Brown

The following personality traits tend to characterize turnaround consultants and leaders.

Tough Minded

Successful turnaround leaders have the reputation for being tough. This assessment is probably accurate to some extent. A turnaround manager frequently has to make difficult decisions and take very unpopular actions, such as closing down divisions, cutting back salaries, laying off long-term loyal employees who are no longer effective, or filing a bankruptcy petition the day before a creditor's lien is scheduled to mature. These are not the types of actions that are going to win popularity with the affected parties.

However, tough minded does not mean that the turnaround consultant is abrasive, arbitrary, precipitous, or insensitive. If he has good negotiating and political skills, he will always take care to explain his actions and persuade those affected that the actions he has taken were necessary.

Action Oriented

Turnaround programs require prompt, decisive action, and because of that, the turnaround consultant is action oriented. He should be able to define exactly what information is required, and how that information will be evaluated in order to make a decision. Once the information is available, he will make a decision and take the appropriate action. A turnaround consultant is the antithesis of a procrastinator. If he makes a decision that does not work out as he planned, he will quickly make another to correct the situation. He knows how to prioritize his efforts, and focuses on the most critical activities first. He is like a lion on the prowl, stalking opportunities for making decisions, and then pouncing on the decision when the time is ripe.

Intelligence and Creativity

Turnarounds are difficult assignments from an intellectual perspective. They demand that the consultant analyze, synthesize, and innovate within tight time constraints. The consultant's challenge is similar to that of an NFL quarterback who gets the ball on his own 10-yard line, trailing by 6 points, with 30 seconds left in the game. There is not a lot of room for error.

The turnaround consultant will have to analyze every aspect of the business to determine where changes are necessary. He must be prepared to innovate. This means he may need to make changes in the equipment, policies, personnel, procedures, organizational structure, distribution outlets, strategy, or compensation of the company. Of necessity, the turnaround consultant must be a quick study, and have the intellectual assets that the demanding situation calls for.

Positive Attitude

The turnaround consultant must be optimistic that things will work out for the better, regardless of how desperate and hopeless the situation appears. This optimism is not designed merely to inspire the people in the company who are scared and are desperately looking for a savior. He must have confidence in what he is doing if he is to have any real chance of succeeding. This self-confidence and optimism will be evident to the stakeholders, who will mirror the tone set by the turnaround manager and continue to strive for the success of the plan.

This does not imply that the turnaround consultant is a Pollyanna or someone who overlooks negatives as a matter of form. The turnaround manager should always be realistic about the probabilities of success or failure. Being in touch with the reality of the situation should be one of his strong points. However, his self-confidence, drive, and optimism will spur him to reduce the probabilities of failure, increase the probabilities of success, and keep looking for better solutions.

Maturity, Status, and Appearance

Maturity in the turnaround manager is very important. The turnaround consultant must have sufficient depth and length of experience to feel confident in his decisions, and to know what the right decisions are, based upon testing them in real crisis situations. He must be able to convince others of his ability to provide reality-oriented solutions. The high-powered 30-year-old entrepreneur who has been fantastically successful may certainly be capable of launching another venture, but is rarely the most appropriate choice as a turnaround manager. An effective turnaround consultant should have 15 to 20 years experience in a variety of business environments. As when hiring a doctor to perform a delicate operation, you do not want to be the doctor's first, second, or third patient.

The Unique Skills of the Turnaround Manager

We now address those special skills that distinguish the turnaround consultant from the other consultants typically hired to accomplish specific functions in the company.

People Skills

> To me, effective consulting means convincing a client to take some action. But that is the tip of the iceberg. What supports that is establishing enough agreement within the organization that the action makes sense—in other words, not only getting the client to move, but getting enough support so that the movement will be successful. To do that, a consultant needs superb problem-solving techniques and the ability to persuade the client through the logic of his analysis. In addition, enough key players must be on the board, each with a stake in the solution, so that it will succeed. So the consultant needs to develop a process through which he can identify whom it is important to involve and how to interest them.
>
> Arthur N. Turner

One of the most difficult and pressing problems for the turnaround consultant is to determine quickly the strengths and weaknesses of the key management employees. He must then decide which employees can contribute to the organization and should remain, and which employees cannot make significant contributions and should be terminated. Employees that have been with the company for a long time know a lot about how things are done, and why they've been done that way.

Some may not be ideal for the positions they occupy, but in many situations, it may be too expensive, too risky, or too time consuming to replace them. Decisions about employees are difficult, and this is another area where the people skills of the turnaround consultant are essential.

The whole issue of people skills is critical to the turnaround manager. It is only through his persuasive communication, judgment of people, and ability to get them to trust him and have confidence in him that he is able to carry out his assignment.

Leadership Skills

> The turnaround man's job is to focus the organization on the right issues, provide the charisma, provide the leadership, and wedge everyone into an effective team that has a commonality of purpose. When he does this, he really becomes an energy force within the company.
>
> Donald B. Bibeault,
> interview with John Thompson

A good turnaround manager is able to transmit energy quite far down the organization. The turnaround consultant must have the leadership skills that are required to revitalize the company, and he must communicate that he does indeed possess these skills. He must be able to clearly state the mission of the organization, communicate that mission, articulate how all the stakeholders will benefit from achieving that mission, and express confidence that success is possible. He must imbue employees with a sense that the situation has changed, the company is now on course, and something positive is going to happen shortly.

Interviewing Skills

> For diagnosticians, the interview is the most effective method of data gathering because it enables the interviewer to engage in thinking, judgements and problem-solving abilities of the interviewee . . . most employees are diagnosticians, and, if two heads are better than one, why not twenty, or fifty—especially when many of the interviewees have an intimate knowledge of the company and its problems. Often they may also develop solutions or at least promising ideas for improvements. If prophets are without honor in their own countries, employees also go unheard in their own companies.
>
> John Quay

One of the ways that a turnaround manager diagnoses a company problem is to talk to the people involved. Someone once defined a consultant as someone who borrows your watch to tell you the time.

Although the image provides a chuckle, there is some truth in it. The turnaround consultant in a company may, in essence, do precisely that—because the person wearing the watch isn't even looking at it. In the interviewing process, the turnaround consultant can determine what knowledge is already present, but has not been evaluated.

The consultant must not only get the facts from managers and staff, but he must also learn about their opinions, attitudes, fears, prejudices, and concerns. He must discover the personnel, systems, and other underlying factors that may have caused the problems. He must also assess what it will take to remedy the company's problems. The employees and management of the company are the best source of this information. True, the consultant will have to evaluate, digest, consolidate, and test it, but first he has to obtain it. That is why excellent interviewing skills will be crucial. The more open and straightforward the responses from informed insiders are, the more accurate his diagnosis, and the more effective his recommendations will be.

The successful interviewer is skillful at establishing an atmosphere of mutual trust and rapport. In such an atmosphere, the interviewee will provide full and spontaneous responses, will not be defensive, and will volunteer information on sensitive matters that he thinks the consultant should know. In the best situation, the turnaround manager can reduce the interviewee's fear of reprisal from the management, so that the responses he gets will not be colored by that fear.

In a turnaround situation the people the consultant interviews may range from truck drivers to bank presidents, from janitors to executive vice presidents. Irrespective of the salary, position, or social station of the interviewee, it is imperative that the consultant establish effective rapport and trust.

Negotiating Skills

Any engagement's usefulness to an organization depends on the degree to which members reach accord on the nature of problems and opportunities and on appropriate corrective actions. Otherwise, the diagnosis won't be accepted, recommendations won't be implemented, and valid data may be withheld. To provide sound and convincing recommendations, a consultant must be persuasive and have finely tuned analytic skills. But more important is the ability to design and conduct a process for (1) building an agreement about what steps are necessary and (2) establishing the momentum to see steps through.

Arthur N. Turner

Extensive negotiating processes occur during a turnaround effort. It will be the turnaround manager's job to spearhead the efforts to gain acceptance for the proposed plan, negotiate any differences that may arise among the stakeholders, and build a consensus and commitment for the plan. To achieve this end, the turnaround consultant must be a skillful negotiator as well as an artful and persuasive politician.

The Experience Base of the Turnaround Manager

One of the most crucial qualities of a turnaround manager is his experience. It is important to know that he has seen your problem, or a variant thereof, in other situations, and that he has devised solutions to it in the past. He is a living compendium of all clients that he has worked with, regardless of whether these situations have had a successful outcome. In fact, a turnaround manager who has attempted to implement a particular strategy and found it unsuccessful will have learned to avoid that strategy in the future, or how to alter it to make it work the next time. It is to your benefit if he has had failures he has learned from.

A successful turnaround consultant will have had the following types of experience:

Entrepreneurial Experience

If he is going to be able to effectively empathize with the plights and problems of his clients, he should have, at one time in his past, been in an entrepreneurial situation where he personally experienced the anxiety, anguish, and loneliness of being in charge of an enterprise.

CEO Experience

If he is going to guide the enterprise from chaos to success, you don't want him learning with your money or with your business at risk. He should have, at some time in his past, been the owner or chief executive of an enterprise.

Insolvency Experience

Since all turnarounds occur on a playing field, the borders of which are established by the bankruptcy system, an effective turnaround manager must have had experience with the bankruptcy system, working with both debtors and creditors.

Operating Management Experience

If a turnaround consultant is to be effective in the implementation phase of the turnaround plan, it is essential that he have had broad experience in operations. If the majority of his career has been spent in staff assignments, or as an analyst or assistant, it is very unlikely that he will have developed the people skills that are essential to the successful implementation of a plan. Broad staff experience will be helpful in the diagnosis, planning, and negotiating aspects of the turnaround effort, but will not be of much use in the implementation phase. He must be used to having power and wielding it.

Turnaround Experience

You don't want your particular situation to be the one on which a new turnaround consultant cuts his teeth. You will want to know that he has had several turnaround experiences prior to the time that he starts work on your problem.

A Good Track Record

No turnaround consultant will have a 100 percent success rate with clients. There are many factors in determining the outcome of a turnaround, as is discussed in Chapter 13, and the turnaround consultant's skill cannot be evaluated on a win–loss basis. He may have worked his hardest and significantly helped a company that ultimately failed. You cannot expect a miracle-worker track record. What is important is that the consultant is aware of his success rate, understands why certain deals did not work out, and is candid about his past performance.

FINDING THE NEEDLE IN THE HAYSTACK: LOCATING A TURNAROUND CONSULTANT

Now comes the question: How do you find a turnaround manager to help with your business? There are a number of sources for finding the names of turnaround consultants.

Referral from Another Business

One way to find a turnaround consultant is to talk with executives in other companies, especially those who have gone through turnarounds. Review your list of business contacts and consider who might know where to find what you are looking for. If you're hesitant to call someone you know because you don't want them to think your business is in trouble, remember: it *is* in trouble, and chances are everyone else knows it. Getting help to get the company back on track is more likely to be viewed by others as a wise move than as an admission of failure. A word of mouth recommendation from someone you know will save you quite a bit of time in finding a consultant.

Referral from a Banker, an Attorney, or a CPA

The bankers on the staff of the workout departments of banks often know of, and work with, turnaround consultants. Bankruptcy attorneys also come in frequent contact with turnaround consultants. Both can provide names of experienced candidates for you to contact.

Your certified public accountant may know and have worked with turnaround consultants and might also give you some names.

Management Consultant Organizations

The following management consultant organizations may offer you a resource to find a good turnaround consultant:

The Institute of Management Consultants
19 West 44th Street
New York, NY 10036
Telephone: (212) 921-2885

Certifies the professional competence of individual consultants and smaller consulting firms.

Acme, Inc.
The Association of Management Consulting Firms
230 Park Avenue
New York, NY 10017
Telephone: (212) 697-9693

Certifies the professional competence of larger consulting firms.

Turnaround Managers Association
Post Office Box 2464
Chapel Hill, NC 27515-2464
Telephone: (919) 967-1724

Provides information about and referrals of the professionals providing turnaround management services.

INTERVIEWING AND EVALUATING THE CANDIDATES

Armed with an understanding of what a turnaround consultant does, and the attributes you should look for in consultants in general and turnaround consultants in particular, you are now in a position to evaluate the candidates you have identified.

Before we discuss the specific criteria that we recommend you consider when hiring a turnaround consultant, it is important that you appreciate just what is at stake. Once again, the medical analogy is applicable. Your company is sick. It has not responded to the tried and true remedies (more of the same), its pulse is irregular, it is running a high fever, and the various systems are starting to malfunction or collapse.

You need a specialist to carry out a delicate surgical procedure that will make the difference between life and death—and it must be done in time. You have identified a number of prominent specialists, and you are going to review their credentials and meet with them in order to make a selection. Considering this framework, the evaluation is not going to be a trivial task. You, as an owner of the business under siege, are faced with one of the riskiest decisions of your business career: that of selecting someone who will help you save your business. A friend, who is chief executive of a mid-sized bank, repeatedly tells his management that the riskiest decision a manager ever makes is when he hires someone into an executive position. Many management professionals agree.

. . . In the purchase of products, alternatives usually offer fractional advantages. Product A may be nine tenths as good as Product B. If A costs eight tenths as much as B and performance tolerance is sufficient, then A is preferable. Comparable options are not open in the hiring of a key executive (or a turnaround consultant). Even at a lower price, nine tenths as good as the best is like swimming nine tenths of the way across the

English Channel. The principles that ought to apply to the purchase of a personal service are those that apply to the hiring of a person; they are not the principles that apply to the purchase of a good . . .

Warren J. Wittreich

When evaluating candidates, we suggest you focus on the following criteria:

What You Know about the Candidate

1. Educational credentials

2. Experience

3. Skills, both those required of the general consultant and those required of the turnaround consultant

4. Track record and references

5. Independence

How You Feel about the Candidate

1. Personality

2. The extent to which he or she relieves your feelings of uncertainty and anxiety

The checklist in Table 9.1 is provided as a guideline to help you in the actual interviewing and evaluation of turnaround manager candidates.

Whom Is He Working for? The Issue of Independence

The turnaround consultant must be truly independent of all other pressures so that he can effectively work for you.

A problem of independence frequently arises due to the relationship between turnaround consultants and secured lenders. Since secured lenders always have a number of troubled loans in their portfolios, they develop relationships, over a period of time, with turnaround consultants whom they frequently recommend to their troubled credits.

TABLE 9.1. CHECKLIST FOR INTERVIEWING/EVALUATING TURNAROUND CONSULTANT CANDIDATE

EDUCATION

Undergraduate school/degree:

Graduate school/degree:

Other relevant studies:

EXPERIENCE

For each section, indicate (at least) whether the responsibility level was decision making, advisory, or assisting.

Insolvency Experience

Company	Responsibilities	Amount of Time
1.		
2.		
3.		

Additional questions (to determine personal empathy):

Has the turnaround consultant had any direct personal experience with insolvency/bankruptcy? (self, relative, friend, business associate)

Comments:

Turnaround Experience

Company	Responsibilities	Amount of Time
1.		
2.		
3.		

Comments:

Entrepreneurial Experience

Company	Responsibilities	Amount of Time
1.		
2.		
3.		

Comments:

(Table continues on p. 150.)

TABLE 9.1. *(Continued)*

CEO Experience

Company	Responsibilities	Amount of Time
1.		
2.		
3.		

Comments:

Operating Management Experience

Company	Responsibilities	Amount of Time
1.		
2.		
3.		

Comments:

PERSONALITY/EMOTIONAL FACTORS

This section is intended to help evaluate your emotional reaction and level of trust in the turnaround manager.

How do I feel about this person?

Do I trust this person?

Do I think he/she understands the problems of the business?

Do I think he/she can help the business?

Do I think other key people in the business will be able to work with this person?

TRACK RECORD/PRIOR PERFORMANCE

What is this turnaround manager's track record?

Number of companies helped: _____
   Number of successful turnarounds: _____
   Number still in progress: _____
   Number of failures: _____

Does the turnaround manager understand why the failures occurred?

TABLE 9.1.   (*Continued*)

INFORMATION FROM REFERENCES/OTHERS

The following section should be completed based on discussions with former clients and professionals who have worked with the turnaround manager.

Quality/Trait	Rating	(Extremely	Very	Somewhat	Not Very)
Tough minded (decisive):					
Action oriented:					
Intelligent:					
Creative:					
Honest:					
Positive (attitude):					
Persuasive:					
Good negotiating skills:					

INDEPENDENCE

What is the turnaround manager's relationship with:

1. The secured creditors (especially the bank) of the business?

2. The unsecured creditors of the business?

3. Anyone with whom the business is involved in litigation?

The senior loan officer of the secured lender will frequently say to the principal of the troubled company: "Look, we both realize that you are in over your head and you need help. You have asked us not to foreclose on the loan in default, and, in fact, you have asked us to extend additional credit. We might go along, *but* only if we get a warm fuzzy feeling about the prospects of the company, and right now our feeling is anything but warm and fuzzy. So I recommend that you hire a workout guy to take a look at your situation and tell us both what kind of trouble you're in, and how you might get out of it. Here are the names of three workout consultants whom we respect. I suggest you talk with them. Any one would be acceptable to us. Or, if you have another alternative, that is O.K. with us, but we would like to see his background."

The secured lender is saying: Get some professional help, tell us what is happening, give us a plan that makes sense to us and to an independent consultant, and maybe we'll go along with your request. However, the secured lender does not want to ever be in a position of telling you to hire Mr. X or listen to Mr. Y, since that could create a potential claim by you against the secured lender for "interfering with the management" of your business.

The names provided by the secured lender are probably very competent; however, their independence is a real issue. If any of the proposed candidates depends on the secured lender for a substantial portion of his business, it is clear that he will not meet the financial independence test. There is a real question as to whether he will pass the test even if he merely expects to get additional referrals in the future.

From the consultant's pecuniary perspective, you, the client, are a one-shot deal, but he expects to have a continuous relationship with the secured lender, regardless of the final outcome of your situation. Obviously, if the consultant is working on your problem with one eye on future referrals from the bank, he is not going to be an effective advocate for you in those matters in which you and the secured lender are adversaries.

I have personally wrestled with this inherent "conflict of interest" problem, since I am frequently referred into situations by certain banks. Moreover, I have been nominated by banks to serve as receiver and trustee in adversarial proceedings brought by the bank.

The way I have resolved this problem in my own practice is as follows. When I am referred into a situation by a secured lender, I advise the client at the first meeting that, if he chooses to retain me, he can rely on the fact that I will do the best I can to promote his interest.

However, I will insist upon full and prompt disclosure to the secured lender of every aspect of the business that I learn, and I will copy the secured lender on all my correspondence and reports to the client. My rationale for this approach is that as long as the bank is fully and promptly informed, senior management can make informed business decisons to protect their interest. Therefore, I am free to do the best I can do for the client, even to the extent that I promote a position that could be interpreted as being adverse to the bank's interest. The bank understands that my relationship with the client obligates me to strive for the best result for the client that I can professionally achieve. The client understands that as a result of the specific contract we have entered, the bank will receive full disclosure. That is the best that one can do in this situation.

Benefit from the Experience of Others: Check References

Talk to some existing clients and ex-clients to get referrals from those that felt he did a good job. What is more important is the direct communication between a previous or present client and you. That previous client has been in your spot, will have empathy with your situation, and will want you to benefit from his experience. Also, check with bankers and attorneys with whom the turnaround consultant has worked.

Feeling Comfortable: Pay Attention to Your Emotional Reactions

You may not like the surgeon who took out your appendix. Your optometrist may be arrogant and rude. Your dentist may keep you waiting for an hour and never apologize. Your auto mechanic may frequently try to put one over on you by selectively padding his bill. Your accountant may never return your phone calls.

Yet, you may continue to use the services of these professionals because you appreciate the fact that they are competent in their specific area of expertise and that they consistently resolve your problems.

However, your relationship with the turnaround consultant will have to be broader and deeper if it is to be wholly successful. It will be more like the relationship between a patient and a psychiatrist than the relationships between client and professional discussed above.

It is well recognized in psychotherapy that therapy will not work unless the patient believes in, and trusts, the therapist. The same can be said of the turnaround consultant. The client must, and will, come to rely upon the perceptions, judgment, insight, and analysis of the turnaround manager. In order for this to occur, your feeling for the consultant must be right.

You have to like him, respect him, and feel comfortable with him—and he must feel the same way about you. You should find your consultant a decent human being: sincere, warm, noncritical, and responsive in an emergency. During your interview with the consultant you will develop some instincts as to whether the two of you "click." If, for one reason or another, you decide that you don't like, can't trust, or feel uncomfortable with the turnaround consultant, pass on to the next candidate.

But before you do that, ask yourself if your lack of comfort is because you are generally anxious and fearful about the process, rather than dissatisfied with the person. You might ask yourself: Do you think this person wants to help you? Do you think he or she can?

Getting Relief from Uncertainty: Some Final Words

If your turnaround consultant has the characteristics that we discussed in the previous section, he should be able to substantially reduce your uncertainty about the problems that you face. He may also be able to reduce your uncertainty about the cost of his efforts by estimating what the total costs may be. However, management consulting to insolvent companies is probably the riskiest and most unpredictable of consulting practices, and you should be prepared for the fact that in some situations his time and effort will be dictated by the circumstances that arise.

Nevertheless, it is reasonable for you to expect that the consultant's fees should fall within a range that the cash flow of the business can accommodate. Concerning the uncertainty as to whether the results are justified by the fees he will charge, keep in mind that you're hiring the turnaround consultant not just to provide a few recommendations, but to develop a strategy to save the business, preserve your assets, and stabilize your company—none of which can happen without the experience and objectiveness he provides.

If the efforts are successful, you have preserved what may be your major financial asset, and, what is even more important, you will have preserved the investment of your shareholders and maximized the recovery of your trade and secured creditors.

If the program fails, your investment will go down the drain, and the recovery of your creditors will be only that which the assets can bring in a liquidation sale. That is why you need the best possible assistance, in the form of a turnaround manager, to increase the chances that the turnaround program will work. Quibbling over fees in this situation is as appropriate as awarding the contract to perform a cardiac bypass operation on yourself to the doctor who submitted the lowest bid in a competitive procurement.

It is important to remain focused on what is really at stake here: the life or death of your business.

THE BUSINESS DIAGNOSIS: ANALYZING A COMPANY IN TROUBLE

A problem well stated is a problem half solved.

CHARLES KETTERING

A consultant called into a troubled business situation must gather the wide range of data needed to diagnose the company's business health status, and these data must be assembled in a very short time. Usually the company is deteriorating rapidly. In all but the simplest business it is very difficult to take significant corrective action until you have some reliable data, an overall feel for how the business operates, and why it got into its present predicament.

To put the problem in perspective, let me offer an example: I was retained by a modest-sized company with revenues of $5 million per year that was losing $5000 a day. Every day that elapsed before we could make informed recommendations to curtail the loss was costing the company $5000. In one week the company would have lost an additional $35,000 if we were not able to find out what was going on, why it was going on, and formulate action plans based on that information.

FOCUS OF THE ANALYSIS

The analysis of a company is directed toward achieving an understanding of the company's qualitative and quantitative history, present condition, and future prospects from the following six perspectives: strategy, finance, marketing, technology (both engineering and manufacturing), organization and control, and human resources and compensation. Through such an analysis, the consultant can identify strategic strengths, weaknesses, problems, constraints, and additional factors that must be addressed. With this information in hand, the consultant is in a position to formulate a coherent insolvency plan.

The various questions that are explored in each of these analyses are briefly reviewed.

Strategy

Past and current strategy of the firm is examined to determine which strategies have proven successful and which have not. The strategy currently being pursued by the firm is examined in terms of the firm's strengths and weaknesses to determine whether the firm has the strengths or key factors of success to compete in its industry. An investigation is made to determine if and how the present strategy differs significantly from previous strategies and whether the present strategy represents a conscious choice or an unconscious evolution. Finally, an assessment is made as to whether the firm's current strategy makes sense in light of the resources it has or can acquire, and the conditions in the industry.

Finance

The finances of the firm are analyzed to determine how the financial performance and the operating accounts have varied over the recent past. Historical monthly and yearly sales, material, labor, selling, and entertainment costs are organized on a spread sheet or graphed to highlight trends, rapid changes, and so forth. The reason for these variations and trends is investigated. The operating statement and balance sheet ratios are calculated at various points in the company's operating history, and these ratios are compared to those of similar businesses. (Such statistics are compiled and tabulated by organizations such as Dun's and Robert Morris Associates.) The performance of the subject business is ranked against published averages, and the reasons for either a high or a low ranking are explored.

A financial analysis of the projected operation of the business at various sales levels will determine the investment required to support operations. The balance sheet of the firm is analyzed to determine the value of the various assets, and the extent to which they are encumbered, so as to calculate the collateral that might be available for a new financing program. The values and sources of the various liabilities are reviewed and categorized (for example, secured/unsecured, delinquent/nondelinquent, contingent/noncontingent). A review of the off-balance-sheet financial resources of the firm is made to ascertain if the assets exist and whether they can be sold to raise capital, or pledged to secure financing. Such assets can include a leasehold interest, pollution credits, computer software, engineering documentation, and so forth. An assessment is made of the company's ability to obtain equity or long-term loans from venture capital groups, present investors in the company, or other sources.

Marketing

The company's marketing strategy is reviewed to determine how the company creates new customers, and how it retains its existing customers. How does the company determine whether its customers' needs are being satisfied? Does the company have any direct way to determine the level of customer satisfaction with its products or services? How effective is the sales force? Is it well balanced or are there a few star performers in a galaxy of mediocrity? What is the thrust of the company's advertising program? How does the company determine if its advertising program is effective?

Technology

The ability of the company to sustain a competitive position in its research and development activities is investigated. How it selects, trains, motivates, and retains its professional staff is addressed. How does it determine the projects that deserve investment and the projects that should be abandoned? How does research and development ensure the company's technological edge? To what extent do marketing considerations dictate the direction of investment in technology?

Manufacturing

The company's manufacturing operation is analyzed to determine the components of its cost structure, the condition of its equipment, the dependability and commitment of its suppliers, its capacity for expansion, and the attitude and motivation of its employees.

Organization and Control

The manner in which the resources of the company are measured and controlled is analyzed. The organization chart is reviewed to determine the manner in which authority, responsibility, and accountability are assigned. Key managers are interviewed to ascertain their views of the organization and their assessments of its strengths and weaknesses. The control systems of the company are analyzed. Are they adequate? Do they actually control what they are meant to control? Are the persons responsible for measuring and controlling key resources competent to do so? Are the systems and hardware adequate for the level of accuracy and timeliness the operations of the company require?

Human Resources and Compensation

The personnel in various departments are surveyed to determine their attitudes, motivation, and job satisfaction. The compensation being paid for various positions is compared with that paid for similar positions in other firms. In what areas is the company overpaying its employees, and in what areas is it underpaying? What is the effect of this on the company's performance? How successful has the company been in attracting and retaining personnel?

GATHERING THE DATA

In gathering the data to evaluate an insolvency situation, we use four methods to accumulate the information for the background report.

Observations

Observations made in plant and store tours are included. Observations provide first-hand information, making it quite reliable. For the expert observer, a brief tour of a facility may provide an enormous amount of information about the business. For example, we were retained by a chain of furniture stores that, among other problems, was exhibiting lackluster sales in certain locations. I suggested to the sales manager that since I was unknown to the store personnel I should independently visit the stores as a "shopper."

The tour was revealing. In one store, where I was the only customer at the time, almost five minutes elapsed before I was greeted by a salesperson; in another, where three salespersons were on duty, I waited while one carried on a protracted telephone conversation and another processed paperwork in the back of the store. The store tour quickly pointed out that the general sales manager, to whom all the store managers reported (and who was a major shareholder in the business), was simply not managing the store managers.

Tours of manufacturing facilities tell the trained observer not only the state of housekeeping, but also the efficacy of the control system, the motivation of the employees, and so forth.

Materials Collection and Review

Materials comprise the documents that are produced by the company in the ordinary course of business. Included are financial statements, schedules of accounts receivable and accounts payable, production reports, minutes of meetings, board minutes, financing statements, organizational charts, and so forth. These materials provide the consultant with information that reflects how the organization functions on a day-to-day basis, the nature of its contracts with its customers, suppliers, and bankers, and what its historical performance has been. With this information, the consultant develops a feel for the business operation.

Surveys

Surveys or questionnaires help determine attitudes and facts as the company as a whole sees them, as opposed to interviews that search for this information on an individual basis. Surveys have the advantage of collecting facts and opinions from many sources simultaneously (which is both convenient and inexpensive), and analyzing the data collected in a rigorous manner to derive conclusions. The climate survey discussed in Chapter 6 is a typical example.

Interviews

Interviews are very important in any situation analysis. They can search out facts, attitudes, and opinions from all of the key participants in the company as well as other important stakeholders. The professional consultant will commit to keeping everything he hears from individual interviewees strictly confidential. Consequently, he will be able to probe successfully very sensitive areas of inquiry and obtain information that has not been available to the existing management. A good interviewer will give individual managers a great deal of leeway in the subject matter the interview covers. In turn these managers will usually be very helpful by not only responding openly, truthfully, and completely to questions, but, also by telling the consultant the questions he should be asking.

Another very important aspect of the interview is the opportunity it provides for the consultant to enlist the help of the employees in his overall problem-solving process. Employees who have lived through the problems of the company for years are usually very interested in offering their ideas about possible solutions to the company's problems. They welcome an accepting and interested listener. They have an intrinsic knowledge of the business and can usually provide meaningful and helpful ideas on how the company's problems should be dealt with.

Because a consultant, like a journalist, protects his sources, he can tap into this reservoir of good ideas, viewpoints, opinions, and evaluations to obtain a broad perspective on the problem and the solutions that are available.

In grappling with the biggest bankruptcy in American history—that of the Penn Central in 1970—turnaround consultant Victor H. Palmieri used such interviews to excellent advantage. He and his consulting team conducted numerous interviews while attempting to rescue Great Southwest Corporation (a Penn Central subsidiary active in real estate and amusement parks). As he explains:

> As pressing as the problems were with creditors and with litigation, and despite the fact that cash was clearly going to be in crisis again, the first thing we did was to begin interviewing people. We spent the first couple of weeks introducing ourselves to (Great Southwest) management groups around the country, telling them that we had taken control; that we meant to save the company and keep it out of bankruptcy; that we meant to do not only that but to rebuild it; and that we thought it was not a real estate

company but a potentially great recreation company. . . . The interviews were not only to learn the character of the people and identify people we wanted to keep but also to collect as much information as we possibly could, and . . . cross-check different perspectives.

Carl Remick

FORMULATING THE ISSUES

As a result of the data-gathering effort the consultant will, given the direction and focus of the analysis, formulate a series of issues that must be addressed in the analysis. To illustrate, the following issues were developed as a result of the internal evaluation of a manufacturing company that was at stage D level of adversity (negative profit, decreasing cash):

1. *Strategic Issues:* Does the business have a "viable core" around which to develop a profitable operation? Does it have a viable strategic business plan for developing the core business, and is the plan being implemented? Is there a workable plan for the principals to be able to phase out of the business?

2. *Marketing Issues:* Does the company have a viable marketing strategy, and is there a workable marketing plan to implement it? Can the business achieve its marketing objectives with present management personnel?

3. *Financial Issues:* What is the realistic evaluation of the company's historical operating performance and current balance sheet? What operating plan will accommodate payments on its present debt obligations? Does the accounting system provide timely and accurate financial information? Does the company have an adequate system of financial controls and reporting to ensure that the business is managed effectively and efficiently?

4. *Organization and System Issues:* Is there a workable production plan in place to support the company's marketing strategy, and is it being implemented? Can the company achieve its production objectives with present management? Are the company's current location and equipment adequate to support production requirements? Does the company have an adequate system of controls

and reporting to ensure that all of the plant operations are effectively and efficiently managed?

5. *Human Resources and Compensation Issues:*   How do the employees perceive the working conditions at the business? Are their perceptions similar to management's? Do the company's rewards and compensation policies provide positive incentives to support development of a viable core business?

PERFORMING THE ANALYSIS AND PREPARING THE FINDINGS

The collected information is then analyzed by the consultant. In performing this analysis the consultant will employ analytical techniques, computer simulations of projected financial performance, statistical analysis, data classification, and so forth. The object of this analysis is to formulate a set of findings that address the issues posed. To illustrate, the following are some of the key findings from the situation analysis of our manufacturing company. It should be noted that the company in question had two independent but related product lines, which we refer to as business A and business B.

Strategic Findings

1. Business A, even in its present deteriorated condition, qualifies as a viable core business. However, business B is *not* a viable core business. In fact, it is a failure that has been and continues to be a millstone on the entire company.

2. There is no business plan for developing business A. There are no stated goals, forecasts, or budgets. As a result, management operates in a day-to-day mode without a clear direction.

Marketing Findings

The primary marketing policy for the company requires that products be shipped on the same day they are ordered. The company does not have the people, systems, or capital resources to adhere to this policy, and attempts to do so create chaos.

Financial Findings

1. The company's operating performance appears to indicate a positive trend over the past two years, with increasing profit before taxes. However, the "profits" have resulted from increases in the inventory of business B, much of which is outdated and obsolete. Adjusting write-off of this inventory would void any book profit over the past two years.

2. Policies, responsibility, authority, and accountability for establishing and enforcing customer credit are unclear and inconsistent. Although the accounting manager performs credit checks in accordance with established procedures and sets credit limits based on past experience, he is often overridden by the chief executive.

Organization and System Findings

1. There is no system for coordinating marketing, production, and inventory management. The company's inventory fluctuates from an overstocked condition to inventory shortages.

2. Present machinery and equipment are outdated or worn out. The maintenance department is inadequate to maintain the production machinery in its present condition.

3. The company's management style is task-oriented. The chief executive admits to being a "firefighter." He tries to be in charge of everything. The production coordinator uses him as a role model; their management styles cause confusion and frustration among their subordinates.

4. Job scheduling is out of control. Scheduling priorities change on a day-to-day and sometimes hour-to-hour basis, often without all persons affected by the changes being informed.

Human Resources and Compensation Findings

1. Employees feel that they are not given sufficient responsibility and are not adequately recognized or rewarded for their efforts and accomplishments.

2. There is frequently a lack of direction as to what is expected of employees, and lines of authority are not clearly drawn.

The Critical Issues

In a normal management consulting situation, these findings would result in a set of recommendations that, when successfully implemented, would eliminate the deficiencies that the consultant discovered in the organization.

However, in an insolvency case, the purpose of the findings is to identify the major strengths of the business and the opportunities available to it. These can serve as the foundation for the turnaround. The findings will also show those weaknesses of the business and threats to it that could either inhibit or even preclude the business turnaround.

A strength is a resource or capacity the organization can use effectively to achieve its objectives; a weakness is a limitation, fault, or defect in the organization that will keep it from achieving its objectives.

An opportunity is a trend or event that could lead to a significant rise in sales or profits, given an appropriate management response. A threat is a trend or event that could result in a deterioration of present sales or profit patterns, and requires a management response to either mitigate or eliminate its effect.

The noncritical weaknesses of the business represent challenges that the management will have to deal with during the future course of the business; however, they will neither break nor make the business. For example, in the turnaround of the manufacturing firm discussed in Chapter 8, the situation analysis revealed the following:

Critical Strengths: Large market share; dedicated and competent work force; loyal customer base

Critical Weaknesses: Large and increasing debt burden of the land development venture; no marketing or promotion program; no effective middle or senior management to lead or control the business

Critical Opportunity: A larger market for the company's products

Critical Threat: The possibility of a competitive product that could greatly curtail the company's market share

Although the analysis revealed many other strengths, weaknesses, and problems, the ones listed were critical to the implementation and success of a turnaround program.

EXTERNAL SITUATION: FARSIGHTED VISION

An analysis of the external situation focuses on three key aspects of the business's world: the customer base, the structure of the competition, the industry, in which the business operates.

The output of this external analysis is an identification and understanding of threats and opportunities facing the business, both present and potential.

Another result of the external analysis is the identification of important areas of uncertainty about a business, or its environment, that must be addressed in formulating an overall plan.

The goal of external analysis is to detect opportunities and threats, suggest effective turnaround strategies for the company, and detect strategic questions that will affect the choice of that strategy.

ANALYZING THE CUSTOMER BASE

The analysis of the company's customers addresses three sets of questions:

1. *Segmentation:* Identify the different customer groups that respond to a competitive strategy. Who are the buyers and users of the products or service? Who are the largest buyers in terms of annual sales volume and profit contribution? What potential customers can be identified who are not currently buying? How is the market currently segmented and how could it be segmented by changing the marketing strategy?

2. *Customer Motivation:* What factors lie behind a purchase decision? What motivates the customer to buy and use the products or services the company offers? What attributes of these products or services are the most important to the customer? What changes in customer motivation are occurring or are likely to occur?

3. *Unmet Needs:* Are the customers satisfied with the products they are presently buying, or do they experience problems that, if solved, would allow the company to command a higher price? Are there unmet needs of which the customer might not be aware?

In analyzing the company's customer base, the consultant will categorize the firm's customers into rational segments, identify the customers' motivations, needs, and capacities, determine how well they are being served by the company and its competitors, and, most important, research how loyal they are to the company and the principals.

A viable core business requires the existence of a customer base that is viable, and able and willing to purchase the company's products and services, assuming they are provided at the price, quality, and service levels of the competition. The nature and condition of the customer base will also influence the company's turnaround strategy. For example, if the company's customers are themselves in financial difficulty, the company is not going to be able to implement a turnaround program based on stimulating sales with liberal credit terms.

The problems of preserving a customer base while a company is deteriorating financially are discussed in Chapter 5. The company's management faces the extraordinary challenge of putting on a "good face" to the customers and attempting to satisfy their needs while the barbarians are storming the ramparts and the company coffers are bare.

The consultant will endeavor to identify the most critical demands on the company, allocate whatever resources are available to stabilize the situation, and incorporate his insight into the analysis of the customer base.

REACTIONS OF COMPETITORS

The common reaction of the competitors of your floundering company is to attempt to hasten your demise using whatever legal (and sometimes illegal) means are available to them. Therefore, the analysis of an insolvency situation must achieve some understanding of the current strategy, strengths, and weaknesses of the competitor. Through such an understanding the consultant might be able to develop a strategy that will avoid threats to the company. In addition, an understanding of competitors will greatly facilitate the prediction of how various competitors might react to a specific company strategy. For example, would a 15 percent across-the-board price reduction by the company, to stimulate sales, likely be met by a matching (or even greater) price reduction by a number of competitors? If so, which ones would be the most likely to engage in a price war?

The actions of a competitor are influenced by the following elements, all of which need to be considered when attempting to ascertain a competitor's behavior:

1. *Size, Market Share, Growth Rate, Profitability, and Recent Market Performance of Each of the Competitors:* The competitors that will be most important to the company are those that are the largest, have the largest market share, exhibit the highest recent growth rate in the industry, and have achieved a recent and substantial increase in market share.

2. *The Competitors' Objectives and Assumptions:* What are the competitors attempting to achieve? Growth? Stable income? To posture a company for sale? Do the competitors strive for technological leadership? A high profile within the industry? What constraints on the management of the competitors are imposed by stockholders, parent companies, and so forth? A knowledge of the competitors' assumptions and objectives provides clues to the kinds of resources a competitor might be willing to invest to increase market share, sales growth, or profitability.

3. *Current and Past Strategies of the Competitors:* Current and past strategies provide insight as to how the various competitors are likely to respond to the company's strategies. Knowledge of a competitor's pattern of new product and new market action plans can help anticipate future growth directions.

4. *Competitors' Organization and Culture:* Are the competitors innovative and prone to take big risks, or are they methodical and bureaucratic in their response to threats and opportunities? What considerations typically dominate their thinking? Is their top management dominated by engineering, marketing, or finance-oriented executives? The organization's culture, supported by its systems, administration, and control, will have a major effect on how rapidly and creatively the competitor can respond to a new situation in the market.

5. *Cost Structure:* A knowledge of the competitors' cost structures vis-à-vis the company's can provide an indication of their probable future

TABLE 10.1. CHECKLIST TO EVALUATE COMPETITOR STRENGTHS AND WEAKNESSES

Innovation
R&D
Technologies
New product capability
Patents

Manufacturing
Cost structure
Equipment
Access to raw material
Vertical integration
Work force attitude and motivation
Capacity

Finance—access to capital
From operations
From net short-term assets
Ability and willingness to use debt financing
Ability and willingness to use equity financing
Parent company's willingness to finance

Management
Quality of top management
Quality of middle management and operating systems
Loyalty, turnover
Quality of strategic decision making

Marketing
Product quality
Breadth of product line, systems capability
Brand names
Distribution
Retailer relationship
Advertising and promotion skills
Sales force
Service
Knowledge of customer's needs

Customer base
Size and growth of segments served
Loyalty of customers

pricing strategies and staying power. Are the competitors' labor costs inherently higher or lower because of where their manufacturing facilities are located? Do they have a high or low debt service? Are they able to purchase raw material more inexpensively? Are their administrative structures inherently more expensive?

6. *Strengths and Weaknesses of the Competitors:* Knowledge of the competitors' strengths and weaknesses can provide insight into the capability of competitors to respond to the strategies the company might pursue. It is the company's objective to develop a strategy that will exploit competitors' weaknesses and neutralize their strengths. Table 10.1 provides an overview of the areas in which competitors can exhibit strengths or weaknesses.

THE BIG PICTURE: INDUSTRY ANALYSIS

There are two major objectives of performing an industry analysis as part of a situation audit of a financially troubled company: first, to determine the attractiveness of an industry to current and potential participants, and second, to identify the key success factors for the industry.

The industry's stability, growth, and current returns on investment will provide an important input for evaluating the probability of success of a turnaround effort. For example, if the industry within which the company operates is capital intensive and experiencing a steep decline, with large numbers of bankruptcies and business terminations, it can be assumed that the competition for business will be fierce. Prices for services within the business will decline rapidly. Those companies with the largest customer base and the lowest debt service will be in the best position to survive. This is precisely what occurred in the oil drilling and oil service industry in the 1985–1987 period. A company in that industry attempting a turnaround would have to contend with those forces.

On the other hand, if the industry is experiencing a high growth rate, is attracting large quantities of venture capital, and is characterized by rapid technological changes so that market share can be rapidly purchased, then a firm with the requisite know-how, strong management, and unique market approach might be an excellent candidate for a turnaround.

The second objective in an industry analysis is to identify the key success factors for the industry. A key success factor is a competitive skill or asset that is particularly relevant to the industry. To be successful in the industry, a company will usually need to have some minimum level of skill or asset quality in each of the industry's key success factors to be a viable competitor. If a firm has a strategic weakness in one of the key success factors, it will not be able to maintain a competitive advantage in the long term, and will soon exit the market.

For example, the key factors for the success of a land developer are (1) the ability to raise equity and debt capital; (2) a skill at locating and optioning desirable properties; and (3) the ability to recruit architects, engineers, designers, and consultants who will contribute to the development of a concept in the hope of being retained if the project should fund.

The key success factors for a chain of retail stores are (1) a consistent advertising program to maintain name recognition; (2) an effective program to recruit, train, and motivate store managers; (3) a dedicated and competent sales manager; (4) an innovative and well-connected merchandise manager; (5) a data-processing system that provides reliable, relevant information on all stores on a daily basis; and (6) good and economical store locations.

Several aspects of the industry analysis that are explored are as follows.

Industry Growth Rate: At what rate is the industry growing or declining? What factors in the economy are driving the growth rate? Is the growth or decline likely to continue? What level of growth will be most hospitable for the firm?

Profit Potential: Who is making money in the industry? Why? To what extent does market share determine profitability in this industry? What are the profit prospects for the firm in the present environment?

Financial Stability: How stable is the industry? Has there been a high rate of mergers and bankruptcies? If so, has the industry stabilized? Is investment capital pouring into the industry or shunning it? How do bankers and venture capitalists feel about the industry?

Technological Know-How: What depth and breadth of technology does the firm need to compete in the industry? How accessible is the technology the firm will need to compete effectively?

Rate of Technological Change: How quickly is the technology changing? How will the rate of technological change affect the ability of this firm to compete? Does the firm have the ability to attract the personnel that will allow it to remain on the cutting edge of technology?

Raw Material Availability: Are the raw materials that the firm will need to purchase readily available or in short supply? How will the firm guarantee its supply of raw materials? Are the firm's sources providing the material at the quality that is required? How much leverage do the suppliers of the material have with the firm and its competitors? How volatile is the situation?

Ease of Entry: How capital intense is the industry? That is, is it similar to the oil refinery industry where a large plant investment is required, or is it like the electronic systems business where the capital investment for entry can be modest? High capital investment discourages new competitors whereas low capital investment encourages them. How important are economies of scale? Does a firm have to establish a large market share in order to be profitable?

Competitive Pressure: How intense is the competition? Is there excess capacity, with too many sellers hunting too few buyers? Is there frequent price cutting? Or are prices relatively stable, with the competitors committed to avoiding price cutting and discounting?

WRAPPING IT UP: THE FINAL ANALYSIS

By the time the turnaround manager has finished the situation analysis, he often knows more about the company than anyone in it. The greater his understanding of what is actually happening within the company and what outside forces are at work, the better he will be able to formulate realistic plans for its survival. The tasks of the turnaround manager and the strategies he uses in a turnaround situation are discussed later. But first, we consider some of the problems that may stand in the way of the company's resolution of its problems.

11 | WHAT YOU *MUST* KNOW ABOUT BANKRUPTCY LAW

Law is not justice and a trial is not a scientific inquiry into truth. A trial is a resolution of a dispute.

EDISON HAINES

In the normal course of business, a company probably doesn't think about the workings of the legal system, unless it is involved in a lawsuit or other legal proceeding. But in fact, the company is always working within a legal framework. Promises to deliver services or products and promises to pay back money borrowed for credit obtained are formalized into written contracts. These contracts are legally binding—thereby placing the company firmly within the rules and regulations of the legal system.

As long as all goes well, the various contracts are simply pieces of paper that define how much money or goods and services are due to whom and when they are due. If the company falls into financial difficulty, however, and can no longer keep all of its promises, the legal system becomes the order of the day.

Problems arise or intensify if the parties who originally agreed to the contract interpret it differently, or for some other reason feel that the other side is not living up to the agreement. If the dispute cannot be settled by mutual agreement, the conflict is brought to the courts to be resolved. That is when the trouble really begins. Neither litigation nor bankruptcy are quick cures for business problems. Once the business brings its problems into the court system, it is entering a foreign and sometimes indifferent environment.

There is, however, no way to discuss strategies for a business in distress without discussing the options and risks of bankruptcy, and there can be no real understanding of the bankruptcy process without first recognizing that bankruptcy is a legal process and, as such, is a specialized part of a much larger legal system. The rules of the legal process are different than the rules of the business world, and if you don't understand the rules you're playing under, you can never win the game.

Suppose you tried to play soccer following football rules. Both are games that involve a ball, and scores are made when the ball makes it into the goal zone. In soccer, however, you're never supposed to touch the ball with your hands unless you're the goalie; in football, you're supposed to do everything in your power to get your hands on the ball. If you don't play by the right rules, you're not even going to be in the game.

The world of bankruptcy and insolvency is very different from the normal business world of risk and profit. The rules are different, the consequences for actions are changed, and for the business thrust into bankruptcy that has never been there before, it is often a confusing experience.

UNDUE PROCESS: THE TRIAL OF MR. K.

Mr. K. was an ordinary man going about his ordinary life. Then one day he woke up, and instead of getting his morning coffee he got arrested. It was with no more fanfare or preparation than this that Franz Kafka introduced his ill-fated character in *The Trial*, a classic tale of the confusion and injustice—and overwhelming indifference—of the legal system.

Mr. K. progresses through a series of court appearances and interrogations with no comprehension of what is happening to him. He never knows precisely what he is accused of. He doesn't clearly know who the various players in the court are, or what they want from him. He is told to appear, but at no particular time; upon arrival, he is chastised for being late. Every action he takes is used against him.

His lawyer, Huld, claims to know the inner workings of the court, but cannot produce any results. Mr. K., uncertain and indecisive, relies on outside help that fails him. He is a man without power, held accountable to rules he cannot understand. The legal machinery marches on, and he is ultimately sentenced to death and executed.

Many a business executive who finds himself in the grip of the court can empathize with Mr. K.'s plight. The legal process is complex and convoluted and riddled with ambiguity. If the person before the court hopes to achieve justice, he is surely doomed to a profound disillusionment. He must rely on his lawyer to guide him through to a resolution, and in so doing may end up the victim of the legal system's version of Russian roulette. His dilemma lies in his lack of choice. The best he can hope for is an honest, competent lawyer who truly knows how to make the most of the situation.

Herein lies the crux of the problem: the legal system is, and always has been, a paradoxical process, attempting to resolve conflict through adversarial battle.

THE LEGAL SYSTEM VERSUS EQUITABLE RESOLUTION

There is a gypsy curse, it is said, that goes like this: "May you have a lawsuit in which you know you are in the right." When dealing with the court system, it may often seem that this is true.

Judge Lois G. Forer, who authored the book *Death of the Law*, suggests that the legal system today does not serve the purpose it was intended to:

> I see that law as a principle by which people conduct their lives is dead, that the entire legal system corrodes any sense of trust or truth. It is a juggernaut laying waste lives, businesses and social order . . . courts exist for the sole purpose of providing a resolution of disputes. Instead, the parties are faced with a lifetime of expenses and irritations as they pursue the mirage of justice through the murky corridors of innumerable courts, countless hearings, appeals and retrials.

The process of resolving a dispute through the courts requires that the parties run a lengthy obstacle course that is so complex and costly that it often defeats those who are not sufficiently strong.

The litigation process invariably becomes a test of the skills of the lawyers who are employed in a "duel" on behalf of their clients. The strengths of the lawyers are rarely equally matched. Very often the different economic and political power of the opponents will have more to do with the outcome of the situation than any other aspect of the dispute, since political and economic might buy the best law firms, expert witnesses, consultants, and computers.

The Role of the Attorney in Dispute Resolution

Lawyers are usually approached and retained by a client as a result of a dispute involving the potential client and another individual, institution, or government agency.

The dispute invariably involves three aspects or components:

1. *The Psychological Aspects of the Controversy:*   The client's perceived needs, motivations, and emotional attitudes to the opponents, himself, the nature of the disputes, the level of trust (or lack of trust) that exists, and the relationships of the parties.

2. *The Business Aspects of the Dispute:*   The money and other rights that are in question; the risks and potential rewards related to the various alternatives; strategies that might be pursued.

3. *The Legal Aspects of the Case:*   The rights of the client as perceived by the attorney; the rights of the opponent as perceived by the attorney; the legal questions involved; the case law; the procedures and costs for securing these rights; the time involved and the probability that the results being sought by the client will eventually be achieved.

The evaluation of the alternatives for resolving any dispute is a systems problem and should be pursued in a dispassionate, objective fashion. It is necessary to analyze the problem, look at the various alternatives to resolve it, and calculate the resources that must be invested to adequately pursue a given situation. The time, energy, money, and psychological stress of the client must also be considered. The attorney should evaluate the risks associated with each alternative and establish a utility curve for the client that will allow him to evaluate the value of the investments, rewards, and risks that each alternative will entail. Then, after this evaluation process has been completed, he would propose a solution and a recommendation of a course of conduct his client should pursue, based upon all the facts available and the client's ability curves. This is what good attorneys do.

Unfortunately it is rarely done this way. Usually clients find themselves in litigations that achieve results which often disappoint the client and appear to be inadequate in light of the money, energy, and time that were invested.

The ultimate resolution of a dispute or controversy depends on four factors: (1) the relative economic power of the parties; (2) the relative skill of their attorneys; (3) the respective merits of their cases; and (4) chance. Sometimes justice prevails and the merits of the case determine the outcome. Chance always plays a part, but usually the relative economic power of the participants and the relative skill of their attorneys have more to do with the outcome than the merits of the case.

THE VITAL IMPORTANCE OF GOOD LEGAL COUNSEL

The legal system, in general, is cumbersome and confusing. The bankruptcy system is even more complex, with a greater need for skill on the part of the attorney. Everything moves very quickly, and there is no time for mistakes when the life of the business is on the line. The attorney must be both experienced and competent. The problem is, as George Bernard Shaw pointed out, "There are not enough competent people in the world to go around; somebody must get the incompetent lawyers and doctors." Try not to let it be you.

Augustine notes that as of 1986, the United States had three lawyers per 1000 residents, and law schools were pouring out 30,000 new lawyers each year. The United States has more lawyers than Iceland has people, 20 times as many lawyers per capita as Japan, and three times as many as England. A Colorado Court of Appeals judge noted that two-thirds of the world's lawyers practice in the United States, that is, 67 percent of the legal population services 6 percent of the world's population, an 11 to 1 ratio. Augustine has commented that since lawyers are a commodity in which we appear to enjoy a vast surplus, an opportunity for a viable export business is lying fallow, awaiting discovery by some energetic entrepreneur.

So, on the basis of these statistics, one might think that it is a relatively simple matter to find a good lawyer to handle a specific matter, right? *Wrong!!*

Finding a mature, motivated, politically astute, and well-respected attorney who is both knowledgeable and experienced in the particular specialty of concern, and who has the intellect, the creativity, and the negotiating and people skills a complex issue requires, is comparable to finding the proverbial needle in the haystack. It's possible, but "it ain't easy."

My own experiences exemplify the difficulty. I once hired an attorney who was mature, motivated, technically knowledgeable, and highly experienced, but whose negotiating and people skills were so poor that the opposition became enraged over his conduct, and what should have been a minor scrimmage escalated into nuclear war.

One attorney I hired had experience and was highly respected in the matter in question, but had personal and financial problems that prevented him from concentrating on my case.

I once hired an attorney who was technically competent to pursue the case through the pretrial phases of litigation, but he fell apart when he had to plead the case before a judge and jury, and he was destroyed by the opposition.

Of the 100+ attorneys who have represented me or my opponents during my business career, I would not consider rehiring 90 percent. My experience is not surprising, considering former Chief Justice Warren Burger's statement: "Up to one-half of the nation's trial lawyers are unfit to appear in court."

A good attorney is a vital ingredient in the resolution of an insolvency matter. It is essential that he thoroughly understand the bankruptcy system, have good negotiating and people skills, be intellectually astute and creative, and work well with the change agent. Although finding and recruiting such an attorney is difficult, it is not impossible. I've done it; but I've also paid my dues in financial and emotional scars accrued during my "learning experiences."

WHAT YOU DON'T KNOW CAN RUIN YOU: WHY A HEALTHY COMPANY NEEDS TO UNDERSTAND BANKRUPTCY

There is a tendency to avoid the topic of bankruptcy in business discussions, or to consider bankruptcy as a last-ditch effort that doesn't need to be talked about until the business is in its death throes. Nothing could be farther from the truth. A solid understanding of the bankruptcy process—and the options it provides—should be part and parcel of the knowledge any business needs to begin operations.

Think of understanding bankruptcy as a kind of disaster preparedness for the business. It is as important as having fire alarms and security systems, or locking the door at the end of the day.

At the beginning of any routine airplane flight, the flight attendant explains what to do in case of emergency. He demonstrates how the oxygen mask will drop down from the panel, and how to secure it to your face, and he points out where the emergency exits and flotation devices are in the aircraft and the additional safety information in the pocket of each seat. First-time travelers listen attentively to the demonstration, because it is information that may save their lives. Even travelers who have heard the speech a thousand times still pay attention to the specific information they don't know—where the exits are on that plane.

Those particularly concerned about safety may do additional reading, and even request certain seating on the plane which is considered most likely to survive a crash. Why do they do this? They want to maximize their chances for survival, and they do it before the flight is in full motion because in the midst of an emergency, there is no time to learn these things.

Picture the airplane in a nose-dive approach to the land. Is that any time to try to catch the flight attendant's attention to ask where the emergency exits are, or to try to change your seat?

The same is true in business. A business should take certain precautions as it is starting up, or in the normal day-to-day operations, to protect itself in case of emergency. Keep in mind that business is a risky venture, and a business emergency could happen at any time. To have effective protection through proper preparation, the business must understand what happens in the emergency—what happens in the bankruptcy system once that process is set in motion. It is much too late to learn about bankruptcy when you're sitting in court, waiting for your case to be called. You don't have time to take protective measures for your business at that point. What you know *now* about bankruptcy may save the life of your business in times of crisis, minimize the damage, and maximize chances for survival.

A REDISTRIBUTION OF ASSETS: PHILOSOPHY OF THE BANKRUPTCY SYSTEM

The purpose of the bankruptcy institution is to provide a vehicle and opportunity for an insolvent firm to "learn" how to adjust its operations to the reality of its business environment, adjust its debt structure (with the agreement of its creditors), or liquidate and exit the field. The bankruptcy institution provides a "no fault" method for the unsuccessful executive to exit from his or her present predicament and, if desired, to start business anew.

Bankruptcy is an intervention in the market processes affecting the business; it is designed to facilitate adjustments that can include the adjustment of debt, payment, and management.

The purpose of the bankruptcy institution is to coordinate many constituents and stakeholders of the firm in an innovative endeavor. As we have discussed earlier, during periods of adversity the inherent conflicts that arise among the various stakeholders become very salient, and are compounded by significant emotional content, making cooperation without the supervision of the court or a pseudo-judicial system very difficult.

Nelson, writing in *Corporations in Crisis*, sums it up very well:

> The necessity of coordinated adjustment, in spite of adversity, creates a need for the special package of arrangements embodied in bankruptcy institutions. Without bankruptcy, unless a firm happened to forge an informal agreement with its creditors, a firm would wither as it tried to fend off grabbing creditors. Businesses would stop operations when they lacked necessary inputs, leaving remaining assets to the most diligent creditors. The bankruptcy institution offers firms a sheltered environment in which to make needed changes. New life can be cultivated, or when necessary, last rites can be performed in an orderly fashion.

In order to communicate clearly the ideas regarding bankruptcy it is valuable to be precise in our use of terms. The word "bankruptcy" will be reserved for the bankruptcy institution, that body of laws and procedures that applies when a company files for bankruptcy.

After a firm, either voluntarily or involuntarily, comes under the jurisdiction of the bankruptcy court it is said to be bankrupt. We will refer to a firm as being insolvent if it cannot pay its debts as they become due and we will refer to a firm as experiencing adversity if its performance and future prospects indicate that it will become insolvent at some fairly predictable time in the future.

The bankruptcy process itself is a more realistic forum for dispute resolution than other legal processes seem to be. This is partly because there is not an unlimited amount of money or time available, and the judge is always watching the legal fees to make sure they make sense. The process forces everyone to be more efficient, and, with its administrative aspects, the bankruptcy process takes some of the emotion out of the proceedings. The problem is clearly defined as a redistribution of assets, and everyone must work toward a solution that makes sense in that context.

Contrary to previous times when the underlying assumption was that default reflects immoral behavior and the bankruptcy processes meted out punishment that would serve as a deterrent, today bankruptcy cases are assigned to a special court with a relatively ameliorative atmosphere, reinforcing the modern attitude that insolvency, in itself, does not indicate moral terpitude nor should it bear the stigma of profligate behavior.

BEFORE BANKRUPTCY: THE DIM VIEW FROM DEBTORS' PRISONS

The total of human misery which was produced over the centuries by the basic illogicality of requiring a man to pay off a debt while at the same time placing him in a position which both increases his indebtedness and diminishes his capacity for gaining money, is enormous.

Christopher Harding

It would be good to keep in mind that bankruptcy law grew out of the desire to create a more humane and practical alternative to the centuries-old traditional treatment of debtors: prison confinement.

Imprisonment for nonpayment of debts, a practice established in England in the late 1200s, was harsh punishment, and gave the debtor no possibility to earn the means to secure his release. If he escaped, the warden in charge of the jail could become liable for the debtor's debt, so a close watch was kept. If an escaped debtor was caught, his sentence began all over again, as though no time had been spent in prison.

One of the early statutes even allowed for the imprisonment of one who managed another's property, which meant that accountants could end up behind bars for their clients' offenses.

Tales of prison conditions for debtors vary from prison to prison and century to century. Prison was, at the very best, a complete loss of freedom and, at the worst, a terrible life of overcrowded, damp cells, starvation, and disease. Years could be spent, and lives wasted, in debtors' prison.

Individuals imprisoned for debt were generally charged for their keep, and their living situation was greatly affected by how much they were able to pay. They were charged for their food, bed, sheets, and blankets, and there was an extra charge if they wanted a bed to themselves. The food was often meager, as at Newgate prison, where the daily allotment was 14 ounces of wheaten bread. It cost extra to get coal to heat the cells. Sometimes debtors were thrown in with criminals, and in a number of cases when the husband was thrown in debtors' prison, his wife and family were thrown in with him.

Debtors had to pay for legal papers filed with the court, and might remain in prison on false charges simply because they didn't have the money to file the paperwork to set them free. A plaintiff could have a debtor arrested without providing any proof that the sum he claimed due to him was in fact due.

Gaols in Scotland where debtors were confined were constructed without courtyards, quite deliberately, according to historian Christopher Harding, since under the laws of Scotland,

> After a debtor is imprisoned, he ought not to be indulged with the benefit of air, not even under guard; for creditors have an interest that their debtors be kept under close confinement, that, by the squalor they may be brought to pay their debt.

Debtors were sometimes tortured, beaten, and starved in attempts to extort money from them—or from their families.

TWO BROTHERS IN DEBT: A TALE FROM THE 1700s

Consider the case, a true story, of two brothers, farmers in Bedfordshire, who were arrested for nonpayment of debts. They were taken into custody, and the bailiffs consented to let one of the brothers go for two hours, to see whether he could borrow the money. If he did not return at the end of that time, they would throw the other brother in debtors' prison.

The two hours passed, and the brother did not return. The bailiffs started to drag the remaining brother off to prison, but he so feared imprisonment that he pulled out a pistol and shot himself. While all was confusion—they had not suspected the desperation of the brother, and had not searched him for any weapon—the other brother returned, with the money to pay their debts in full. This is just one example of the many tragedies in the past, before bankruptcy law became the legal process for debtors who could not pay their debts.

TODAY'S LAWS: THE FOUR BANKRUPTCY CHAPTERS

Fortunately times have changed, and so have the laws that govern the treatment of debtors unable to pay their debts. Under the current U.S. Bankruptcy Code, there are four basic bankruptcy processes that businesses and individuals can use to deal with insolvency. These are:

Chapter 11: Under this bankruptcy chapter, normally used for business bankruptcy and reorganization, corporate owners usually remain in control of the business and attempt to either restructure its finances so that it can continue to operate, or liquidate in an orderly manner. The goal of a Chapter 11 reorganization is to formulate and confirm a plan of reorganization that will establish how much creditors will be paid, in what form, and over what period of time.

Chapter 7: Under this chapter, the affairs of the corporation or the assets of an individual are turned over to a trustee who marshals all the assets, liquidates them (that is, converts them into cash), and distributes the proceeds to the creditors of the corporation in order of priority.

Chapter 13: This chapter, intended for personal bankruptcy, allows an individual with regular income and secured debts of less than $100,000 and unsecured debts of less than $350,000 to develop and perform a plan for the repayment of his creditors over an extended period of time so that he can support himself and his dependents while repaying his creditors. Unlike a Chapter 7 case, an individual is allowed to retain property and protect assets by agreeing to pay for them over time.

Chapter 12: This is a newly added chapter of the Bankruptcy Code, intended to assist family farmers. Chapter 12 combines most borrow-oriented features of Chapter 11 and Chapter 13 and provides a quick and inexpensive means for a family farmer to confirm a plan of reorganization. Chapter 12, which became effective in November 1986, allows an eligible family farmer whose debts do not exceed $1,500,000 to retain his property, even if there is no equity in it, and make periodic payments to the secured creditor, which respects the "value" of the property, and to compromise with his unsecured creditors as in a Chapter 11 plan.

THE ROAD TO THE COURTHOUSE: WHY BUSINESSES END UP IN BANKRUPTCY

In general, people would rather stay out of bankruptcy court and resolve their financial difficulties in some other fashion. Out-of-court agreements and reorganization plans are preferable to spending time and money in court. However, there are certain situations in which the filing of a Chapter 11 petition is the only way for the business to survive and successfully reorganize.

1. Secured or unsecured creditors who have been frustrated in their efforts to collect from the troubled business may join together and force the company into bankruptcy by filing an involuntary petition. This action is sometimes taken when the creditor wants to ensure that its security interests do not erode due to the carelessness or errors of the company's management.

2. Unsecured creditors with substantial claims against the troubled business may independently seek writs of attachment as a way of enforcing collection of the debts owed to them. If the assets so attached are crucial to the operation of the business, the company will have to file bankruptcy in order to release the attachment.

3. In attempting an out-of-court reorganization plan, the company may find that it cannot convince certain creditors to accept its proposal. If the company then seeks protection under Chapter 11, the Bankruptcy Code provides that a simple majority of creditors, who represent two-thirds of the dollar amount of debt, can approve a Chapter 11 plan. This is an effective method for dealing with individual creditors or small groups of creditors who disagree with the majority and attempt to block an out-of-court reorganization plan, since the Bankruptcy Code holds that they must accept the plan if it provides them more payback than if the business were liquidated.

4. If the insolvent company's primary secured lenders decide to stop advancing funds or choose to foreclose on the collateral necessary for the operation of the business, such as inventory, equipment, or accounts receivable, the business may seek protection of the bankruptcy court simply to be able to continue to operate. The Bankruptcy Code allows the debtor to get a court injunction, a "stay," which prohibits creditors from enforcing their claims. The stay allows the debtor time to develop a plan.

The temporary relief provided under Chapter 11 gives the business breathing space to try to reorganize for future financial health. However, it is important to understand that bankruptcy does not solve the basic financial, marketing, or operational problems of the business. It is simply a legal tool that provides a structure for negotiating deals between the business and its creditors, and an opportunity to avoid the potential liquidation of the company.

THE TWO BROTHERS IN DEBT: A 20TH CENTURY UPDATE

What difference does it really make, you may wonder, whom you owe or how your debt is structured? Don't you owe the same amount of money, no matter what?

The answer is no. How your business approaches bankruptcy, and who is holding the bills, can make a crucial difference between disaster and simply wiping the slate clean to begin again. To illustrate this, let's return to the two brothers of our earlier tale.

Suppose those two brothers lived now, in the 1980s. Suppose, once again, they end up in debt. There is no threat of debtors' prison facing them, but they are at the highest level of adversity in their business. Failure is staring them in the face. Bankruptcy is just a filing away.

Only this time, for the sake of discussion, suppose they have separate businesses. Each one has the same amount of assets and the same total dollar amount of debt. But they have handled their money differently.

The shrewd brother, the one who dashed off to get funds while his brother was held fast by the bailiffs, has been very, very careful with his business. He has made sure that he keeps current with his payroll taxes to the IRS. If he couldn't make the taxes from the company's profits, he either delayed paying his employees until he had enough funds, or he laid off employees.

Meanwhile, his brother, a nice guy with a great rapport with his customers and on personal terms with many of his creditors, is also struggling along with his business. When he's unable to make payroll taxes, he lets that slide, figuring he'll make it up the next time around. It only costs him a small penalty to pay taxes late, and he views it almost like a loan from the government. Business is declining, but he just hates to let any of his employees go. He uses the money he owes to the government to finance his losses.

Each of the brothers has signed a guarantee with the bank. The shrewd brother works diligently to make sure that the bank's collateral is secure. He figures that it is in his own best interest for the bank to be paid on time. He has no uncovered guarantees.

His brother, however, likes the feeling of having unencumbered assets, and tries to minimize the bank's security. He also signs guarantees to suppliers, and even to his landlord. He signs a five-year lease to get reduced rent on his office building, and smugly figures that he is secure.

While the shrewd brother pays all of his little creditors because he figures he shouldn't have too many bills, his brother placates the big creditors and doesn't pay the small ones anything.

The shrewd brother is aware that the State Board of Equalization can put him out of business for nonpayment of sales tax, so he makes sure he collects sales tax and reports and pays it as required. His brother, on the other hand, in an effort to placate his customers and increase his business, often doesn't charge them sales tax. He figures it is a way to give them a discount without taking money out of the firm. He rarely reports sales taxes to the State Board of Equalization, and when he does, he understates it so he can pocket the money and use it somewhere else.

The shrewd brother maintains excellent records on the day-to-day operation of his business. He knows exactly where the money is going, and he keeps track of his bank balance. As a result, he knows his business is in trouble and worries about the decline.

The nice brother thinks his brother worries too much. In his own business, he doesn't "waste" money on endless recordkeeping. When he wants to know how much money he has on hand, he simply calls the bank and asks for his balance. He never balances his checkbook and never knows how much money he has. But he sleeps easier than his brother.

That is, until they both decide they have no choice but to declare bankruptcy. It might be assumed, at first glance, that with the same amount of total debt liability and assets, each brother would receive the same treatment in the bankruptcy courts. If anything, the nice brother expects that the bankruptcy judge will appreciate his efforts to keep all of his employees on board.

But the two brothers are not equal in the eyes of the bankruptcy court. The nice brother discovers that since he hasn't protected the bank, his largest secured creditor, the bank is very uncooperative. Since he owes back payroll taxes, the IRS springs to action, placing liens on his accounts to protect what is owed to them. The State Board of Equalization revokes his sales tax license, so that he is no longer able to ship. All of his smaller creditors, whom he has not paid in quite some time, panic and start harassing him day and night. Although he will get some relief from this once he has completed his bankruptcy filing, his records are in such bad shape that he cannot even file a list of creditors. When he files a reorganization plan, no one has confidence that he will be able to carry it out.

The shrewd brother faces a much easier time of it. The bank is fully secured, so it doesn't have a high level of anxiety. He's not at risk with the IRS, since his payroll taxes are current. He's in the good graces of the State Board of Equalization, so his sales tax bond stays in effect, and he can continue to do business as usual. When things get tough, he only has to negotiate with his major vendors, because all of his small creditors are paid. His records, up to date and complete, inspire confidence in his ability to fulfill the reorganization plan he proposes.

This story, though fictional, illustrates the importance of understanding how bankruptcy law views the debts of the business. You may never end up in bankruptcy court, but it is wise to take precautions. Remember the risky nature of business. You are never completely "safe." If fate and bad luck put you at the mercy of the bankruptcy system, you'll want to make sure that the way your business was conducted allows you to use the law in your defense.

12 HEALTH IS A RELATIVE TERM: INSOLVENCY OBJECTIVES, STRATEGIES, AND PROCESSES

Our plans miscarry because they have no aim.
When a man does not know what harbor he is
making for, no wind is the right wind.

SENECA
14 B.C.–A.D. 65

Once management and ownership have accepted the fact that the business is insolvent, and that intelligent and decisive action is necessary to deal with the company's problems, efforts to achieve some type of solution can begin in earnest. In this chapter we will establish a framework for these efforts. What kinds of plans are possible, which are practical and can be achieved realistically, what are the risks, and how can these risks be controlled and minimized?

It is important to distinguish between the overall strategy for dealing with an insolvency situation and the strategy for the turnaround of a business. An insolvency case may involve a number of aspects that are not specifically related to the business per se, but are certainly impacted by it.

The following example should clarify the situation. A company was in the business of manufacturing products for the home leisure market. It was a public company with about 250 public shareholders, but the majority of the stock was held in a trust controlled by the founder. The company, which reported sales on the order of $10,000,000 per year, was insolvent with liabilities of $3,250,000 exceeding assets of $1,500,000. The company's debts included obligations of $450,000 to the IRS and the state taxing authorities, 55 percent being nondischargeable.

The company had loans of $1,000,000 with a bank, of which approximately $500,000 was secured by real property of the founder. The founder had intentionally executed guarantees of almost $500,000 to unsecured creditors of the corporation in order to acquire various products and services for the corporation.

Finally, the founder and his family had established another corporation to market the company's products on a retail basis. The retail corporation was managed by many of the same family members who participated in the management of the manufacturing concern. Moreover, the retail corporation had run up unsecured obligations with the manufacturing corporation for products that they had not paid for. The manufacturing corporation had also executed, and was liable for, a number of leases on the retail establishments. To further complicate matters, the founder, who was the driving force behind the corporation and responsible for its very high growth rate, was seriously ill and suffering from stress. In this particular situation, the overall insolvency strategy had to deal with the following issues:

1. The viability of the manufacturing corporation

2. The financial situation of the founder, whose continued services were necessary to rehabilitate the corporation, and whose property outside the corporation might be required to fund the rehabilitation

3. The effect of the nondischargeable obligations on the founder and other members of his family

4. The interests of the public shareholders and the effect of all of the previous insider transactions on their interests

5. The viability of the retail corporation, which owed the manufacturing corporation $500,000

As can be seen from this example, the issue of the turnaround of the manufacturing corporation is only part of the problem and is subsumed within the larger insolvency context.

SETTING THE FRAMEWORK FOR DEALING WITH INSOLVENCY

In order to deal with a complicated insolvency situation, such as the one described above, it is helpful to have a framework to address and evaluate the various issues that are involved. In formulating an overall insolvency strategy, six issues have to be taken into account. They are briefly described below and illustrated in Figure 12.1. The first four issues are discussed in more detail later on in this chapter.

1. The hierarchy of objectives of the principals, major shareholders, and board members for the business and the principals

2. The needs, wants, capacities, and capabilities of the principals

3. The various strategies that can be employed in an insolvency situation to meet the objectives

4. The various processes that are available to implement the strategy selected

5. The internal situation, including the financial, legal, and economic aspects from the viewpoints of both the business itself and the principals

6. The external situation, including the customer base, the competitive conditions, the conditions within the industry, and the overall business environment

These six issues provide the framework for the structure of an overall insolvency plan.

THE HIERARCHY OF OBJECTIVES: WHAT DOES THE BUSINESS REALLY WANT?

Objectives are defined as the targets that we are attempting to achieve. The primary purpose of an objective is to guide strategic decision making.

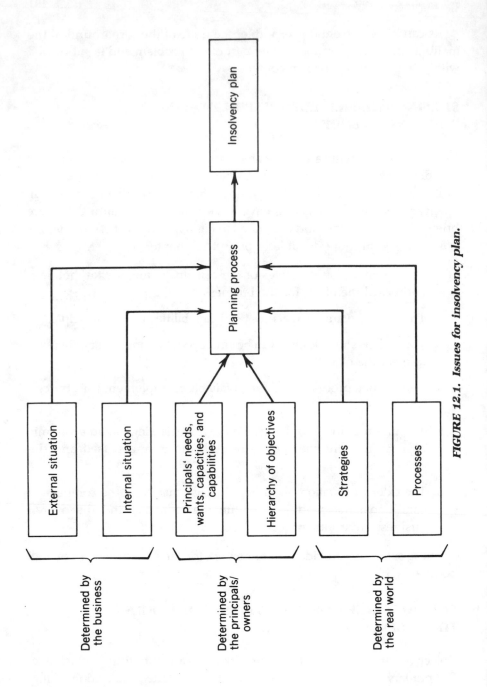

FIGURE 12.1. Issues for insolvency plan.

Specifically, objectives provide the basis for choosing, from among the strategies and processes that are available and viable, those specific ones that will be used to implement the plan.

Although the specific objectives of an insolvency plan may differ from one case to another, they are all derived from the generic types briefly outlined in the following.

1. *Preserve the earnings of the business.* The objective is to maintain the business as an operating entity to generate future profits and shareholder value. In medical terms, this is equivalent to keeping the patient alive so that it can enjoy some quality of life in the future.

As long as a business can continue operations and preserve its identity, market, technology, and employee base, the number of options for formulating a successful financial solution for the principals is maximized. An operating business can provide continuous income for the principals, pay for the professional services necessary to formulate and implement solutions to the company's problems, and search out an effective long-term solution (which could include sale or merger), without its management being subjected to the intense pressure that invariably accompanies a "shut-down mode."

2. *Preserve the assets of the business.* The assets of a business, or a personal household, include the types of property listed on the schedules that are filed with the Bankruptcy Court, as presented in Table 12.1.

When a business is no longer operating, extraordinary steps must be taken to preserve the assets. As a business starts to fail, there is a tendency for the valuable assets of the business to begin to disappear. Employees, ex-employees, and even managers engage in double dealing and collusion with future employers or benefactors. The failing business is viewed as a carcass to be plundered. Ethics, legal niceties, and so forth are ignored or suppressed. Employees and creditors to whom money may be owed engage in a ritual of rationalization and justification as they attempt to "right" the wrongs that they experienced at the hands of the failing company and its principals. We have seen instances of a client's car being severely damaged with sledgehammers; the client's property vandalized; substantial quantities of fixed assets stolen by ex-employees and creditors acting in concert; trade secrets, drawings, and specifications copied on a wholesale basis and surreptitiously removed from the company's premises.

TABLE 12.1.   PROPERTY TYPES LISTED ON BANKRUPTCY SCHEDULE

Real property
Cash on hand
Deposits
Household goods
Books, pictures, and collections
Wearing apparel and personal possessions
Automobiles and other vehicles
Boats, motors, and accessories
Livestock and other animals
Farming supplies and implements
Office equipment and supplies
Machinery, equipment, and supplies used in business
Inventory
Other tangible personal property
Patents and other general intangibles
Bonds and other instruments
Other liquidated debts
Contingent and unliquidated claims
Interests in insurance policies
Annuities
Interests in corporations and unincorporated companies
Interests in partnerships
Equitable and future interests, rights, and powers in personality

In many situations involving substantial amounts of valuable personal property, equipment, and inventory we frequently post round-the-clock guards until the property can be disposed of. Strange as it seems, property still disappears occasionally.

3. *Maximize the net future realizable earnings of the principals irrespective of the disposition of the business.* In many instances, a business has constituted the major asset of an individual entrepreneur. It has provided him employment and a good standard of living. When the business fails, it's tantamount to his employer firing him. Unless the principal has been able to accumulate and retain substantial assets outside of the business that could support him in the manner to which he has become accustomed, he will have to face up to the unhappy prospect of working under different conditions. This can certainly be a major trauma for even the most emotionally stable ex-entrepreneur. What happens to ex-entrepreneurs who have not been successful, are at mid-life, and must continue to work to put "beans on the table"? Unless they drop out of society, they will have to go out into the community and seek gainful employment or start another business. In either case, it is important that the principals retain, to the maximum extent possible, their reputations. The community's view of their honesty and integrity should not diminish as a consequence of the insolvency plan.

There are instances in which the principal of a business is worth more working for someone else than inside his own business. We have had a number of clients with distinctive skills (such as doctors, auto mechanics, and psychologists) who have struggled for years attempting to build a business or practice in their specialty and were barely able to eke out a living. When we pointed out to them that they were actually earning less than what their skills could command in the open market, they liquidated their business and achieved two to three times their previous net income working for someone else.

4. *Preserve the assets of the principals outside of the business.* If the business is a corporation, the individual's assets can be separated, except to the extent that the principals are obligated under guarantees to secured and unsecured creditors or the federal and state governments for penalties. In many instances principals no longer have either the interest, the capacity, or the stamina to manage their business, and their primary interest is in maximizing their assets outside of the business.

5. *Eliminate, to the extent possible, the nondischargeable obligations of the principals, should they have to file personal bankruptcy.* In many situations where principals are obligated to several entities under guarantees, and where aggressive creditors pursue the principals under theories of alter ego, there may be no practical way for the principal to escape personal bankruptcy. If that appears to be the case, the minimum objective to be pursued is to ensure that either the nondischargeable obligations of the principals are paid, or there are sufficient assets in the bankruptcy estate to pay them.

6. *Eliminate, to the extent possible, the stress, anxiety, and uncertainty of the principals caused by their financial situation.* In striving for this objective, the principal is, in effect, saying that he is willing to give up both control over the disposition of his business and a certain amount of assets, in order to escape from the stress and uncertainty that may have plagued him for a substantial period of time.

The priority in which each of the above six objectives is placed is a function of the needs, wants, capacities, and capabilities of the principals. We discuss these considerations later in the chapter.

Frequently the wants of the principal will be inconsistent with capability, financial capacity, or the realities of the marketplace. For example, an owner of a failing business insisted that the business be saved at "all costs," that is, he was insisting that preserving the business was his first-priority objective. However, the market for the services he was offering was declining rapidly, and he was indebted to the IRS for $250,000 of unpaid withholding taxes. He had no significant assets outside the business to pay the withholding tax obligation and, with the market decline, no realistic prospect that the business would generate sufficient profits to pay the tax obligation. The only asset he possessed that could be liquidated was the good will of his company, which was of interest to a competitor. He refused to consider a sale and his business eventually closed, leaving him indebted to the IRS.

PRINCIPAL CONCERNS: THE PRINCIPAL'S NEEDS, WANTS, AND CAPABILITIES

Henry David Thoreau wrote that "The mass of men lead lives of quiet desperation." Henry must have had the principals of troubled businesses in mind. "Quiet desperation" usually describes the state of mind of a principal who is wrestling with insolvency.

We have discussed the mental and emotional states of the firm's principals. Irrespective of the client's physical and emotional states, the turnaround manager must quickly determine what the principal wants or needs from the business, what he is willing and able to give to the business, and what the principal's needs and wants are, apart from the business.

Sometimes the principals want to "cut and run," leave the scene, disappear. In other instances they want to save the business but do not have the skills to manage it even if it were stabilized. Some clients want to limit their loss and get on with their lives in a new endeavor. Others want to avoid bankruptcy "at all costs." Some want to see their creditors "paid in full," others are simply too exhausted to care any longer.

The issues regarding the needs and wants and the capacity and capability of the ownership are addressed by asking the following questions, either rhetorically or directly.

Control: To what extent do the owners wish to control the affairs of the business?

1. Full control.

2. Limited control.

3. No control.

Management: To what extent do the owners have the desire to contribute to the ongoing management of the business?

1. Ownership wants to be involved full time.

2. Some limited involvement.

3. No involvement.

Management Capability: To what extent do the owners have the capability to contribute to the ongoing management of the business? Capability can include skill, intellectual capacity, and physical capability.

1. Ownership has the skill and capability to contribute on a full-time basis.

2. Ownership has the skill and capability to contribute on a limited basis.

3. Ownership lacks both the skill and the capacity to contribute on any basis.

Management Requirement: To what extent are the owners of the business essential to the survival and growth of the business?

1. Ownership has unique distinctive skills that are not easily replaceable and without which the business cannot survive or grow.

2.   Ownership has unique distinctive skills that are replaceable with some difficulty.

3.   Ownership does not possess any distinctive skill that is essential for the business's survival or growth.

Financial Support: To what extent do the owners need to look to the business to provide them the income needed to maintain their standard of living?

1.   Owners need the income from the business to sustain them.

2.   Owners need some income from the business.

3.   Owners do not need any income from the business.

Financial Capability: To what extent are the owners willing and able to provide funds that the corporation will require to accomplish a turnaround program or to sustain the business until an orderly liquidation or merger can be accomplished?

1.   Owners have resources available to fund the full turnaround program.

2.   Owners have resources available to partially fund the turnaround program.

3.   Owners have limited resources, that is, they can provide funds or guarantee the payment of professional fees that will be required by consultant, lawyer, and accountant.

4.   Owners have no resources.

Status: How strongly does the principal feel he wants to maintain the status of himself or the business?

1.   To what extent are owners willing to go (financially) to avoid bankruptcy of the business? Personal bankruptcy?

2.   To what extent are owners committed to preserving the identity of the business and their identity with the business?

3.   To what extent are owners anxious to clean the slate, put the past behind them, and start a new beginning through personal bankruptcy?

By addressing these issues in a candid and forthright manner, we can create a spectrum of *realistic* desires and objectives for the principals, which will constitute a vital ingredient in our planning process.

GAME PLANNING: STRATEGIES FOR DEALING WITH INSOLVENCY

Before we discuss the strategies for dealing with insolvency, it is important to distinguish between what we mean by strategy, as opposed to process. A strategy is your overall plan to achieve a set of objectives. A process is the means and procedures—the method—by which you carry out your strategy. In an insolvency situation, you may have turnaround of the business as your strategy. You may implement that strategy through the bankruptcy process or through other processes. Table 12.2 shows how strategies compare to processes in dealing with insolvency.

There are six primary strategies for dealing with an insolvent business or personal situation. These are briefly outlined in the following.

1. *Turnaround:* The turnaround of the business via operational and financial changes is aimed at making the business a viable and self-sufficient enterprise at some point in the future. As part of the turnaround, the existing debt of the corporation is restructured or modified to the satisfaction of the creditors.

2. *Sale of the Business:* Sale to another party who will either incorporate the business unit into an existing enterprise or will effect a turnaround of the business is another strategy. The proceeds of the sale are used to satisfy the claims of the creditors to the extent of the funds available.

3. *Dump and Buy Back:* In this strategy the owners of the business will assign the assets, with creditor approval, to an independent trustee who will liquidate the assets in a commercially reasonable manner, as described above, and make an overall settlement with creditors. However, in this case, the original owner will attempt to buy back the assets that he wants from the trustee and restart his business, or some modification of it, free and clear of the liabilities.

TABLE 12.2. INSOLVENCY STRATEGIES AND PROCESSES

| Strategy | Bankruptcy Processes | | | | Nonbankruptcy Processes | | |
	7	11	12	13	Assignment	Compromise	Receivership	Walk Away
Turnaround		√	√	√		√		
Sale		√				√	√	
Dump and buy back			√		√			
Controlled liquidation					√	√	√	
Uncontrolled liquidation	√							
Abandonment								√

4. *Controlled Liquidation:* The owners of the business marshal all of the assets of the corporation that have value and sell them off piecemeal, or in bulk, through negotiated private sales or at auction. The funds received are used to satisfy creditors' claims to the extent funds are available.

5. *Uncontrolled Liquidation:* In this case, the liquidation of the business assets is managed by an entity that is not controlled by the owners. It can be a trustee or receiver appointed by the court, or a trustee appointed by a creditor or group of creditors.

6. *Abandonment:* The owners merely abandon the business and its assets to the secured and unsecured creditors. This strategy is also known as "Throw the keys on the table and turn out the lights."

The viability of each of the strategies will of course depend on the particular business and owner situations as discussed earlier in this chapter. However, we can briefly review the types of situations in which the various insolvency strategies are effective.

STRATEGY 1: TURNAROUND

Turnaround is usually the preferred strategy, because it will preserve the earnings and assets of the business, and it will usually maximize the value of the owner's equity. Whether or not a turnaround can be achieved will depend on many issues. Turnaround may not be feasible because the prospects for the business are not very attractive, the owners are unable to raise the capital required to implement a turnaround plan, or the creditors are unwilling to accept the plan.

Moreover, there are cases where the owners, in light of their assessment of the probability of a good result, may decide that available plans place them at too great a financial risk. Given the alternative of either selling or liquidating the business to limit their financial loss or attempting a turnaround program that could conceivably increase their loss, they may opt to sell or liquidate.

STRATEGY 2: SALE OF THE BUSINESS

A sale of the business can be an effective strategy, provided the proceeds of the sale are used to pay those debts that are critical to the owner's financial survival, such as guarantees and nondischargeable obligations to the taxing authorities. It can, perhaps, provide the owners with some future involvement in the business, and income from that future involvement. However, the sale of a business requires a willing and able buyer, and they are always in short supply when a business is failing and needs to sell. The sale of an insolvent business will require the approval of the secured and unsecured creditors that will be impacted as a result of the sale, that is, receive less than full value for their claim.

Finding prospects for the purchase of a failing business poses yet another difficult and frustrating problem to the owner and his team. A buyer candidate must be prepared to make a long-term investment in the business and assume the risk and burden of operating the business, in the hope that the investment will yield a reasonable return. Since the business is failing, and presumably no buyer is interested in a business that has perpetually lost money, it will be a prerequisite of any sale to educate the buyer as to why the business has failed and what actions the buyer can take to make his investment successful.

Selling a business involves five major tasks. These are summarized below.

1. Preparing a proposal or presentation that describes the characteristics of the business that is being sold, its history, assets, customer base, market structure, and so forth

2. Locating prospective buyers

3. Educating the prospective buyers as to the characteristics of the business being sold

4. Negotiating the sale

5. Implementing the sale, that is, preparing the closing documents, transferring personnel, vacating premises, and other tasks

Selling a business is a tremendously time-consuming and emotionally draining process. It is extremely difficult for the owner, who must usually spearhead the efforts to sell. He is invariably torn between his intellectual understanding that he must sell in order to preserve his personal financial situation, and his emotional desire to preserve the business to which he has devoted a significant portion of his adult life and all of his emotional energy.

The first part of the process (preparation and presentation) is relatively straightforward and can usually be accomplished within a one- or two-week period, depending on the size of the business. The second step, locating prospective buyers, is considerably more difficult. The prospective buyers of the troubled company will come from the company's stakeholders or be strangers brought to the company by brokers, investment bankers, company advertisements, or news releases. They will include present or past employees, competitors, customers, suppliers, investors, and others. The most effective procedure is to publicize promptly that the company is interested in a sale and flush out the available prospects as quickly as possible.

The ease and speed with which prospective buyers can be educated about the company to raise their level of interest is a very sensitive function of their familiarity with the industry and the market. Employees will require very little education, and as a result often allow a sale to be achieved rapidly. Competitors require slightly more education, customers even more, and suppliers have probably no greater familiarity with the business than would a stranger who saw the company's ad in the *Wall Street Journal*.

The speed with which a deal can be negotiated and implemented will rely greatly on the previous relationship of the prospect to the company. The more knowledgeable the prospect is about the business and the personnel of the selling company, the more he will be able to rely upon his own capability in making the crucial decisions and evaluations that go into the purchase of a business, and the more quickly he will be able to make those decisions. Prospects who are relative strangers to the business will have to rely upon consultants, accountants, and other experts to provide the vital data that they will require, which adds both time and risk to the buying decision. It is for this reason, and our experience bears it out, that the most likely prospects to purchase a business in adversity are its former and present employees, its competitors, and its customers.

STRATEGY 3: DUMP AND BUY BACK

Dump and buy back is an effective strategy for resolving all the debts of a business and starting up again free and clear of previous liabilities. It will be very effective if the owners have the benefit of the corporate shield for all the debts of the business (no guarantees and no nondischargeable obligations), can raise the cash necessary to buy back the assets from the liquidating trustee, and will not be adversely affected by the interruption of the business.

STRATEGY 4: CONTROLLED LIQUIDATION

Controlled liquidation is employed when none of the previous strategies appears viable and the owner's future financial health is highly dependent on the aggregate proceeds realized from the liquidation of the assets. For example, assume that an incorporated manufacturing business fails owing $1,000,000 to a creditor who is secured by receivables, inventory, and capital equipment having a book value of $2,000,000. Receivables are valued at $1,200,000, inventory at $300,000, and capital equipment at $500,000. The corporation's other debts are $100,000 owed to employees for wages, $350,000 owed to the IRS and state taxing authorities for withholding taxes, and $550,000 owed to unsecured creditors. The secured creditor's loan to the corporation has been guaranteed by the owner, who has also pledged the equity in his home (valued at $200,000) as additional collateral.

If the owner is to avoid a call on his guarantee, the business assets will have to be liquidated for $1,000,000. If the owner is to ensure that all the debts of the corporation that may create a nondischargeable obligation for him are paid, he will have to achieve net liquidation proceeds of at least $1,450,000 ($1,000,000 to the secured creditor, $100,000 for employee wages, and $350,000 for taxes). Therefore it is in the owner's interest to maximize the liquidation value of the business in order to minimize his own financial exposure.

Maximizing the liquidation value of the estate requires a dedicated effort. Receivables owed to failing firms are notoriously difficult to collect; inventory, other than raw material, is difficult to sell. Work in process has no value unless someone finishes the products, and even finished products are difficult to move to other than certain existing customers or discounters, since the product will be identified with a manufacturer that is quitting business and will not be available to support the product. The liquidation value of the capital equipment will be very sensitive to the size of the market for the equipment, how unique it is, and whether the industry in which the equipment is used is growing so that it can absorb the equipment from a failing competitor.

One of the most difficult aspects of any liquidation program is to estimate the likely results at the outset. Appraisers are frequently hired to estimate the fair-market wholesale value and the auction value of equipment and inventory. My experience indicates that appraisals of frequently auctioned equipment, such as trucks, cars, and so forth, are relatively accurate, with results within a few percentage points of predictions, while appraisals of infrequently auctioned equipment, such as specialized parts, can be off by as much as several hundred percent.

Another major factor that determines the net proceeds of a liquidation is the cost of the process itself. The collection of receivables will require clerical and accounting support and someone to staff the telephone and plead with recalcitrant debtors; the inventory and capital equipment will have to be inventoried, sorted, guarded, and tagged. If an auctioneer is employed, he will require funds for cataloging the material to be auctioned and advertising the auction. In addition, certain equipment items may not be operable, and repairing such equipment may be in the best interest of the business to maximize the proceeds. All of these costs add up and reduce the funds that can be used to pay creditors.

Tables 12.3 and 12.4 analyze two hypothetical liquidation results for a sample manufacturing firm, illustrating the points made in the previous discussion.

In the example of a good liquidation, shown in Table 12.3, the liquidation results in the payment of all of the secured debt, all of the wages, and all of the taxes and even provides a small return to the unsecured creditors. The owner has no personal obligation for any of the debts of the corporation. In the example shown in Table 12.4, the liquidation only provides enough funds to pay the secured creditor, the unpaid wages, and a small part of the taxes; $313,000 of the taxes will remain unpaid, and the unsecured creditors will receive nothing. In this case the owner will have substantial obligations to the taxing authorities, amounting to 55 percent of the unpaid taxes, or $172,150.

Banks and other secured creditors who have the primary lien position in the assets believe that the owner of a business is frequently in the best position to achieve the maximum value from a liquidation program. Often this is not the case. Although the owner may be the most knowledgeable person with respect to how to maximize the assets of a company, he may be the least capable of actually liquidating the business that he has spent years building. The owner may not be able to be motivated to do "what it takes," namely, apply very aggressive collection methods against his former customers, negotiate with his competitors for the sale

TABLE 12.3.   GOOD LIQUIDATION RESULT
_____

Revenue
Receivables collected $1,100,000
Inventory sold   150,000
Capital equipment   300,000
   Total proceeds $1,550,000

Less: Costs of selling
Accounting/clerical   10,000
Guard service for 2 months   12,000
Repair of equipment   1,000
Yard labor to clean inventory equipment for sale   500
Auctioneer fee   30,000
Advertising, catalogs   10,000
   Total expenses   63,000
Net proceeds available $1,487,000

Disbursements:
Secured creditor   1,000,000
Employee wages   100,000
Taxing authorities   350,000
   Subtotal $1,450,000
Available to unsecured creditors $ 37,000
Premium to unsecured creditors = $.074/$ owed.
_____

of inventory and capital equipment, recruit and negotiate with auctioneers, and negotiate with former employees to whom he still owes wages so that they will work on an hourly basis to help market his inventory and equipment.

Such activities are not pursued enthusiastically by entrepreneurs. Better results are often achieved if the owner hires a professional or a former employee to manage the liquidation for some type of incentive compensation. This approach ensures both the bank and the owner that a dispassionate and professional effort will be made to maximize the liquidation value of the business.

STRATEGY 5: UNCONTROLLED LIQUIDATION

An uncontrolled liquidation of a business occurs when a corporation files under Chapter 7 of the Bankruptcy Act and a trustee is appointed by the court to liquidate the estate. An uncontrolled liquidation also occurs if a receiver is placed in charge of a business with instructions to manage the business or liquidate it as he sees fit.

The risk to the owner of the uncontrolled liquidation is that he has no say in any aspect of the liquidation proceedings, and he is literally at the mercy of the trustee. Trustees run the gamut from those who strive very hard to do a professional job to those who are inadequate, inept, and even senile. A trustee gets paid a percentage of the funds that he recovers and is not paid any type of hourly fee. Therefore he is clearly motivated to get as many dollars as he can in the shortest amount of time, and he cannot be expected to invest a substantial amount of his time selling difficult-to-move merchandise or pursuing nonpaying creditors who owe small balances.

An uncontrolled liquidation strategy is appropriate when the owner is at either extreme on the financial exposure spectrum: if he has absolutely no personal exposure and nothing to gain from maximizing the proceeds, or if even the most wildly optimistic liquidation would not have any material effect on his dismal personal financial situation.

TABLE 12.4. POOR LIQUIDATION RESULT

Revenue		
Receivables collected	$ 900,000	
Inventory sold	100,000	
Capital equipment	200,000	
Total proceeds		$1,200,000
Less: Costs of selling		
Accounting/clerical	10,000	
Guard service for 2 months	12,000	
Repair of equipment	1,000	
Yard labor to clean inventory equipment for sale	500	
Auctioneer fee	30,000	
Advertising, catalogs	10,000	
Total expenses		63,000
Net proceeds available		$1,137,000
Disbursements:		
Secured creditor	$1,000,000	
Employee wages	100,000	
Subtotal		$1,100,000
Available to taxing authorities		$ 37,000
Shortfall for taxes		$ 313,000
Funds available to unsecured creditors = $0.		

STRATEGY 6: ABANDONMENT

If an owner determines that he cannot turn around or sell the business, is not interested in restarting the business through a dump and buy back strategy, and has nothing to gain from and is not interested in participating in liquidation, only two options remain available: uncontrolled liquidation or abandonment. To implement the process of an uncontrolled liquidation, the owner has to either file under Chapter 7 of the Bankruptcy Act or arrange to turn over the assets of the business to a trustee.

The owner may not want to take either of these actions. First, he might want to facilitate the recovery of a secured creditor with whom he has a close relationship and merely abandon the assets to the secured creditor, pack up his books and records, and leave the scene. Second, he might want to avoid any trustee's careful examination and reconstruction of certain business transactions that might expose him personally. Third, the owner might want to start up a similar or identical business using the same customer base as the now defunct business and will want to avoid the possibility of a trustee examining his future actions and possibly bring a theft of trade secret action against him. In three instances abandonment of the business and its assets is a viable strategy.

SHARING THE LIMITED WEALTH: PROCESSES FOR REDISTRIBUTION OF ASSETS

Processes for accomplishing the redistribution of assets in an insolvency can be classified as either bankruptcy or nonbankruptcy processes. These processes are illustrated in Table 12.2.

Bankruptcy Processes

There are four basic bankruptcy processes to deal with insolvency:

Chapter 11 usually allows the corporate owners to remain in control of the business and to attempt either to restructure its finances so that it can continue to operate, or to liquidate in an orderly manner.

Chapter 7 is a liquidation under which the affairs of the corporation or the assets of an individual are turned over to a trustee, who marshals all the assets, liquidates them, and distributes the proceeds to the creditors of the corporation in order of priority.

Chapter 13 is designed for individual, personal bankruptcy. The individual is allowed to retain property and protect assets by agreeing to pay for them over time.

Chapter 12 is for family farmers and combines most borrower-oriented features of Chapter 11 and Chapter 13 with a quick and inexpensive means for a family farmer to confirm a plan of reorganization.

Nonbankruptcy Processes

There are three basic types of nonbankruptcy insolvency processes: compromise agreement (also referred to as a composition agreement), assignment for the benefit of creditors, and receivership.

Compromise Agreement

This is the process by which an insolvent debtor enters into a new contract with his secured or unsecured creditors to restructure the obligations that he cannot service into new obligations that he believes he can service. The compromise agreement defines the amount, nature, terms, and conditions of the restructured debt.

Debtors enter into compromise agreements in an effort to avoid the costs, uncertainty, and stigma of a bankruptcy. Creditors agree to a compromise agreement rather than forcing a debtor into bankruptcy because they feel the debtor is worth more "alive" than "dead" in terms of future business, to avoid either classifying the loan or writing off the debt, and (like the debtor) to avoid the legal costs and uncertainty of a bankruptcy.

Compromise agreements are terrific when they work. They require a few hours of work by an attorney, some letter writing, and some stamps. An insolvency problem can be cured with the stroke of a pen (or several pens, depending on the number of creditors). The hitch is, it can be very difficult to accomplish since it requires essentially 100 percent cooperation among your significant creditors (significant means that you cannot afford to "buy them out" for either economic or political reasons). Any hostile or recalcitrant creditor who does not wish to cooperate and pursues litigation and writs of attachment inevitably will upset a compromise plan.

Frequently debtors who are considering implementing a compromise agreement need the same unsecured creditors to continue to ship to them after the plan is in place and to continue to offer some type of credit. Unsecured trade creditors will divide themselves into those who will or will not sue, and those who will or will not ship on credit terms.

In our experience we have found that:

1. It's a fair bet that virtually no creditors will sue and continue to ship. When it does happen, it's because the creditor's internal control system has broken down—but it does happen.

2. Most creditors will go along with the compromise if they feel that they have been fairly dealt with, that there is full disclosure of the company's situation, and that the executive responsible for the account in the creditor's firm does not have a high emotional involvement in the debt.

3. The vast majority of creditors will agree to the compromise but will not ship on credit; they will demand COD terms or even cash in advance.

Consequently, it is usually wishful thinking to plan on implementing a compromise agreement and getting a substantial majority of your vendors to extend you more credit.

Assignment for the Benefit of Creditors

An assignment is a method by which assets are assigned to a trustee to be liquidated. The trustee can either be proposed by the debtor, subject to the agreement of the creditors, or selected by the creditors. In this process the trustee shuts down the business, sells the assets for the highest value he can achieve, pays the costs of shutdown, and then pays the claims against the business in the order of bankruptcy priority. The creditors must agree to the settlement whereby they will, in effect, compromise their claim against the debtor for whatever proceeds they receive from the trustee. It is quite rare (I've never seen it) that the creditors receive the full value of their claim.

The key to a successful assignment is the trustee who, whether he is nominated by the debtor or by the creditors, is both competent and independent.

Receivership

A receiver is a trustee, appointed by a judge of the state court to whom he is accountable, to perform certain functions for the estate of an insolvent debtor. The appointment of a receiver is typically sought by a secured creditor who is concerned that the collateral, which is security for the loan, is being dissipated. The secured creditor will therefore petition the state court to appoint a receiver to marshal the collateral; preserve, protect, and insure it and prevent any further dissipation.

A receiver could also be sought by a junior or silent partner of an insolvent business who is concerned that the active partner is mismanaging the business, dissipating its assets, and creating liabilities for the junior or inactive partner. In this situation the inactive partner could petition the court to appoint a receiver to take over the management of the business from the active partner.

THE LADY OR THE TIGER: WHICH CHOICE TO MAKE?

There is a tale of a young man and a beautiful princess who fell in love. As is often the case in these stories, the king was not pleased when he found out. He condemned the young man to the arena, where he would have to choose his own fate.

Behind one door was death in the form of a very hungry tiger, behind the other was a beautiful woman—not the princess—who would become his wife. The princess found out which door had which fate, and she signaled her lover to choose the door on the right. The question was, did she love him well enough to give him to another woman in marriage? Could he trust the choice she told him to make?

The executive of a business in financial distress may feel like the man in this story. The choices presented seem clear cut, but who can he believe? How can he choose?

In this chapter we have presented a number of choices that can be made when a business faces insolvency. Clarifying the objectives of the business and its principals is of primary importance. Together with a realistic assessment of the company's current condition and its likely prospects, this crucial step will help guide you toward the most realistic and appropriate plan of action.

13 | WILL THE PATIENT LIVE? KEY FACTORS IN COMPANY SURVIVAL

The best of seers is he who guesses well.

EURIPIDES

Picture this scene from a dramatic, tearjerker movie. A very ill, pale-faced man sits in his doctor's office facing the white-coated doctor, who has a stethoscope dangling from his neck. An X ray is lit up on the wall. The patient, who has undergone a series of tests for some rare, usually fatal, disease, is waiting to hear the good or the bad news. The doctor explains, in excruciating and precise detail, the results of the tests and the need for some very delicate and risky surgical procedures.

The patient, who has sat quietly through the long explanation, reaches out to grab the doctor's arm and asks the only questions he really wants the answers to: "Doctor, what are you saying? What are my chances for pulling through the operation? Will I live?"

These questions have no guaranteed answer. The doctor can quote percentages, survival rates, and other statistics, but there is really no way to predict the future. He doesn't know the answers for this particular patient, at this particular time.

The same is true in a business turnaround. The ailing company faces an unknown future, even after the turnaround manager has established a treatment program. What the business executive really wants to know is: "Will this turnaround work? Will the business survive?"

Answering this question is even more difficult for the turnaround consultant than for the medical doctor. The doctor's adversaries are a limited research base for his diagnosis, the patient's will to live, and the quirks of nature. The turnaround consultant's list of adversaries can include creditors, employees, managers, bankers, the government, the complexity of the business, the economy, the industry, and the business executive's willingness to work toward a realistic solution.

In addition, the conduct of business is in itself a stochastic process: results are determined by the interaction of random variables rather than by strict cause and effect. None of the processes that are involved in a turnaround effort is deterministic. An assessment of a situation is made based on the best information that the turnaround manager can acquire. He formulates a plan, attempts to implement the plan, and then works like hell and prays a lot that it will succeed. Sometimes he is very successful and the business is rehabilitated, sold, or liquidated on terms that are very favorable to the client. Sometimes the whole program collapses and both the business and the client wind up in a Chapter 7 bankruptcy proceeding—usually because one of the key elements hasn't worked out in accordance with plan. A program that was considered risky proves to have been too risky.

In his book *Corporate Turnaround*, Donald B. Bibeault tells the story of a conversation between Robert Wilson, who was negotiating to take over as president of a foundering Memorex Corporation, and Tom Clausen, president of the Bank of America, Memorex's principal secured lender. Wilson had established a reputation as a turnaround manager as a result of his success with Collins Radio. Tom Clausen purportedly asked Wilson, "Do you think you can walk on water twice?" "Yes," Wilson replied. This is the kind of self-confidence that the turnaround business requires, the kind that miracle-working turnaround managers seem to be able to pull out of the hat.

However, despite the confidence of the turnaround manager, predicting success of a turnaround effort is a high-risk enterprise, with substantially higher risk than predicting the success of a new business. Even the brightest, most skillful and experienced turnaround manager can only play the cards he's dealt. All things being equal, a competent and experienced turnaround manager has a substantially better chance to turn a "sow's ear into a silk purse" than the average businessperson or even the experienced professional manager. But all things are rarely equal.

Sometimes the best that even the most skilled turnaround manager can do is not enough.

But how can you tell? The problem remains, how do you assess the likelihood of the success of a turnaround effort, and what things can be done to improve that likelihood?

A number of management researchers have recently been examining, on a detailed level, what elements are prevalent in successful turnarounds. This research is international in scope, based on studies of firms in the United States, Europe, Great Britain, Japan, and India. The research has yielded results that are quite consistent with our own experience.

In this chapter we employ their research and attempt to analyze and quantify those factors that contribute to the success of turnaround. This will allow the various stakeholders in the company to decide if they want to endure the risk, grief, and effort that a turnaround entails.

In order to deal with the myriad of factors that affect the success of a turnaround and evaluate them in a systematic manner, we will introduce a model based on probability theory. We have found this technique very useful in our practice. It establishes a logical and consistent framework for making a realistic and dispassionate assessment of the probability of success in a turnaround effort.

THE ABC'S OF A SUCCESSFUL TURNAROUND

We have found that the factors that affect the success of a turnaround fall into three distinct categories. These elements are the ABCs of success for the turnaround.

1. *The A Elements—Additions from the Turnaround Team:* These elements must be created during the early stages of the turnaround program through the efforts of the turnaround team.

2. *The B Elements—Business Basics:* These elements must be present in the firm, certain basic strengths that the firm must possess and be able to provide to the turnaround effort.

3. *The C Elements—Crucial Concerns:* These elements critically contribute to or detract from the probability of success of the turnaround.

THE B ELEMENTS: BUSINESS BASICS

First we discuss the four key elements that the business must possess so that there can be any reasonable prospect for a turnaround. Later we explore the A elements, which develop due to the efforts of the turnaround team. However, the business must already have:

B1. A viable core business

B2. Skilled and loyal employees to do the work that is required to sustain the core business

B3. Sufficient competent and loyal management personnel to provide direction to the employees and perform the essential administrative and control tasks of the business

B4. Cooperative and honest ownership

Without these four cornerstones of the business in place, there is virtually no chance that the turnaround will be successful. Each one of these elements is now discussed in detail.

B1: The Viable Core Business

A viable core business can be said to exist when an enterprise possesses the following attributes:

1. Gross Profits Are Greater Than Fixed Operating Costs

There must be sufficient demand for the products or services so that the company makes money rather than loses it. In other words, the business is able to make enough profit to cover its fixed costs and the cost of money. Let us take a look at how this is quantitatively calculated.

The variables needed for the calculation are:

g = gross profit on each item of goods or services that the company sells

N = number of items of goods or services that the company sells during its accounting period, for example, per month

F = total of the fixed costs that the company sustains each month to "stay in business," that is, its rent, administrative salaries, utilities, telephone, insurance, and advertising during its accounting period

I = debt service during the accounting period, that is the money the business must pay its lenders to comply with its loan agreements

E = earnings that the owners and investors will require to maintain their lifestyles and justify the investment risk

In quantitative terms, if the core business is structured so that the following equation for gross profit is satisfied, then the business is viable:

$$g \times N > F + I + E$$

For example, suppose the business is a shoe store, which typically sells 500 pairs of shoes per month at a gross profit per shoe of $20. It must sustain an inventory of $100,000, for which it pays interest of $1000 per month, and in addition it has incurred a debt service obligation on its fixtures of $500 per month. The owners, who are the only investors, require $2500 per month to sustain their personal lifestyles.

Since, in this example, we have a value for all of the variables except fixed costs, we will rewrite our basic equation:

$$F < g \times N - I - E$$

Inserting the values from our example, g = $20, N = 500, I = $1500, and E = $2500, in the previous equation,

$$F < (\$20 \times 500) - \$1500 - \$2500$$

$$F < \$6000$$

This shoe store will be a "viable core business" if it can be organized so that all of its fixed costs are less than $6000 per month. If this basic inequality relationship cannot be satisfied, there is no core business. For example, you cannot build a business on volume (where N is high) if gross profit is low, while the period cost of being in business and the cost of money are both high.

This is a common trap of the "entrepreneur salesperson" who believes he can incur losses but "make it up on volume." Also, independent of how high the gross profit per item and how low the cost of doing business are, a viable core will not exist unless you have some minimal customer base. A brain surgeon may charge $50,000 per operation, but if he chooses to set up his practice in the Marshall Islands in order to reduce his fixed operating expenses, and people don't flock to that remote location, he may soon be bankrupt for lack of customers.

2. Distinctive Competence or Valuable Resource

The business must possess a distinctive competence or own a valuable resource that can be relied upon to generate or maintain a sustainable competitive advantage. A distinctive competence is something the business does extremely well and that has a strategic importance to the business.

For example, a small refinery that saw the majority of its business disappear when oil was deregulated in 1981 created a business unit based on the owner's skill in reclaiming "junk oil."

A valuable resource is an asset of strategic importance that is strong relative to competitors. This asset can be a leasehold, a patent, or even just a strong name in the industry. The valuable asset of a chain of waterbed retail stores, for instance, was its name recognition that had been developed through 15 years of radio advertising. If a business does not have a distinctive competence or a valuable asset that will allow it to create a marketing program to convince the market that there are real or perceived advantages in buying from it, the company does not have a viable core business.

B2: Skilled and Loyal Employees

A business attempting to achieve a turnaround simply cannot afford the time and cost to start hiring, training, and integrating large numbers of employees to carry out the day-to-day activities of the company.

Of course, there are instances in which a labor dispute accompanies a company turnaround, as in the acquisition of TWA when the flight attendants went on strike. The company was able to tap a large pool of trained attendants and management personnel to fill the void.

In most instances, however, if the employees do not measure up to the minimum standards of competence required to compete in the industry, or are apathetic or even hostile to the company and its ownership, the turnaround effort will probably be unsuccessful.

B3: Competent and Loyal Middle Management

In his book *How to Solve the Mismanagement Crisis,* Ichak Adizes identifies four management roles that need to be performed in a business for the long-run effective and efficient operations of an organization. These roles are:

1. Producers who achieve results or produce services that are equal to or better than those of the competition. In order to perform this function, the producer manager needs to have the knowledge of both the technology and the market within his field and industry (manufacturing, engineering, marketing, accounting), and must have the necessary drive to see that the final results are produced.

2. Administrators who schedule, coordinate, and verify implementation of the business's short-term objectives. They see to it that the system works as it was designed to work.

3. Entrepreneurs who generate goals, objectives, and plans for the enterprise, communicate these plans, and set up the mechanism to see that they can be carried out.

4. Integrators who provide the leadership and coaching to convert the goals, objectives, and plans of the enterprise into goals, objectives, and plans for the individual employees.

Individuals differ in the extent to which they have the capacity to carry out any of the above roles. There are managers who are primarily producers, and are extremely weak administrators, entrepreneurs, or integrators. A troubled company, poised for a turnaround, must have competent producer managers and administrator managers if the turnaround effort is to be successful. It can get by without entrepreneur managers and integrator managers in the short run, since these skills can be provided by the turnaround consultant, his staff, or the newly hired personnel.

However, the producer and administrator managers are essential. Someone has to make sure that the work of the business gets done and gets done right, and someone has to make sure that the control system continues to function. In addition, the producer and administrator managers who will keep the core business operating must be loyal to the company. If they begin to leverage the ownership in an effort to achieve a better deal, initiate disloyal acts, participate in company-bashing bull sessions with other personnel, or actually harm the company in an attempt to improve their own situation with competitors, the turnaround effort is likely to fail.

B4: Cooperative and Honest Ownership

Several years ago during a discussion with the executive vice president of a once successful, but now seriously troubled service company, I was expressing my frustration over my inability to motivate the owner/president to take even the most primitive actions to deal with the very serious problems in the company. After listening to me for a few minutes, the vice president smiled at me, implying that he'd heard this all before, and said, "But you're forgetting, it is *his* diamond mine, and if he chooses to use his rock crusher to destroy the diamonds that we have so laboriously mined, that's *his* prerogative."

If the business owner refuses to do, or allow others to do, those things that are necessary to rehabilitate the business, then obviously whatever efforts are expended in the turnaround attempt will be fruitless.

During the initial years of my practice I would expend considerable effort, both intellectual and emotional, arguing, convincing, pleading, and cajoling business owners who had to be dragged, literally, kicking and screaming through a turnaround program. I soon found that even my efforts were in vain, since at some point the principal of the company would simply refuse to cooperate further, causing substantial problems for all of the other participants in the turnaround effort.

Enthusiastic cooperation of the owners is a must for a turnaround program to have any hope for success.

As far as the requirement for honesty is concerned, it should be self-evident that in an atmosphere of doubt, distrust, disappointment, and frustration with which the company and its owners are invariably viewed (as discussed in Chapter 5), there simply is no place for anything other than candor, directness, full disclosure, and professionalism of the highest order. Any hint or smell of deceit, evasion, or surreptitious actions on the part of the owners will rapidly undermine and destroy any turnaround effort. In a turnaround, not only is honesty the best policy, it is the *only* policy.

THE A ELEMENTS: ADDITIONS FROM THE TURNAROUND TEAM

In addition to the basic elements the business must have in place, there are five key elements that must be added to the business for it to have a reasonable prospect for a successful turnaround. These are:

A1. One or more powerful change agents

A2. The cooperation of the company's principal secured lender

A3. Bridge capital to sustain the day-to-day business until the situation can be stabilized

A4. Competent and mature legal counsel with extensive bankruptcy experience and good negotiating skills

A5. Competent accounting support

A1: The Change Agent

The turnaround process involves second-order change. As we discussed, it is unlikely that a successful turnaround can take place without a powerful change agent. The change agent needed to implement a turnaround plan could be a turnaround consultant, a new chief executive officer or chief operating officer, or a previously uninvolved owner or member of the board of directors who has not had much involvement in the day-to-day business of the company. No matter who the change agents are or where they come from, they must exhibit many of the characteristics of a turnaround consultant if they are to be change agents in fact, as well as change agents in name.

A2: Cooperation of the Company's Secured Creditors

As the creditor who is usually secured in most, if not all, the collateral of the company (receivables, inventory, and capital equipment), the bank's cooperation is absolutely essential for a successful turnaround program.

For our purposes we will define the bank as any financial institution that holds security in assets that are necessary for the company to carry out its business, and is in a position to call a default in the obligation and foreclose on the collateral. In some cases the company's bank is a commercial finance company or a leasing company.

If the business is in default in its agreements with the bank, the bank has two options. It can sue and foreclose on its collateral, with the objective of liquidating the collateral to pay its loan in part or in full, or it can decide to cooperate with the company in a workout plan.

In order to gain the bank's cooperation in the turnaround plan, the company will have to persuade the bank that:

1. The management that will be running the company has integrity, will be honest both in actions and in statements, will avoid obfuscation or stonewalling, will be ethical in its dealings, will provide full disclosure on the condition of the company at all times, and will realistically evaluate the prospects for the future.

2. The management has a viable and realistic plan for achieving a turnaround, rather than a low-probability "escape hatch."

3. The management is competent to carry out the plan; it is a good operator and will implement the plan with a level of professionalism that the banker can respect.

4. The bank's position, as measured by the value of the underlying collateral and guarantees versus the outstanding loan balance, either will continue to improve, such that if the plan fails, the bank will not be worse off, or will have suffered a deterioration in its position that will not exceed a preagreed amount.

One of the major objectives that the change agent is expected to accomplish is to persuade the bank to cooperate. The credibility of the company's existing management has probably suffered substantial deterioration as a result of the financial difficulties the company has experienced. There is usually an understandable lack of confidence in any plan that the management proposes. The banker is likely to say, "In view of the fact that you have failed to meet your minimum plan during the past two years, that your sales are running 50 percent of your projection, and that your net worth has eroded to nil, is there any reason we should believe that you can meet this new proposed plan?" This is a difficult question to answer.

That question will not be posed to the change agent, since he has no connection with the past and represents a fresh approach. He brings instant credibility to the plan. His stature, as well as his analytical and persuasive skills, will be major factors in securing the cooperation of the secured lender.

A3: Bridge Capital

Assuming the company has the cooperation of its secured creditors and they have agreed not to foreclose, the company will have to deal with the critical issue of bridge capital.

Bridge capital is the cash the company will need to survive until it is stabilized and generating a positive cash flow. The bridge capital will be comprised of the following components:

1. Cash to fund the losses the company will incur until it achieves a positive cash flow

2. Cash to pay for the professionals that the company will hire to assist it in the turnaround effort, such as the turnaround consultant, the bankruptcy lawyer, outside accountants, and appraisers

3. Cash to solve those "problems" with its unsecured and government creditors that are critical to its very existence

The first two items are fairly straightforward. The company's turnaround plan may contemplate losses for a period of time and these losses must be funded. The company will have to hire professionals, and these professionals will have to be paid in a current fashion so that they do not become unsecured creditors of the business. This would result in a loss in both their interest and their effectiveness.

The turnaround plan will usually contemplate paying interest only to the secured creditors for a period of time, and paying nothing to the unsecured creditors for their "old" debts. The plan will anticipate paying for "new" supplies and services on a COD basis. Most unsecured creditors will usually agree, if somewhat reluctantly, to the above terms and will continue to ship to the company on a COD or cash-in-advance basis.

However, some unsecured creditors are in a substantially stronger position than others to leverage the company and insist on a different accommodation.

The amount of capital that will be required to bring the business to a positive cash flow condition will be determined using sales forecasts and expense projections based upon the model of the firm. An analysis is made of the operating results of the business during the most immediate relevant period to determine the volume-sensitive and period-related operating ratios. These ratios are then adjusted to reflect the cost reductions and organization changes that are to be implemented during the turn-around process. The capital that will be required is the investment necessary to fund the maximum negative cash balance.

Obviously, the estimate of the required capital is only as good as the reliability of the sales forecasts and the expense projections. Therefore, it is prudent to make both the sales forecasts and the expense projections conservative. There is simply no point in being optimistic, obtaining insufficient funds, and then having the business fail again because it ran out of cash.

In some situations, if the business is relieved temporarily of an onerous burden of debt service, it can develop adequate capital to sustain its operation and does not need an infusion from an outside source.

For the business that cannot, there are very limited sources for bridge capital. They are:

1. The secured lender, who may invest bridge capital in the hope of retrieving an existing undercollateralized position

2. The principals of the firm, who may invest to preserve their equity in the business or to keep the business operating so that it will be able to pay delinquent taxes and loans that they guaranteed

3. Collateral lenders, also called "hard money" lenders, who will lend to a business based upon their estimate of the minimum value of the liquidation of the assets (receivables, inventory, and fixed assets)

4. Venture capitalists, financial institutions that lend or invest in the hope of a meteoric rise in the value of the business

5. Related entities, individuals, or other companies who may invest in order to protect their existing asset position, or to protect themselves from a contingent liability that would mature into an actual liability should the business fail

6. Government entities, which may make grants or loans to the company in order to preserve an industrial base or jobs (as was done in the Chrysler case)

This list does not include potential purchasers who make an investment in the business in order to obtain an option to purchase the entire business or a controlling position, because they would be regarded as purchasers.

After the size of the required investment has been determined, the potential lenders have been solicited, and their interest ascertained, it usually becomes quite clear whether or not the bridge capital to effect the turnaround will be forthcoming. Then an assessment of A3 can be made.

A4: Legal Counsel

Good legal counsel is worth its weight in gold, platinum, or any other precious metal. As we discussed in Chapter 11, it is difficult to find a good lawyer, especially one who is skilled, mature, understands the bankruptcy process, and is a good negotiator.

A5: Competent Accounting Support

My friend Arnold Goldstein, a turnaround expert and author, writes in his book *How to Save Your Business*:

> My first official act in many (insolvency) cases? Firing a client's existing accountant. No apologies. If the accountant wasn't doing his job, I conclude he can't change overnight into an effective member of the turnaround team. It's a recurring theme. Businessmen everywhere can't tell you whether they're making or losing money. Books and records either don't exist or lie in shambles. In over 70% of my cases I'm lucky if I can obtain an accurate list of creditors. There may be thousands of accountants, but few know how to keep score.

Unfortunately our experience is very similar to Arnold's. Despite the myriad numbers of accountants, computers, and software packages, we find that the businessperson who knows the score is a rarity. The personnel complement responsible for maintaining the company records generally falls into one of the following categories:

1. Fully staffed internal accounting department with periodic reviews (typically yearly) by an outside CPA firm

2. Partially staffed internal accounting department (clerks and book-keepers) with all of the professional accounting functions performed by an outside CPA firm

3. All accounting functions performed by an outside CPA firm that operates directly from source documents

Our experience indicates that regardless of who is doing the books for the troubled company, the results are the same. The accounting records are not timely, not accurate, and not relevant. Reports are not provided to management in a time frame in which they can be used to make effective management decisions. They are not consistent or accurate, are frequently rife with errors, and therefore do not reflect the true values of the physical assets and liabilities. The receivables do not represent what can be collected, and the inventory does not represent the value of what can be sold.

We have concluded that there are four major reasons that the accounting records are so poor:

1. Incompetent personnel within the businesses themselves, resulting from the fact that the businessperson or the chief executive is so unfamiliar with the accounting process and mechanics that he does not know how to hire, supervise, and motivate the personnel he needs.

2. Neither the businessperson nor the outside CPA fully understands the operation of the business. As a consequence, they are unable to construct an accounting system that will reflect accurately both what happens in the business and the information that the businessperson must have to be able to monitor and control the operations.

3. The outside CPA firm and the client "conspire" to create an accounting system that will obfuscate, confuse, and bewilder the taxing authorities in order to minimize the federal and state income taxes that the company pays. As an example, one of our clients distributed his business transactions over five separate companies, each with a different year end. Although his business consisted of distinct strategic business units, he would run the transactions for a single strategic business unit through several of his corporations.

Whether or not these machinations actually resulted in his paying less taxes is a conjecture. What was certain was that neither he nor his CPA firm ever really knew the "score."

4. The outside CPA firm and the client engage in the process of "creative accounting" to show the best face to the company's secured creditors, stockholders, and trade creditors.

Management comes to rely upon the mountains of schedules and spreadsheets generated by the modern computer for its "information" and does not develop a keen appreciation for the real information it needs to manage the company.

Computer babble allows the management to believe that it really understands the company's performance, despite the fact that key critical aspects of the performance of the business are ignored. I recall an instance where a CPA firm was providing an oil-drilling contractor with a monthly financial statement that was approximately one-half-inch thick. The statement contained a detailed analysis of the operation of every single rig and auxiliary item of equipment, including the costs of fuel, maintenance, and depreciation. However, what the CPA firm did not provide was a consolidated financial statement for his several businesses. The consolidated statement would have shown that, although the oil-drilling business appeared to be profitable, it was financing a losing construction company. The loans, while classified as assets on the oil-drilling balance sheet, would never be collected.

Clearly, the level of accounting performance that we have just described is inadequate for a turnaround program. The credibility that the company will be able to command from its secured and unsecured creditors will depend, to a considerable extent, on its ability to produce timely, accurate, and relevant financial data. To achieve this objective, the business will have to recruit competent accounting support.

We discussed in Chapter 3 the type and quality of information that is required to control a business enterprise. The troubled company demands even better information than the stable, solvent, ongoing business because it starts in a credibility hole and there is no time or opportunity for trial-and-error learning. The turnaround will require a scorekeeper who is proficient in cost accounting, cash flow projection, budget preparation and analysis, asset evaluation, and forecasting, and who can communicate with the other managers in the company so that his financial reports are relevant to the business. Such an individual is a rare but essential commodity. You simply cannot afford to play the game without a competent scorekeeper.

THE C ELEMENTS: CRUCIAL CONCERNS

Assuming that a turnaround situation includes all of the B elements and that all of the A elements can be provided through the efforts of the change agent, the most important factors that will influence the probability of success of the turnaround are as follows:

C1. The amount of time available to effect the turnaround

C2. The simplicity of the business

C3. The accuracy of the financial information available at the beginning of the turnaround process

C4. The ability of the business to reestablish and sustain an acceptable market share

C5. The condition of the industry and the environment in which the firm competes

C1: Time

Theophrastus (278 B.C.) stated "Time is the most valuable thing a man can spend." That famous quote could be rephrased by the turnaround manager: "Time is the most valuable commodity in a turnaround program." In a situation that is deteriorating rapidly (a company in level F adversity), crises abound and options diminish. There is almost no time to analyze, evaluate, discuss, formulate plans, and implement them. However, given adequate time, the turnaround team has the opportunity to be creative, and to devise and explore unique solutions to the company's problems. Given time, the external world may also offer solutions.

We struggled for many years working with a client who owned a small refinery that had become obsolete after the decontrol of oil in 1981. We had succeeded in negotiating a substantial reduction in his personal exposure through a confirmed Chapter 11 plan of reorganization. The company remained alive, though limited. However, it continued to have some contingent obligation to the secured creditor. The amount of this personal obligation would depend upon how much money the secured creditor received from liquidating the remaining assets.

Five years after we became involved with the company, a large petrochemical firm decided to construct a new facility in the immediate vicinity of our client. The petrochemical firm determined that its overall cost of construction would be materially reduced if it could purchase our client's pollution credits. An agreement was negotiated, giving the buyer an option to purchase these credits over a period of time, in return for a series of payments to our client.

An even more dramatic example of the benefits of "staying alive" is offered by the case of a client whose personal service firm became obligated to the Internal Revenue Service for unpaid payroll tax benefits in excess of $250,000. This obligation carried with it the potential of a 100 percent penalty assessment against the principal.

The company filed Chapter 11 bankruptcy. Against all odds, and through truly herculean efforts during the bankruptcy proceedings, the company survived. The IRS did not assess the penalty, and the company was eventually able to propose a plan of reorganization. At one time during the period of survival, all the employees of the company were laid off, the offices of the company vacated, and furniture stored. The principal took a position with another firm. Yet only one year later, the company's annual sales were approximately $300,000 and the business was profitable, with the prospects for a relatively bright future.

How much time is enough time? The adequate amount of time for a successful turnaround depends on many factors. It is a function of the complexity of the company, the uniqueness of the situation, the caliber of the professionals involved, and the complexity of the debt structure.

If no time is available, in other words, if the creditors are clamoring for immediate payment or liquidation, the probability of a turnaround is zero. At the other extreme, if the creditors are very cooperative or even passive, then there is an endless amount of time available for a turnaround.

The shortest time constraint that we find tolerable to accomplish a turnaround successfully is one year. Three years should be adequate for all but the most difficult and complex cases.

C2: The Simplicity of the Business

Thomas Mann wrote: "Order and simplification are the first steps toward the mastery of a subject—the actual enemy is the unknown." In business, complexity tends to increase the chances for confusion and error. The simpler the business, the easier it will be to diagnose and to formulate and implement a plan of recovery. The more complex the business is, the more difficult, time consuming, and resource depleting it will be to accomplish every aspect of the turnaround plan.

The factors contributing to the simplicity of a business include the following:

1. *Number of Products:* A single line of products is the highest simplicity. As you add related products, then unrelated products, simplicity decreases. A complex and diverse number of products indicates low simplicity.

2. *Complexity of the Technology of Individual Products:* Products can range from a simple design to multiple components, increasing in complexity. If the products are highly intricate, technically sensitive, or complex systems, this is high complexity.

3. *Degree of Forward/Backward Integration:* Integration, in this context, means the number of steps involved in manufacturing and distributing the product. High integration means that there are many steps, all of which the company controls. For example, in the oil industry a major oil company controls exploration as well as development, oil transportation, refining, wholesale distribution, and retail distribution.

4. *Rate of Innovation:* The faster the rate of innovation and change in the product process and technology, the higher the product complexity is.

5. *Geographic Scope:* If the business has only a single location for its production and marketing, it is relatively simple in this area. The most complex geographic scope for marketing and operations would be one involving national and international locations.

6. *Distribution Channels:* A single distribution channel is the simplest. As the company adds channels, it increases in complexity toward a multiple, complex system of channels.

7. *End-User Groups:* The simplicity ranges from a simple, well-defined group to multiple and diverse groups.

As change is made, the simplicity of the business is reduced—and so is the probability of a successful turnaround. One of the great advantages of a simple business is that the various stakeholders, who must cooperate to effect the turnaround, can more easily understand some of the details of the turnaround process, will feel more involved, and may be more inclined to support the plan.

C3: The Accuracy and Reliability of Financial Information

When the turnaround manager arrives on the scene, one of the first things he must do is determine, as accurately as possible, the recent operating history of the company and the condition of the company's balance sheet. He will need to know the historical performance of the company to be able to determine the reasons for the company's recent poor performance and what steps might be taken in the short term to reverse any negative trends.

He will also need to know the values of the various assets and liabilities on the balance sheet, so that he can determine what assets are available and can be converted to cash in the short run, or used as collateral for new borrowings; what are the relative positions of the various secured and unsecured creditors; to what extent the estimated liquidation values of the various assets would cover any guarantees that the principals have executed for the benefit of the various secured and unsecured creditors; and so on.

If this information is not available, the turnaround manager has no way to determine the company's financial position and will be unable to project a plan for a recovery effort. Furthermore, there is usually no time, money, or personnel for the massive accounting effort that is required to reconstruct the books and records of the company in order to figure out where it has been, where it is, and where it might be going.

To illustrate the problem, we were retained by a client who manufactured products for the leisure industry. The company was five years old and had grown to a sales level of approximately $12 million per year. The company was founded by a supersalesperson who placed little value on the information or integrity of the accounting information.

The company's receivables were stated as $1,560,000. This wasn't as good as it looked on paper. Approximately $350,000 was owed by insiders and was clearly uncollectible; $1,000,000 was in excess of 90 days old. Moreover, customer-by-customer reconciliations had not been done for over a year.

The inventory was stated as $1,900,000. This figure had its problems, too. The company's year-end physical (which was purported to be accurate) totaled only $1,050,000. In attempting to resolve the discrepancy, we talked with a number of people within the company. Finally, several company employees admitted that there had been numerous transactions in which product was moved "out the back door," that is, sold for cash. What can you do in such a situation?

Not much. Why should any banker believe that your cost projections have any basis in reality if your year-end physical inventory is only one-half your book inventory? Why should the banker believe that any of your receivables are collectible if you haven't bothered to reconcile them for over a year? Why should any creditor trust you if your employees freely admit to the fact that product has been sold for cash and was not recorded in the books and records of the corporation?

The answer is that they shouldn't and won't. In the situation described above, the probability of a successful turnaround is also close to zero. This is a worst-case scenario. Most situations we see are somewhere in the middle ground between the most precise, accurate, and relevant accounting records and financials with missing data. On the whole, as described previously in this chapter, accounting records are usually inadequate, and this increases the difficulty of the turnaround manager's job significantly.

C4: The Company's Competitive Position

The stronger the company's competitive position, the greater is its probability of effecting a successful turnaround. For example, if the company manufactures a unique product for which there is no immediately available substitute, then the company's competitive position is very strong. This will result in a high probability of turnaround. On the other hand, if the company's products are sold into a highly competitive market where the customers are fickle and replacements readily available, then the company's competitive advantage, and therefore the probability of its accomplishing a successful turnaround, will be low.

The various factors that determine the company's competitive advantage were discussed in Chapter 10. As a result of this analysis, sufficient information can be developed about the company and its competitors to evaluate its competitive position.

The factors that contribute to the company's competitive advantage are:

1. *Market Share:* If the company has a high market share with no strong competitors, it has a high competitive advantage.

2. *Product Quality:* If there is excellent quality control, this also puts the company in a high competitive position.

3. *Product Life Cycle:* If the product is new to the market, this increases competitive advantage. If the product has been in existence for many years competitive advantage is lowered.

4. *Product Replacement Cycle:* The slower customers are to replace existing products with new products, the higher the competitive advantage.

5. *Customer Loyalty:* If customer loyalty is high and customers are unlikely to switch to the products or services of another company, this greatly improves the company's competitive position.

6. *Competition Capacity:* When competitors are operating at maximum capacity and there is room in the marketplace for additional competitors, a new company will have a high competitive advantage.

7. *Technological Know-How:* The higher the level of technological know-how required, the greater an existing company's competitive advantage.

8. *Vertical Integration:* This is the number of different steps between raw materials and retail distribution in which the company is involved. The more stages, the higher the competitive advantage. This factor is similar to the forward/backward integration factor under C2, simplicity of the business. The oil company example applies here as well.

C5: The Strength of the Industry

Achieving the turnaround of a company in a declining or sick industry is quite difficult. Unfortunately, when an industry gets sick and goes into decline, all the marginal performers within the industry experience financial difficulty and become candidates for turnaround, sale, or liquidation.

On the other hand, if the industry is basically strong and the particular company under consideration experienced financial difficulty because of unique circumstances, the probability of a successful turnaround of that business will be substantially greater than if the industry were in decline.

The various factors that determine the viability of an industry were discussed earlier. As a result of this analysis, sufficient information about the industry can be determined to evaluate the strength of the industry in which the company is operating. The following factors contribute to the overall industry's strength:

Growth Potential: When the growth potential of the industry is high, the industry attracts considerable venture capital and the overall industry strength is high. This creates a favorable environment for turnaround success. A weak industry with low growth potential spells trouble for the turnaround.

Profit Potential: The profit potential, like the growth potential, is important in attracting venture capital. Profit potential is high when the industry is strong.

Financial Stability: If the industry is characterized by a high rate of bankruptcies and firms exiting the market, the industry is unstable.

Raw Material Availability: When the raw materials required for the industry are scarce, competition for those materials will be intense and the industry may be at risk.

Technological Know-How: If the industry requires a high level of technological know-how that has already been developed, the industry is stable.

Rate of Technological Change: A rapidly changing technology will affect the strength of the industry, since the potential for technological advances and breakthroughs may create new opportunities.

Ease of Entry: When the industry requires a high capital investment for entry, this discourages new competitors and strengthens the position of existing firms.

Competitive Pressure: An industry that is highly competitive may experience frequent price cutting, which weakens the profit potential and may require a larger market share for profitability.

PROBABILITY THEORY: AN INTRODUCTION

The probability of an event is a measurement of the uncertainty of that event occurring. If it is certain that an event will occur, then the probability is equal to 100 percent, or $P = 1$. If there is only a 50 percent chance, then $P = 0.5$, if only a 20 percent chance, then $P = 0.2$, and so on. For an impossible event, $P = 0$.

If the event of interest is the result of an "experiment" that can be repeated, such as rolling a die, the probability can be calculated as follows:

$$P(E) = \frac{\text{number of ways } E \text{ can occur}}{\text{total number of possible results}}$$

For example, the probability of rolling a "6" is:

$$P(6) = \frac{1 \text{ (number of times "six" occurs on the die)}}{6 \text{ (total number of possible sides)}}$$

$$= .167 = 16.7\%$$

Business decision makers, especially those in marketing, banking, finance, and research and development, frequently are faced with unique problems, namely, problems that have not previously occurred and are unlikely to occur again. Since the "experiment" is not repeatable, the probability of an event occurring can not be easily calculated. If the decision maker is unable to predict the outcome of such a unique situation, he may find it convenient to view the outcome as a chance event. The probability concept permits quantitative estimates of the uncertainty associated with such problems.

As commonly understood, the word "probability" often refers to unique situations. Examples are statements such as "The probability that a Democrat will be elected president in the next election is 0.47" and "The probability that the Los Angeles Raiders will win the football game on Sunday is 0.75." Since all the factors that determine the outcome of an election or a football game cannot be repeated, the associated probabilities cannot be interpreted as relative frequencies.

Instead, we say that probability is being used to express one's degree of rational belief. Probabilities assigned in this manner are often referred to as *personal or subjective probabilities* in that they reflect an individual's intuition and belief. Decision makers often have strong intuitive feelings about the likelihood of a particular outcome that is determined by chance. The assignment of subjective probabilities to such outcomes provides the decision maker an opportunity to quantify his feelings about them.

Calculating Probabilities of Independent Events

A fundamental law of probability theory states that if two events are independent, that is, if the occurrence of one will have no effect on the occurrence of the other, the probability that they will both occur is equal to the product of the individual probabilities.

Therefore, to calculate the probability of two independent events A and B occurring, you would use the following formula:

$$P(A \text{ and } B) = P(A) \times P(B)$$

As an example, the probability of rolling a 12 (6 on each die) with the throw of two dice is

$$P(12) = P(6 \text{ on die 1}) \times P(6 \text{ on die 2})$$

$$= 1/6 \times 1/6$$

$$= 1/36, \text{ or } 3\%$$

Let's take a more complicated situation. Suppose you lived in Los Angeles and were considering going to Las Vegas to see a particular show. A friend of yours who lives there says he thinks there is an 80 percent chance he can get tickets for you. So you decide to take your chances—you could always play blackjack if you can't get into the show—and go to the airport. You find that the plane you have to catch in order to get there in time for the show is full, but there is a 75 percent chance that you'll be able to get on the flight. You add your name to the stand-by list and sit down to wait. What is your probability of making it in to see the Las Vegas show?

Using the probability formula;

$$P(\text{tickets}) = 80\% = 0.8$$

$$P(\text{making the plane}) = 75\% = 0.75$$

$$P(\text{seeing the show}) = 0.8 \times 0.75 = 0.60, \text{ or } 60\%$$

As you're waiting, you remember that your friend has a very unreliable car, which only starts half the time. The probability his car will start is 50 percent. How does this affect your probability of seeing the show?

$$P(\text{car starting}) = 50\% = 0.5$$

Now the probability of seeing the show is

$$P(\text{seeing the show}) = 0.8 \times 0.75 \times 0.5 = 0.30, \text{ or } 30\%$$

As you can see, adding the third factor decreases the probability of the event (seeing the show) taking place. Every time you add a factor having a probability that is less than 100 percent, the overall probability decreases.

A MODEL FOR ASSESSING THE PROBABILITY OF A SUCCESSFUL TURNAROUND

Now that you have a basic understanding of probability, let's move away from the gambling house and the Las Vegas show and back into the business world. What we want to do now is apply probability theory to estimating the chances of success in a turnaround.

The probability of a successful turnaround is a function of the existence and values of the ABC elements of the turnaround: the A elements, the B elements, and the C elements. If we define a successful turnaround as S, and the probability of a successful turnaround as $P(S)$, then the equation for assessing the probability of a turnaround can be written as

$$P(S) = P(A, B, C)$$

The probability of the turnaround can be calculated by multiplying the probability of each of the groups of elements. Therefore, using the probability formula,

$$P(S) = P(A) \times P(B) \times P(C)$$

In our experience, each of the A elements and B elements must exist for a turnaround to work. The business either has the basic B elements it needs, or it doesn't have them. The probability is either 100 percent for each individual B element that exists, $P = 1$, or zero when the element is not there, $P = 0$.

Suppose, for example, that the company does not have a cooperative and honest management (B4), even though all of the other B elements are present. Then the probability of B4, written as $P(B4)$, is zero. The probability of each of the other B elements is $P(B1) = 1$, $P3(B2) = 1$, and $P(B3) = 1$.

Look what happens, in this case, to the overall probability of the B elements, $P(B\ elements)$, using these values in the probability formula,

$$P(B\ elements) = P(B1) \times P(B2) \times P(B3) \times P(B4)$$

$$= 1 \quad \times \quad 1 \quad \times \quad 1 \quad \times \quad 0$$

$$= 0$$

The same is true for the A elements. The turnaround team either can marshal the necessary resources or it can't. If any element is missing, it severely hampers any turnaround effort. Suppose, for example, that all of the A elements exist except that the secured lender refuses to cooperate (A2). Therefore, $P(A1) = 1$, $P(A2) = 0$, $P(A3) = 1$, $P(A4) = 1$, and $P(A5) = 1$. Using these values in the probability formula,

$$P(A\ elements) = P(A1) \times P(A2) \times P(A3) \times P(A4) \times P(A5)$$

$$= 1 \quad \times \quad 0 \quad \times \quad 1 \quad \times \quad 1 \quad \times \quad 1$$

$$= 0$$

The question will undoubtedly be asked whether it is possible to have a successful turnaround if one or more of the A elements or B elements are missing—there is no change agent or if the bank is uncooperative so that a legal battle ensues—of course it is.

Companies attempt turnarounds all the time without change agents, without competent accounting support, lacking adequate legal counsel, lacking adequate bridge capital, and dealing with a hostile bank. Occasionally they are successful and survive. However, based on our experience, we feel the probability of effecting a turnaround under such circumstances is so slight that it cannot justify the risk on the part of the unsecured creditors. We believe that without the five A elements plus the four B elements the risks of failure will simply be too great.

THE CRUCIAL FACTORS: IMPORTANCE
OF THE C ELEMENTS

The C elements, you will remember from the earlier discussion, are time (C1), simplicity of the business (C2), accuracy of financial data (C3), competitive advantage (C4), and industry strength (C5). Each of these crucial elements can have a critical effect upon the success of the turnaround. In a turnaround effort, assuming the presence of all the A elements and all the B elements—which we have indicated are essential—the C elements will determine the ultimate outcome.

The probability for each C element cannot be calculated precisely. Any estimate is a judgment call. What is certain is that the higher the probability for each C element, the higher the chances of success for the turnaround.

If the probability of the C elements is high, then probability of turnaround will approach 1, or 100 percent; if the probability is low and falls below the 50 percent level, the turnaround faces rough times.

In employing this model in a practical situation we convert our qualitative or quasi-quantitative estimates of the "values" of the elements into probability estimates as follows:

Qualitative Value of C Element	Assigned Value of $P(C)$
Very high	1.00
High	0.75
Medium	0.50
Low	0.25

We will illustrate the use of the model using the example of the Widget Shop.

The Widget Shop

The Widget Shop is a small firm that is in the business of making widgets. We will estimate the probability of each of the C elements as follows:

C1 (Time): There's only a 75 percent chance that this company will have enough time to survive through the turnaround. Their creditors are growing increasingly impatient with the company's inability to pay bills. It might be noted that none of the creditors owns widgets, and they consider them useless items. This increases their impatience for payment; C1 = 0.75.

C2 (Simplicity): The making of widgets, however, is simplicity itself. The Widget Shop is a single-product firm, and the widgets they produce are neither high-tech nor intricate, just your basic widget. They only have the one shop, and their marketing strategy is to have people come and choose from the available widgets, so that, too, keeps things simple. The probability that the business is simple enough is very high, so C2 = 1.

C3 (Accuracy of Data): Here the company is not in a very good position. Everyone in the shop, including the head of the firm, would rather make widgets than keep books. As a result, their financial data are hardly complete, and there is only a 50 percent chance that it will be enough to reassure the creditors; C3 = 0.50.

C4 (Competitive Advantage): This is what the company considers to be its strongest ace. There simply aren't very many widget makers out there, and they make the best. They have a corner on the market, a high-quality product, strong customer loyalty, and a slow product replacement cycle—people who buy their widgets are not likely to switch to another widget maker. So their competitive advantage probability is C4 = 1.

C5 (Industry Strength): Unfortunately, although they are the best in the business, there isn't much of a business marketplace. People simply don't buy widgets the way they used to. Sales are down for all widget makers, and the industry slump gives them a C5 = 0.50.

Calculating the Probability of the Turnaround

The probability equation for a successful turnaround, $P(S)$, is written

$$P(S) = P(\text{A elements}) \times P(\text{B elements}) \times P(\text{C elements})$$

Assuming that all of the A elements and B elements exist, this means that $P(\text{A elements}) = 1$ and $P(\text{B elements}) = 1$. Therefore

$$P(S) = 1 \times 1 \times P(\text{C elements})$$

$$= P(\text{C elements})$$

Since

$$P(C) = P(C1) \times P(C2) \times P(C3) \times P(C4) \times P(C5)$$

the probability of a successful turnaround for the Widget Shop is

$$P(S) = 0.75 \times 1 \times 0.50 \times 1 \times 0.50$$

$$= 0.19, \text{ or } 19\%$$

How would a change in any of the variables affect the overall chances of the turnaround? Suppose the Widget Shop had kept accurate records, so that C3 = 1,

$$P(S) = 0.75 \times 1 \times 1 \times 1 \times 0.5$$

$$= 0.38, \text{ or } 38\%$$

This one element alone could double their chances of a successful turnaround. Also, if their financial data were in good shape, it might very well reassure their creditors, and therefore increase the time available for the turnaround. Suppose it were to improve the probability that there would be enough time to effect the turnaround to 90 percent, so $P(C1) = 0.9$. Then the probability of a successful turnaround would be

$$P(S) = 0.9 \times 1 \times 1 \times 1 \times 0.5$$

$$= 0.45, \text{ or } 45\%$$

These are significantly better odds for the Widget Shop's future.

The real value of this model for evaluating the probable success of the turnaround is that it can help the participants in the turnaround process focus their attention on the real issues. Once they address the key elements that affect the turnaround process, they stand a much better chance of making it successful.

In the next chapter we discuss how the turnaround manager deals with the various elements we have discussed, and the tasks he faces in effecting a turnaround. We examine how he allocates his time during the different stages of the turnaround treatment—from the emergency stage to a return to normalcy—continually working to keep the company alive and to improve the probability of the turnaround's success.

14 INCREASING LIFE EXPECTANCY: TASKS OF THE TURNAROUND MANAGER

Force has no place where there is need of skill.

HERODOTUS

Managing a turnaround is a very complex and demanding activity. As we discussed earlier, it requires a set of skills, disciplines, and experience that neither the average executive nor the consultant possesses.

> Because of their training and experience, operating managers seldom have the special skills needed to manage a turnaround. They function in a hieratic environment designed to solve daily problems efficiently. Restructuring a company to reverse a situation which may already have caused severe damage is simply beyond their mandate and experience (and skill).
>
> Peter J. Irvine

The turnaround manager often comes into a situation with no historical background of the company, its products, or the industry in which it competes, and he must quickly accomplish a number of objectives to keep the situation from deteriorating further: assess the situation, formulate an insolvency strategy (turnaround, sale, or liquidation), negotiate the strategy with key stakeholders, and so forth.

The degree of success that the turnaround manager achieves will be a function of the elements that we discussed in the previous chapter—the A elements, B elements, and C elements—and the skill and capabilities of the turnaround manager.

The purpose of this chapter is to provide the reader with some insight as to what happens in a turnaround program. In doing so we will make the assumption that there is a change agent on the scene: a new executive who has been charged with the responsibility of achieving a turnaround, a turnaround managment consultant, or some other person whose purpose is to direct the turnaround effort. Our focus in this chapter is not to provide "how to do it" information, but rather to explain what a turnaround effort usually entails, and what happens during the turnaround process. We will explore the turnaround process from the following five perspectives.

1. The tasks that must be accomplished as part of the turnaround effort—what the turnaround manager does

2. The issues that the turnaround manager must deal with in most turnaround situations

3. The typical stages in a turnaround effort

4. The manner in which the turnaround manager allocates his time among the tasks that he is charged to accomplish

THE TASKS AT HAND: RESPONSIBILITIES OF THE TURNAROUND MANAGER

A turnaround manager must be prepared to carry out six major responsibilities when he becomes involved with a company.

1. He must establish a climate of mutual trust with the principals of the firm, the board of directors, the key management personnel, the lenders, and other key stakeholders in the business.

2. If the company is experiencing a financial or other major crisis, he must provide the guidance to manage it through the crisis with a minimum of deterioration in the assets or operations of the business.

3. He must perform a situation analysis of the company and its principals.

4. He must formulate an insolvency strategy that is appropriate to the situation, and if that strategy includes the turnaround of the business, he must also formulate the turnaround strategy.

5. He must take the lead in presenting the proposed plan to the key stakeholders of the corporation, and try to gain their acceptance through persuasion and negotiation.

6. He must direct the implementation of the plan.

The turnaround manager does not perform these tasks sequentially. Instead, the six tasks that the turnaround manager performs during the course of the turnaround program can be viewed as occurring on six separate tracks. As the turnaround progresses from the early emergency and crisis stages to a more stable situation, the amount of time the turnaround manager spends on each task will change.

Before we discuss the tasks in detail, we address the issues that confront the turnaround manager, the stages in the turnaround process, and how he allocates his time among the several tasks.

IN SEARCH OF AN INSOLVENCY STRATEGY

Every workout situation is different. I have personally been through over 50 different situations, and each one was unique. Although there may be similarities in debt structure, secured lender attitude, business operations, or other aspects, these similarities are usually small in comparison to the differences that exist. Since the situations are different, the workout strategy and tactics are, of necessity, also different.

It is the responsibility of the turnaround manager to spearhead the search for a realistic strategy that will achieve as many of the objectives of the owners as is possible. In accomplishing this, the turnaround manager will mentally review all of his past turnaround experiences and his knowledge of the management literature, both theoretical and practical. He will then apply his creativity to construct a strategy, and a set of tactics for implementing that strategy. This activity will usually be accomplished in collaboration with the company's insolvency attorney.

A turnaround manager enters each new situation with three primary objectives: (1) to ensure the survival of the business; (2) to stabilize the company's operation; and (3) to make the company worth something for its owners. As the turnaround manager becomes more knowledgeable about the situation of the company, the owners, the industry, the competition, the bankers' attitudes, the company's tax obligations, and the owners' personal exposure, these objectives may change and he may determine that for the particular situation at hand the only feasible options are a sale of the business or, failing that, to liquidate it.

The formulation of an insolvency strategy in a specific situation is complex and depends on a myriad of legal, business, and personal factors that are unique to that case. It is beyond the scope of this book to discuss the "how to" of insolvency strategy formulation.

However, the issues that the turnaround manager must consider are common to every insolvency situation, and it is appropriate that we briefly review them, since they will provide some insight into what the turnaround manager needs to know and why he needs to know it.

THE TWELVE BURNING ISSUES: KEY QUESTIONS OF THE TURNAROUND MANAGER

The turnaround manager must determine the answers to the following 12 important questions in order to be able to develop the most appropriate insolvency strategy for the business.

1. *What is the stage of adversity?* The stage of adversity determines how much time and effort will have to be spent on crisis management, and how much time is available to analyze the situation, formulate plans, and negotiate with stakeholders before Armageddon occurs.

2. *What is the status of the present and near-term cash position of the company?* Cash is to the turnaround process what gasoline is to the automobile. Without gas the car won't go; without cash, the turnaround process will not get started. Cash is required to pay for the professional services (turnaround consultant, attorney, CPA, appraisers, and so forth), to keep key utilities in service (phone, gas, electricity, water), to keep the landlord at bay, to keep employees on staff, to keep the doors open, and to keep merchandise shipping.

If the company is operating in the later stages of adversity, cash will be short. Therefore it will be necessary, as Gerald Meyers says, to "make love to your cash. Find it, protect it, enhance it, and control its flow."

If sufficient cash is not available to continue operations in a normal fashion, operations will have to be cut back. In a turnaround, "cash is king."

3. *What are the critical issues that need to be addressed immediately in order to ensure the continuation of the business?*   In the history of every financially troubled company there are always certain pending crises which, if not addressed promptly, may severely impact the company's ability to operate, rehabilitate, or both. These problems must be addressed and handled to the extent possible so that the company's future prospects are not adversely affected.

Examples of such crises include the threatened lapse of important insurance coverage, the potential attachment lien by a creditor, the imminent seizure of assets by the IRS, the pending revocation of business operating permits, the inability to pay for key materials that are needed for a major contract shipment, the prospect that there will be insufficient funds to meet the payroll, and so forth.

4. *What is the liquidating value of the balance sheet?*   If the business were terminated immediately and the company filed a Chapter 7 petition, what is the anticipated liquidation value of each of the asset accounts and of the off-balance-sheet assets, such as leaseholds? What amounts remain for the unsecured creditors after the secured creditors have received the value of their secured claims, that is, the liquidation value of the underlying collateral up to the value of the remaining loans?

The liquidating value of the balance sheet establishes the baseline for evaluating various insolvency plans. Both secured and unsecured creditors will have to be convinced that there is a significant benefit to them, over what they would achieve in a Chapter 7 liquidation, if they are to support any alternative insolvency plan.

5. *To what extent are the principals or key managers of the firm exposed to secured creditors on their guarantees or to taxing agencies for nondischargeable obligations?*   The extent of this exposure will have a major influence on the types of insolvency plans that the company can consider. If the principals are seriously exposed, and that exposure would be exacerbated by a turnaround effort, it would be prudent to pursue an insolvency plan that involves a sale or liquidation—if such a plan would eliminate the obligation. If, on the other hand, the principals have no exposure to either secured creditors or taxing authorities, the company can pursue a turnaround program since it is using the "house's money," that is, the investments of the secured and unsecured creditors.

6. *What are the objectives and characteristics of the principals and owners?* The turnaround manager will have to assess quickly the principals of the firm, since this assessment will have a significant bearing on the practicality of any proposed insolvency plan.

7. *What is the recent historical performance of the company?* The recent historical performance of the company will provide some insight as to the level of confidence with which profitable performance in the near future can be predicted. For example, if the company has been exhibiting a steady sales performance in the past and there are no factors that should interfere with that performance, then selective reductions in expenses might bring about profitable operations that could be counted on.

On the other hand, if historical sales have been sporadic and unpredictable, and there is no reason to assume that future sales could be predicted with any degree of certainty, then profitability may be difficult to both predict and achieve unless expense cuts are extremely severe.

8. *What is a realistic forecast for the company's profitability and cash flow?* The immediate future prospects of the company as manifested by profit/loss and cash flow forecasts will either provide comfort for, or underscore the hopelessness of, the rehabilitation efforts. To be meaningful, the forecast will be based on historical data, management's current assessment of the business, information provided to the turnaround manager by employees, vendors, customers, and other stakeholders, and the turnaround manager's judgment. The forecast should, of course, be both conservative and realistic.

The forecasts will indicate the rate at which losses are diminishing or increasing and the capability of the company to operate without additional capital.

9. *Are there potential product breakthroughs, technological breakthroughs, or other imminent miracles?* Does the company have emerging products or technological development programs that could, if brought to fruition, create new opportunities for the company? Has the company developed and launched a new marketing program that is about to result in soaring sales? Has a well-known "rainmaker" (supersalesperson) recently joined the company and brought along the major accounts of the company's biggest competitor? Is there a "great white hope" lurking in the shadows that could realistically save the company?

A product or technological breakthrough that has potential for creating a new future for the company can rekindle the hope of weary secured creditors and can even open the door to new capital.

10. *What is the status of the B elements?* We have discussed the B elements, or basic business elements, that should currently exist in the business and their effect on the probability of a successful turnaround. Each of these elements presents an issue that the turnaround manager must consider in formulating an insolvency plan. To review, the B elements are:

1. Is there a viable core business in the company?

2. Are the employees skilled and loyal?

3. Is the middle management personnel competent and loyal?

4. Are the principals or owners honest and will they be cooperative?

A strong negative answer to any of these questions would indicate a very low probability of a successful turnaround and would suggest an insolvency plan based on a sale or liquidation.

11. *What is the status of the A elements?* The A elements, also introduced and discussed earlier, are those that the turnaround manager must provide for the business. As in the case of the B elements, each A element presents an issue for the turnaround manager to consider.

1. The change agent presumably is embodied in the personage of the turnaround manager. However, can the business afford to pay for him and his staff through the duration of the turnaround effort? If not, is there an alternative change agent that can be mentored by the turnaround manager so as to reduce the financial burden to the company?

2. Will the secured creditors cooperate with the company in a workout effort as opposed to foreclosing on the loan?

3. Where will the bridge capital come from? Can the company self-finance? Are there unsecured assets that can be sold to provide the required working capital? Will the secured creditor expand

the credit he is providing the company? Can the principals contribute capital or provide additional collateral?

4. What attorney capability does this situation require? Is this going to be a highly complex and contested case requiring a "star" or a very prestigious firm, or can we get by with a competent, mature, and politically astute attorney who may not enjoy name recognition?

5. How are we going to get control and maintain control of the records? Is there anyone in the firm who can, with adequate direction, perform the accounting function? If not, whom can we bring in? Are the accounting systems adequate? If not, how quickly can a system be implemented that will get us by?

12. *What are the probability estimates of C elements?*   The C elements pose the following issues for the turnaround manager to consider.

1. How much time do we have to propose and confirm a plan, and how long will the creditors wait before they start to see any money?

2. How simple is the business? How long will it take us to understand what is going on in the various strategic business units? How many people will it take to dig out the information that we need?

3. How accurate is the financial information? Can we rely on it? Can we arrange to verify it? Has anyone else checked it?

4. How strong is the company's competitive position? Is it holding on to its customers? Are the customers worried? Will the business be able to hold on to its customers if it files a bankruptcy petition?

5. How strong is the industry? Is it growing, stabilizing, or declining? Is it attracting new money, or are investors running for the hills?

The answers that the turnaround manager determines for these questions will influence the formulation of the insolvency plan. The higher the values of the C elements, the higher the probability that a turnaround effort will succeed; the lower the values of the C elements, the lower the probability that a turnaround program will be successful.

As the turnaround manager evaluates the company's situation with respect to the above 12 issues, he will come to a conclusion with regard to the insolvency plan that offers the best prospects for the company and its principals. As we discussed in Chapter 12, the plan will be based on one of the following strategies: turnaround, dump and buy back, controlled liquidation, uncontrolled liquidation, or abandonment.

Having determined the key strategic thrust for the insolvency plan, the turnaround manager will begin to formulate the specifics of the plan in cooperation with the principals and the management as well as the insolvency attorney, and ultimately, will negotiate the acceptance of the plan with the relevant stakeholders of the company. He will then implement the plan, which may involve filing a bankruptcy petition.

In the remainder of this chapter we discuss the turnaround manager's activities under the assumption that the insolvency plan involves the turnaround of the financially troubled business.

THE FOUR STAGES IN THE TREATMENT OF BUSINESS ILLNESS

Every turnaround program passes through four distinct stages: emergency, stabilization, recovery, and return to normalcy. Each stage is characterized by a set of circumstances, attitudes, and perceptions. In addition, each stage has a medical analogy that is descriptive of the gestalt associated with that stage, and there is a relatively clear-cut demarcation between stages. Table 14.1 summarizes the principal characteristics of the four stages of a turnaround plan.

Stage 1: Emergency

This stage is initiated when the management or ownership of the business realizes, during a rare moment of lucidity (also referred to as the moment of truth), that the business is in serious trouble and that its very survival might be in question. Up to this point, the management of the company may have viewed signs of trouble, such as a sales slump or inventory accumulation, as one of the "bumps in the road" that all companies experience from time to time. Successful managers have a difficult time gauging the likely depth and duration of a downturn. In addition to "explaining the problems away," management may have attempted corrective actions that were inappropriate or inadequate for the underlying problems the company faced.

TABLE 14.1. STAGES IN THE TURNAROUND

STAGE	Focus of Management Actions	Typical Events	Perceptions of the Outside World	Employee Attitudes	What Marks the Beginning
Emergency	Cope with the crisis Stop the bleeding Control the damage Rally the troops	Crises abound Checks are returned for insufficient funds Collection agencies are hounding the company IRS liens company's bank accounts Customers defect to competitors Company is unable to meet payroll Bank threatens to send demand letter Landlord delivers notice to pay rent or quit premises	Company will probably not survive	Fear, anxiety	Management/owners accept that there are serious problems that must be addressed
Stabilization	Repair the damage Resume operations Formulate recovery plan Negotiate with creditors	Company is generating cash and paying for new goods and services as they are received Customers start to place orders Vendors start to ship on COD terms rather than cash in advance	Company will probably survive in the short run; not convinced it can make it in the long run	Hope, ambivalence	Filing a Chapter 11 petition Getting creditors to back off Management gets control of actions

		Some employees change their minds about leaving Management begins to discuss options for generating cash and revenue in the short term			
Recovery	Plan strategy Invest in personnel, equipment, and systems Focus on profitability Perform to the plan	Employee salary cuts are restored New management employees are hired Management is actively discussing new marketing and product development plans Vendors now provide open lines of credit in limited amounts	Company may survive for a while; not sure it can perform to plan; not sure it will ever be worth anything	Commitment to success	Plan of arrangement approved Company starts to perform
Normalcy	Achieve growth in revenue Improve return on investment Strengthen the balance sheet	Management is actively working on five-year plans Full company fringe benefit programs are reinstated Stock options are taken seriously Company stock is relisted	Company has made it; it's a money machine	Enthusiasm, pride	Bankers and investors begin to court company

In small companies, the moment of truth usually coincides with the occurrence of a liquidity crisis. There simply is no money to pay trade creditors, taxes, or even employees. If the company's liquidity crisis can be resolved by a quick trip to the "friendly banker," the moment of truth may be delayed until the next liquidity crisis.

In medium and larger companies, the moment of truth tends to coincide with a visit from the company's primary banker, who expresses concern over the continuing losses the company is sustaining and the deteriorating condition of the balance sheet, and advises the management that it is unlikely that the bank will renew or extend the loan agreement.

Once the company accepts the fact that it has serious problems, the process of rehabilitating the business can begin. Even though the company may continue to decline, the potential for a turnaround has been created with the introduction of a change agent. The level of adversity the company is in when the ownership experiences its "moment of lucidity" will determine the nature of the efforts that are called for to deal with the company's situation: the higher the level of adversity (for example, stage E or F), the more severe are the measures that must be taken to ensure the survival of the firm.

If the emergency stage is characterized by crisis conditions as described previously, the turnaround manager will have to deal with unpleasant surprises and ambiguities. However, independent of the nature and extent of the crisis, he must take five steps as quickly as the company's resources and his time permit.

1. Take control of the cash, including directing its accumulation and disbursement.

2. Find out the score—how the company has been doing on an operating basis during the recent past, and what the liquidating values of its balance sheet accounts are.

3. Stop the bleeding. Halt the oozing outflow of cash, which is the company's lifeblood. Examine every significant cash drain and shut off those that are not absolutely necessary to the business.

4. Establish a climate of mutual trust and cooperation with the significant stakeholders in the corporation.

5. Establish himself clearly as the leader to whom everyone will look for direction.

The actions and activities undertaken during the emergency stage are, of course, a function of the specific situation and conditions of the company. However, they will always be focused on keeping the business alive, determining the extent of the problems, and limiting the damage.

Frank Gristanti describes what he does during this stage:

> The cash flow plan carries with it what I call purchase-order surgery and manpower. You first put a hold on the corporate structure. Stop anything from coming in. Put a freeze on the payment of all accounts payable until you can analyze where you stand. You have to control what goes into the pipeline in order to control what comes out. Automatically freeze all purchase orders and take control of purchasing.
>
> After you have put moratoriums on payments, perform surgery on payroll. Lop people off in a wholesale fashion, not arbitrarily, but by analyzing the segments of the business and relating income to outgo. You work fifteen, eighteen, twenty hours a day during that period, because in many cases you have to ask somebody for a payroll on Friday and you have to have a good check to clear that account.
>
> Donald B. Bibeault,
> interview with Frank Gristanti

It is critical that the turnaround manager implement, as quickly as possible, some changes in the organization which the employees feel are indicative of the fact that something really is changing and the future does hold promise.

Typical things that I have done are: terminated the son of the founder, who was drawing a large salary and was extremely disruptive to the business; terminated all company credit cards and sold all company automobiles; eliminated expensive golf club memberships for management; abandoned a vacation condo that had no equity; and eliminated a company policy for "same day shipped as ordered," which was disruptive to the organization and, in any case, was not adhered to.

The analogous situation in a medical setting is the performance of critical surgery on a very sick patient. As long as the patient's life is at risk, the patient is considered to be in an emergency situation, and everything that can be done is done to preserve the patient's life. That may include amputating a limb or removing some organ that may have a negative effect on the future quality of life enjoyed by the patient. The focus of the surgical team is to preserve the patient's life.

Preserving a company's life requires that the enterprise continue to exist—even if operations are temporarily suspended. To the extent that the company's customers, suppliers, personnel, lenders, managers, employees, facility, and equipment can be maintained, the trauma of the emergency stage can be mitigated. Sometimes this is not possible, and the company will suffer the loss of key stakeholders and even see its operations placed on hold or its facilities closed before the situation can be stabilized.

Stage 2: Stabilization

The stabilization stage begins when it appears that the company is no longer in immediate danger of failing. When the emergency is over, the objective of the turnaround manager is to stabilize operations and attempt to return the business operations to normal. In this stage there is a high probability that the company will continue in operation on a day-to-day or week-to-week basis, although its ability to survive in the long run is still very uncertain. However, the management can at least enjoy the relative calm after the turmoil of the emergency.

Once the company is in the stabilization stage, the turnaround manager will have the opportunity to assess the existing management staff in a more leisurely manner to determine who will be effective in guiding the company through its problems, and who can be eliminated. Invariably, some key positions are not adequately staffed and he will have to hire new personnel. Frequently it is difficult for a company in an unstable situation to attract managers with the skills the company needs, so the turnaround manager will use consultants to fill the positions on an interim basis.

During the stabilization stage, the turnaround manager is focused on making those changes that will increase profitability in the near term, staffing the organization with the skills and experience it will need to grow, reassuring customers, reestablishing relationships with suppliers, and working out terms for a repayment plan with secured and unsecured creditors.

The turnaround team also reexamines the various reasons why the company got into trouble and begins implementing policies, procedures, systems, and staff changes to correct these shortcomings. In addition, the management will begin to invest serious effort into rethinking the overall strategy of the company. It will begin asking whether the strategy that it had been pursuing makes sense in terms of the current reality, and how the distinctive competences and valuable resources of the company can be leveraged to ensure a better fit with its present and future environment. In short, the management will begin to focus on the question: *Now that it appears that we may have saved the business, what do we do to make it valuable to the owners?*

The stabilization stage is usually characterized by intense negotiations with the various creditors as the company attempts to formulate, and get acceptance of, a plan of repayment. A company cannot move out of the stabilization stage to the recovery stage until there is an agreement between the company and its creditors, within or outside of bankruptcy, as to how the company is going to accommodate their claims. Until the time of that agreement, the company operates as if it were going to survive, plans for the future, and attempts, through negotiations with its creditors, to ensure that it has a future.

The stabilization stage for a company can be compared to the state of a patient who has just undergone an operation and is in a condition ranked as "stable and serious." The patient has survived, is out of immediate danger, and is expected to recover. But we are not out of the woods yet.

Stage 3: Recovery

The recovery stage commences if and when the creditors approve (and, in the case of bankruptcy, the court confirms) a plan of arrangement, and it appears that the company has a reasonably high probability of performing according to the plan. Once this occurs, a serious and dangerous cloud lifts from above the company, and it is given control over its own future. The management can, without having to secure creditor approval, go forward with its long-range plans, purchase the needed capital equipment, and hire the professional and management employees needed to carry out its plans.

Strategy reformulation, organizational changes, and implementation of new control systems can now proceed without the tentativeness that characterizes various management actions during the stabilization stage. The company has survived, it has been stabilized, and the creditors have agreed to the plan. The question that now remains is: *Can the company perform to the plan and will the company be worth anything in the future?*

The recovery stage for a company is analogous to the recovery stage for a patient: the operation was successful, the patient survived his hospital stay, and now he has returned home for the four to six weeks of rest he will need to regain his strength so that he can carry on with his life.

Stage 4: Return to Normalcy

A patient who has undergone surgery is considered to have returned to normalcy when he goes back to work, resumes his Sunday golf outings, and starts playing racquetball again on Wednesday evenings.

A company is considered to have returned to normalcy when the management, investors, bankers, creditors, and vendors all begin to believe that the company will perform according to its plan of arrangement, and the business's future is assured. The "we made it" banners go up around the company premises, the beer kegs are broken out, and celebrations begin. The bankers start again to refer to the company as "the customer" rather than "the debtor."

In the normalcy phase, efforts to figure out how to make money from the business intensify. Management will search out opportunities to make investments in equipment, personnel, and systems that will allow the company to increase its margins. The company will search for ways to expand its market areas and customer base and to improve its sales programs so that it can achieve growth in revenues. Investments in equipment, personnel, and training can be made with the expectation that the company will be around to both profit from these investments and be able to pay for them.

Finally, in order to make the company attractive to potential investors and buyers, and to improve its ability to withstand the unpredictable downturns in the economy, the management will focus its efforts on improving the company's return on assets and equity, and strengthening the balance sheet.

WHEN TO DO WHAT: THE TURNAROUND MANAGER'S ALLOCATION OF TIME

When a turnaround manager becomes involved in a client situation, he must achieve a balance between the time and energy he has available, the tasks that he is charged to accomplish, and the stage of the turnaround in which he is operating. For example, if the turnaround manager is retained when the company is in the last two stages of adversity (E and

F), a majority of his effort will be devoted to managing the crisis. The remainder will be directed toward establishing a climate of mutual trust with the stakeholders and performing the situation analysis.

If, on the other hand, the turnaround manager is retained during the early stages of adversity (C and D), then very little of the turnaround manager's time will be involved in crisis management.

As the company moves out of the emergency stage into the stabilization stage, he will complete his situation analysis and then turn his attention to formulating and negotiating a recovery plan. He will also begin to implement key aspects of the plan to the extent possible. When the company is in the recovery stage, the majority of the turnaround manager's time will be directed toward implementing the plan. It is also common for the turnaround manager to continue to negotiate, with key stakeholders, certain aspects of the implementation that are ambiguous or contingent on subsequent events. When the company returns to normalcy, virtually all of the efforts of the turnaround manager are directed toward implementing the plan. Once the company has progressed to this stage, it can be said to have executed the turnaround program successfully.

The board can then decide to retain the turnaround manager as the chief executive for the company, as was the case when Wickes retained Sigaloff, or it can replace the turnaround manager with another chief executive.

The circle graphs in Figure 14.1 illustrate a typical allocation of the turnaround manager's time as a function of the turnaround stage.

A WARM CLIMATE: ESTABLISHING TRUST AND COLLABORATION

One of the most important tasks of the turnaround manager is to establish a climate of mutual trust and companionship with the principals and to create, to the extent possible, a spirit of collaboration for the resolution of the company's problems. The turnaround of a business is a joint search to discover and implement realistic and workable solutions. The more creative the participants drawn into this process, the higher the likelihood of a good result.

The principals are a very important part of this process. Often they are the most knowledgeable about the market and the industry, and can contribute in precisely those areas where the turnaround manager is

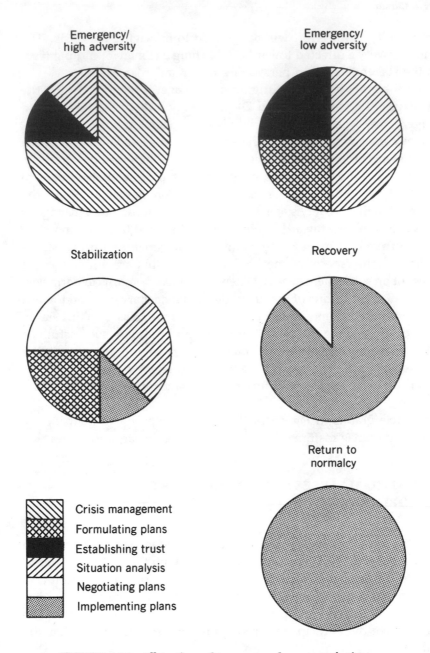

FIGURE 14.1. Allocation of turnaround manager's time.

least informed. One major by-product of this climate of mutual trust is that the principals will be able to learn certain skills and behaviors from the turnaround manager in a nonthreatening environment—giving the executive a sense of regaining power or control, which had faded as the business faltered.

As the executive feels better about himself and more confident of his abilities, he and his managers may be able to relieve the turnaround manager of certain specific tasks. The key concept here is that the turnaround is accomplished in a spirit of teamwork, where the executives' strengths are maximized, and their weaknesses minimized, due to the turnaround manager's presence.

The turnaround manager will similarly have to establish rapport and mutual respect with the key representative of the secured lender. When the turnaround manager enters the picture, the banker will have already been concerned about the loan and his collateral position for some time. If he has not lost all confidence in the principals of the company and the chief executive, he will at least be apprehensive. He will be looking for someone who feels competent to cope with the problems of the company, and who has the experience and skills to warrant that self-confidence. It will be up to the turnaround manager to provide the banker with a level of comfort that will allow him to decide to work with the company in a cooperative manner rather than act as an adversary of the company.

The turnaround manager must similarly establish contact and a relationship with other key stakeholders, whose cooperation and support must be acquired early in the turnaround effort. These entities can include key employees, partners of the principals, investors, collection agents from taxing authorities, large unsecured creditors, and the company's landlord.

The turnaround manager's message will be clear: I am someone who has the skills, experience, and competence to address the problems of this company, and I will do the best that can be done under the circumstances.

PUTTING OUT FIRES: CRISIS MANAGEMENT

A crisis situation is one in which events take on the following characteristics.

1. *Surprise:*   Events occur that were not predictable.

2. *Ambiguity:*   It is not clear what the full dimensions of the problem are.

3. *Overload of the Decision-Making or Management Capability of the Company:*   The demands being made on the management cannot be accommodated by the present staff.

4. *Telescoped Time for Making Decisions:*   Decisions must be made on a time scale that precludes careful research and deliberation.

5. *Competence Overload:*   Management is confronted with events, information, and the necessity to make decisions in areas where it has no experience or competence.

In addition, in the crisis situation these events or their immediate consequences are:

1. Escalating in intensity

2. Falling under close media or government scrutiny

3. Interfering with the normal operation of the business

4. Jeopardizing the positive public image currently enjoyed by the company or its officers

5. Damaging a company's bottom line

When a business enters stages E and F of adversity, crisis abounds. Let me illustrate, with an example of a company in crisis. We were referred by a CPA to a meat packer that was experiencing some financial problems. The CPA was only casually familiar with the company; one of his clients was a major creditor of the company. We met with the major stockholder of the firm, who was 75 years old, in poor health, and suffering from extreme stress. During the first few days of our involvement, the following events occurred:

1. Their two largest grocery chain customers advised the company that they would no longer be purchasing products because of poor quality control.

2. A truckload of beef the company had ordered arrived. The driver announced that since the company was behind in payments, he

would not unload unless he received payment for at least two loads ($40,000). At that point in time, the bank account was overdrawn by $20,000.

3. We discovered that the company was not current in its fees to the meat storage company, and that the storage company would not release any material until it was brought current. The company did not have the means to make the required payment.

4. A major unsecured creditor obtained a writ of attachment without notice, and liened the company's bank accounts, effectively precluding the company from operating.

5. The company's knowledge of its manufacturing costs was minimal, and there was not, and had not been for the history of the company's existence, adequate cost accounting. Thus there was no way of knowing immediately whether the incoming orders were going to contribute gross profit or merely accelerate the losses.

Most of the elements that define a crisis were present simultaneously—surprise, ambiguity, overload of management decision-making ability, and telescoped time for making decisions.

These five events were followed by similar events escalating the situation, events that interfered with the normal operations of the business, jeopardized the public image of the owners, and damaged the company's bottom line.

Crises have an enormous impact on the company's top executives. The functioning of a senior-level executive in a crisis may be like this:

> The senior executive can find that his perception of time becomes somewhat distorted; it can appear to be passing more quickly than it really is. He develops a compulsion to make quick decisions, often limiting the search for alternatives and the depth of cost benefit evaluation. There will be a tendency to make decisions before adequate information is available. The results can be higher rates of error from decisions, decisions which are more random, and often based on overly simplistic assumptions. As the pressure mounts, senior executives may resort to primitive decision patterns drawn from quite different situations in the past where they produced success.
>
> Henry C. Knight

There is extensive research material indicating that crisis situations can bring about psychological pressures that result in counterproductive decisions and actions. (Some of these research efforts are referenced in the bibliography for this chapter.)

The objectives of the turnaround manager when the company is immersed in a financial crisis is to identify quickly the source of the crisis, to isolate or quarantine the source in order to keep it from "infecting the company at large," and then to attempt to manage the crisis and limit the damage to the extent possible.

The turnaround manager will attempt to manage the crisis to the extent that it is manageable. In some cases, as in the meat-packing business described, managing the crisis involved locating and retaining a competent bankruptcy attorney and filing a Chapter 11 petition to stay all of the collection and foreclosure activities that were being pursued by the creditors.

When a crisis is in progress, there is no opportunity for learning by trial and error. A decision is made, a path is taken, and then events unfold based on that decision. Taking the path on the right has precluded you from taking it on the left, which may have worked out more favorably. However, as in the story of the lady or the tiger, the choice faces you, and a choice must be made. Some action must be taken, and it is fervently hoped that the information you are working with is true and accurate.

SITUATION ANALYSIS: THE FACT-FINDING TASK

As we discussed in Chapter 10, performing a comprehensive situation analysis is a crucial task of the turnaround manager. In doing the situation analysis, he has worked to evaluate the internal and external realities of the business.

You will remember that to gather data regarding the internal situation, the turnaround manager does not rely solely on materials collection and review—often a herculean task in itself—but also on information obtained through surveys, interviews, and direct observation. This sum total of information allows for the formulation of internal issues, the analysis and preparation of findings, and the identification of critical issues.

The second component of situation analysis, that of determining the external view, involves a careful examination and analysis of the company's customer base, its competitors, and the industry within which it operates.

Without a well-founded situation analysis, there can be no intelligent and informed development of strategies to see the company through the rough times ahead.

15 | CHOICES FOR SURVIVAL

The art of progress is to preserve order amid change and to preserve change amid order.

ALFRED NORTH WHITEHEAD

Once the company has opted to attempt a turnaround under the guidance of the turnaround manager, strategies for achieving a turnaround can be developed. In this chapter we describe the major strategic paths involved in the turnaround process, and we discuss what the turnaround manager does to formulate, negotiate, and implement turnaround plans.

MAKING CHOICES FOR SURVIVAL: THE STRATEGIES OF A TURNAROUND

The basic strategies by which turnarounds are implemented fall into five major categories: management change, operational strategies, growth strategies, strategic restructuring, and financial restructuring. Turnaround plans are implemented using one or more of these strategies.

Management Change Strategies

These strategies involve change in top management personnel, that is, executive vice president and above. These include a switch in chief executive officers and the formation of new top management teams. In these strategies it is typical that an executive outside the organization is recruited to lead the revitalization effort, and this new executive typically will bring on board an entire new management team to support him.

Typical examples are the recruitment of Lee Iacocca at Chrysler and Sandy Sigaloff at Wickes.

Frequently, bank lenders will insist on a change in top management as their price for cooperating (that is, not calling their loan) or providing bridge capital. This is particularly the case if the lenders feel that the existing management has not been forthright in disclosing the problems of the company, or uncooperative with the efforts of the bank to assess the extent of the company's problems.

Management change strategies are based on the following reasoning. First, the present management got the company into its present difficulty, and they are either not experienced managers, or they are great managers who unfortunately are no longer operating at peak capability. Since a turnaround needs top-notch managers, the present management must be replaced. Second, present management has created and is responsible for the programs, decisions, staff, and investments that brought about the problem, therefore they will not be able to review their past decisions objectively and reverse them if necessary. They will find it difficult to split with the past.

If the board decides to make a leadership change, sometimes it need not go outside the organization for a new leader. If the new leader is recruited from inside the business, he will have the advantage of being familiar with the industry, the technology, and the market, and may represent a lower-risk choice than an outsider. However, if an insider is chosen, it is essential that he not be tainted with past errors; otherwise his failure is virtually assured.

Kenneth B. Schwartz and Menon Krishnagopal performed research on changes of chief executive officers in financially troubled firms. Their research showed that firms that appeared headed for bankruptcy changed their CEOs at about 2½ times the rate of healthy firms. Furthermore, firms suffering from business adversity tend to find CEOs from outside the firm. The research revealed that 65 percent of the failing firms recruited CEOs from outside the business versus 44 percent reported by the healthy control group. This research is certainly consistent with our discussion of the role and qualifications of a change agent.

Operational Strategies

Operational strategies, also referred to as cutback or retrenchment strategies, include those actions that focus on reducing expenses and increasing the revenue of the current operations. These strategies usually involve tactics that the executive can implement without soliciting agreement from entities outside the management team. Typical examples of such tactics are:

1. Revenue can be raised by increasing prices on products where the company has large market share; increasing prices on services and products not subject to competitor retaliation (such as spares and service contracts); hiring salespeople and distributors from competitors; opening additional distribution centers where appropriate; conducting off-price sales for slow-moving or discontinued items.

2. Direct labor costs can be decreased by terminating marginal or unproductive personnel; trading off high-priced labor for lower-priced labor; reducing employee hourly rates; requiring increased hours of labor from exempt personnel for the same weekly compensation; reducing fringe benefits such as insurance.

3. Direct material costs can be reduced by finding alternative sources of supply; reducing quality to be consistent with pricing; instituting budget constraints to control the purchase of supplies and services.

4. Overhead, sales, and administration costs can be reduced by reducing personnel to a level consistent with the size and gross profit of the business; reducing salaries and fringe benefits of overhead personnel; reducing travel, business conference, and entertainment expenses and subjecting them to budget control; terminating leases on all equipment and vehicles that are not absolutely essential to the conduct of the business; relocating operating facilities to reduce rent expenses; restructuring telephone services to bring them in line with the needs of the company; reducing or eliminating professional services that are not absolutely necessary for the continuation and survival of the business.

An important factor that must be kept in mind in implementing an operational turnaround strategy is to "avoid throwing the baby out with the bath water." In this case the "baby" is the key professional skills that the company will depend upon to achieve its long-range objective. These skills may be encompassed in a few key executives who are not "carrying their weight" and appear to be expendable. Conventional wisdom may dictate the lopping off of unneeded heads; however, management must proceed with caution. If certain individuals have distinctive skills, or the ability to exploit a valuable asset, terminating the relationship in the hope that the skills can be replaced at some future time ignores the reality that uniquely competent individuals are difficult to find.

Growth Strategies

These actions are designed to promote substantial increases in the firm's revenue by aggressively promoting existing products and services to the firm's existing market, introducing the firm's products and services to new markets, or developing new products or services for the firm's existing markets. A typical example of a growth strategy would be a retail firm that had a strong market identity and profitable locations in a given region, deciding to roll out its regional strategy to address a national market.

Another form of growth strategy is one that is dependent on a new product which may exploit an emerging tendency in consumer taste; or on a new technological breakthrough that may create a product family that did not exist previously. Growth strategies based on either new products or new technologies are grist for the venture capital mills, since the implementation of plans that depend on new products and new technologies requires risk capital that bank lenders will usually not provide.

Although, according to Bibeault, product breakthrough turnarounds are rare (accounting for only 4 percent of the turnarounds he surveyed), they are important in that, if they are successful, they can cause a quick and significant reversal in the company's fortunes.

Strategic Restructuring

In strategic restructuring, the effort focuses on the asset side of the balance sheet and the business aspects of the profit and loss statement. Whereas in a growth strategy the effort focuses on selling more of what we have, in an operational strategy the effort focuses on squeezing more cash out of current operations. Strategic restructuring is concerned with the search for the viable core "needle" in the firm's "haystack." Typical issues are the extent, speed, and intensity of any downsizing of the business, including the divestiture of nonessential or weak elements (the so-called "dogs") and of promising but nonperforming business units, to free financial resources and ease the cash bind.

The principal objectives of strategic restructuring are to:

1. Capitalize on the company's strengths

2. Minimize vulnerability due to the company's weaknesses

3. Put the company in a position to take advantage of opportunities

4. Insulate the company from threats

5. Establish a mix of products and services that will allow the company to gain a decisive competitive advantage in its target markets

6. Ensure that the company possesses the key marketing, technology, finance, and production capabilities to compete for resources and customers

Common restructuring and asset redeployment efforts can involve any of the following activities: selling a money-losing strategic business unit; leasing unused facilities; licensing a product or product line rather than manufacturing it; selling surplus equipment; purchasing a related business that can contribute gross profit, or that can share in the overhead and sales and marketing costs; changing the method of selling from an organization of independent distributors to an organization of direct captive salespersons or vice versa.

Financial Restructuring

This strategy is concerned with achieving relief on the liability side of the balance sheet through concessions and accommodations with the company's existing creditors, or achieving new agreements with new creditors. Development of a strategy demands interaction between the company and its various creditor groups while it tries to formulate and sell a plan that will grant the company relief from the pressures of the debts it cannot fully service.

Virtually all financial restructuring strategies seek to keep the many creditors of the company at bay, reduce debt service burdens to the level that the company can service out of its minimum predictable cash flow, and bring in new cash from the principals, potential partners, or secured creditors who are at risk.

According to Charles M. Williams, an analysis of major financial restructuring reveals the following main concessions that management attempts to secure from its lenders (secured creditors) in roughly ascending order of intensity.

1. Further advances from lenders; if existing lenders are unwilling to help, management may ask them to permit new lenders to come in on a priority-secured basis, ahead of the old lenders.

2. Deferment of interest payments to reduce cash outflows for a time.

3. Concession of interest payments due the lenders; this has a positive direct impact both on cash flows and on the profit and loss statement and, indirectly, on the borrower's equity position.

4. Easing of restrictive covenants that permit the lenders to accelerate maturities or otherwise bring pressures on the borrower.

5. A de facto freeze on further repayments of maturing loans, which commonly is later converted into a formal extension of the maturities of the various debts.

6. Conversion of interest payments or principal due into the equity securities of the borrower, or into securities that represent calls on equity in the future. This produces a double-barreled improvement in the balance sheet by cutting debt and boosting net worth.

7. Outright concessions of principal due to lenders, which also cut debt and boost net worth.

In negotiating with unsecured creditors, the company will attempt to achieve the following.

1. Place a moratorium on the payment of "old accounts payable" until the corporation is able to achieve certain milestones and obtain some credit for new purchases.

2. Convert the accounts payable balance to a note, the terms of which would accommodate the company's cash flow (that is, paying interest only for a period of time).

3. Schedule the payment of accounts payable over an extended period of time.

4. Tie the payment of "old accounts payable" to new purchases. In other words, the company would pay for the new purchases on a COD basis plus 10 percent against the old balance.

5. Convert accounts payable into some form of company security.

Choosing the Appropriate Strategy

Every turnaround program involves one or more of the substrategies described above. Some involve all of them. Which strategies are most appropriate for a specific company at any given time will depend upon what the situation analysis reveals.

The substrategies that will be selected for implementation will be affected by a number of factors, including the competitive position of the company, where the company's products or services are in their life cycle, the nature of the industry in which the company competes, and the severity of its current financial situation. For example, if the company has a strong competitive position, that is, enjoys a relatively high market share in a growing but mature market, there would be little point in attempting to implement a growth strategy. In such a situation, implementing operational strategies that would increase profitability and redeploying assets to provide more resources for the promotion of the key product line would make more sense.

On the other hand, if the company is struggling to increase its share in a rapidly growing and emerging market, operational (cutback) strategies might adversely affect the company's ability to compete. A growth strategy to increase market share and a financial strategy to fund the loss until the company is profitable may be more appropriate.

When the company has a strong competitive position (high market share), it can reasonably be assumed that the major strategic decisions regarding that business have been correct (market share being the reward for past correct decisions) and that the current decline can be reversed by reemphasizing the firm's message.

For a firm with a moderate share, a growth strategy might be appropriate and yield a high payoff.

If a firm has a very weak market position, it is unlikely that a growth strategy would be successful. In such a situation emphasis on operational strategies and restructuring to make the best "polyester purse out of the sow's ear" might be all that can be hoped for. It simply may not be worth the risk to try to grow from a low share position and weak financial condition in the face of stiff competition, unless a substantial amount of new risk capital is brought into the company.

The lowest risk turnaround programs are the ones where the company has management that is capable, a product or service with a good market share, and does not require either strategic or financial restructuring. In such a situation the company can often be restored to profitability through the implementation of operational strategies.

The most difficult and most risky situations are those in which management change, strategic restructuring, and financial restructuring must all be accomplished for the company to survive.

When a company must implement a number of strategies simultaneously to meet its objectives, the interrelationships and interdependences of the substrategies must be taken into account. Since strategic business restructuring and a growth strategy would both affect cash flows and the need for financing, the company's planning must be based on financial realities, that is, the company's ability to attract the required capital.

On the other hand, the ability of management to achieve either growth or a restructured business that is more congruent with the company's current realities is critical to management's ability to convince its lenders that there is a reason to support the company, that there *is* "light at the end of the tunnel."

SELLING THE SURVIVAL STRATEGY: ISSUES FOR FORMULATING AND NEGOTIATING THE PLAN

Once the turnaround manager has formulated a plan and that plan has been accepted by the company owners (shareholders) and the company's insolvency attorney, it will be necessary to "sell" the plan to the company stakeholders: the secured, unsecured, and government creditors; the employees, both management and labor; and others who have some stake in the business performance. To accomplish this objective, the turnaround manager must activate his persuasive, negotiating, and political skills. This effort may be accomplished either outside or within the bankruptcy system. If the negotiation is attempted outside the bankruptcy system, it is, as a practical matter, necessary to achieve agreement and cooperation of 100 percent of the stakeholders, because any one creditor can block the plan by bringing a civil lawsuit against the company or its principals. If the turnaround team cannot convince the recalcitrant creditor to cooperate, then the company will have to negotiate and sell its plan under the protection of the bankruptcy system.

There are a number of issues that must be considered in formulating all restructuring plans. They are discussed in some detail in the sections that follow.

1. The trade-off between the concessions management asks of its creditors and its ability to get the creditors to accept the plan.

2. How to treat several secured creditors to maximize the probability of gaining acceptance of the plan and achieving the optimum concessions for the company. Treating all creditors alike has the advantage of simplicity and allows the creditors to share their pain "equally." However, the philosophy of the standard give-up disregards important variations in the characteristics of the loans, such as their underlying security, the size and strength of the financial institution that made the loan, and the form and terms of other various loans.

3. The third issue deals with how much "sacrifice" the lender will ask of employees, management, dealers, distributors, and other stakeholders in the company as their "price" for supporting the plan. The more the secured lender feels that the burden is being shared on a broad base, so that he is not the only one holding the bag if the plan fails, the more inclined he may be to support the plan.

4. The fourth issue and potential source of conflict during the negotiations between the company and its creditors is the question as to how best use the cash (if any) generated as a result of any substantial divestitures. There are always competing demands for cash. The company needs the cash to fund its working capital requirements, capital acquisitions, and new marketing programs. The creditors are anxious to see their loans paid down as quickly as possible.

These issues are discussed in greater detail in the following section.

THE ART OF PERSUASION: NEGOTIATION TASKS

There are five aspects to negotiating the plan with the various stakeholders. We discuss each of them in some detail.

Negotiating the Plan with Major Lenders

The process of formulating a restructuring plan and negotiating it with the major lenders can be frustrating, stressful, and demanding for the members of the turnaround team engaged in the process.

The core issue for the company is to convince itself and its major creditors that the company has a reasonable prospect to recover and pay its debt obligations as a consequence of its proposed turnaround strategy. The creditors must be given a reason to believe that the company will not fritter away their collateral position in a futile attempt to survive and protect management's jobs and perks. Most important, the company's turnaround plan must offer the creditors a better alternative than liquidation.

The process typically proceeds like this: after the situation analysis is performed, and the turnaround manager has some appreciation for the type of debt repayment plan that the company appears to be capable of accomplishing, he will formulate a proposed structure and then discuss it with the apparent leaders or the most influential representatives of the creditor groups. Assuming that a consensus on terms and conditions can be reached, he will then convert the broad outline of the plan to a specific proposal, review it with the same lenders, and attempt to achieve both an agreement on the terms and conditions and an endorsement for the plan. If he achieves the agreement and the endorsement, he will attempt to gain acceptance of the proposal plan from the remaining creditors.

The turnaround manager accomplishes this objective through three activities.

1. *Presentation*:   A presentation describes where the company was, where it is not, why it is in the condition that it is in, where it expects to go in the immediate future, how it expects to get there, and what concessions it will need from the various stakeholders to get there.

2. *Selling*:   The benefits of the proposed plan must be "sold" to each of the key stakeholders by pointing out to them the benefits they will accrue if the proposed plan is successful, and why the alternatives to the plan, which might result in the demise and dissolution of the company, will be less attractive.

3. *Negotiating Differences in Position (Dispute Resolution)*:   The resolving of differences between the positions of the company or principals and that of the stakeholders to achieve a mutually acceptable resolution is most important.

If a restructuring plan is attempted outside of the bankruptcy system, then agreement of substantially all of the creditors will be required or, at least, of all of those creditors who are holding claims that are material (in the sense that the company either could not afford or would not be successful in defending against the claims). If the restructuring plan is being proposed and implemented within the bankruptcy system, then the necessary creditor support is substantially less, namely, one-half of the claimants in number and two-thirds in amount of the claims they represent, for any given class of claims.

The company can always expect that certain creditors will be unwilling to go along with the proposed plan, for a number of reasons. Some will attempt to play the "spoilers role" holding out for a substantially better deal, consuming management's time and energy, in the hope that they can exhaust the company's patience so that they can be paid off to be gotten rid of.

Unfortunately the company jeopardizes the integrity of its plan if it does not treat all creditors of a given class (as it has chosen to define the "class") in the same way. So management is faced with the dilemma: if it pays off the recalcitrant creditors to get rid of them, and the word gets out (as it always does), it may undermine the entire plan as other creditors are encouraged to play the "spoiler's role." On the other hand, if the company continues to hold fast and not deal with the recalcitrant creditor, the available time that the company has may run out and other creditors, whose agreement has been tentative, may desert.

Some creditors will find themselves in the position of having "bet their company" on your business, and may feel that if they agree to your proposal it may be necessary to meet with their own bankruptcy attorney.

Finally there will be those creditors who were personally responsible for having granted the company the credit that is now the subject of the restructuring agreement. Depending upon the institution or firm they represent, they may be feeling extreme pressure to resolve satisfactorily a problem with which they are personally identified. In this type of situation, where a creditor has a high emotional involvement in the debt, it is often very difficult to deal with the creditor in a rational manner.

Another common problem encountered in negotiating a creditor agreement arises from the fact that the financial information, cash flows, sales projections, and so forth, on which the company bases its proposal, may, with the passage of time, have proved to be unrealistic. So the company finds itself with a proposal that while accurate and "realistic" at the time it was presented, becomes obsolete before the creditor agreement can be nailed down.

As time passes, and the discussions with creditors continue, apparently without any end in sight, the company is faced with the problem of updating its financial information, which may cause some creditors who have already "signed up" to defect. If the creditors begin to believe that management's forecasts are inherently optimistic, or are being purposely "hyped" in order to sell the plan, credibility of the management will erode and the entire plan will be jeopardized.

In order to combat these tendencies, which are inherent in any financial restructuring or debt composition arrangement, the turnaround team must develop a comprehensive program to mobilize available pressures and influence to achieve agreement in the shortest amount of time. During the process, it must keep the key lenders and creditors accurately informed of the company's performance, status, and prospects.

Achieving a successful debt restructuring agreement requires a high degree of personal commitment and skill.

Over time, if the company's problems prove intractable, primary players may become weary or bored and "decision making by exhaustion" is threatened. Key people involved in the slow, tiresome restructuring processes of several companies have emphasized the importance of the personal effectiveness of those leading the management and banking groups' efforts . . . The financial restructuring efforts are inherently likely to represent a major distraction and a severe physical and emotional drain on the energies of the main people involved.

Charles M. Williams

As we discussed in the previous section, it takes a good deal of skill and lots of practice to formulate creditor plans and negotiate agreements.

Dealing with Secured Creditors

Reduced to its bare essentials, the usual dominant philosophy of the secured creditor in dealing with the debtor can be summarized as follows:

Cash rather than promises

More rather than less

Sooner rather than later

As we discussed earlier, secured lenders will want to believe that the company's management is honest, in touch with reality, and competent to carry out the plan that has been proposed, and, most importantly, that the banker's exposure will not grow beyond a predetermined and acceptable level.

If several banks are involved, a decision will have to be made as to how to deal with them in an organized, prudent, and consistent manner. The banks will undoubtedly have different security positions, and will certainly have different agendas and aspirations with respect to any restructuring negotiations. Paying off one or more secured lenders will certainly antagonize the remaining banks when they realize that other creditors have been paid off with the "their" money.

Dealing with Unsecured Creditors

If the secured creditors can be accommodated in the plan, the next major issue that the company has to deal with is the unsecured creditors. The unsecured creditors, organized and represented by a competent bankruptcy attorney, can wield a good deal of clout in the bankruptcy court, especially if the company winds up with a pro creditor judge. The creditors will always be looking to get paid earlier rather than later, even if they have to take a deep discount in the amount that they are owed. The company will be looking to stretch the unsecured creditors out as long as possible, and to preserve the working capital for the growth of the business.

The unsecured creditors will always be searching for their "white knight," who will make an offer to purchase the company on terms that will pay the unsecured creditors early. The company will always be doing its best to stave off such offers in the hope it can find a better deal; one that will provide both the management and the shareholders somewhat more than the "white knight."

How this all ends up is a function of the relative skills of the two attorneys; the determination, organization, and leadership of the management team; the leverage each side can exert over the other; and the propensity of the bankruptcy judge to be procreditor or prodebtor.

For example, if the debtor finds himself in a position where his officers and directors may be personally liable for withholding taxes, and are subject to the 100 percent penalty, prudence dictates that he must achieve some kind of a deal that will guarantee that the withholding taxes are paid, irrespective of what happens to the company. Otherwise the debtor will be exposing himself to large risks. Since the taxes have the lowest priority in the priority debt, the company needs a buyer or investor who will pay off all the priority debt and the administrative expenses for the principals to escape the 100 percent penalty.

On the other hand, if the company is in the position where it can sustain operations with the cooperation of a secured creditor or will, in a Chapter 7 liquidation, pay virtually no premium to unsecured creditors, it is in the position of substantial leverage.

Dealing with Employees

Several years ago, a trucking company that was involved in the oil industry was experiencing problems. The trucking industry had been decontrolled in 1980 and rates had begun to drop precipitously. The company had been poorly managed, had squandered its resources, had rarely shown a profit, and had been losing money steadily since the rates had declined. After a brief analysis of the situation, it became clear that if the company was going to stay in business, it was going to have to reduce its costs in order to be profitable.

After reducing overhead and expenses to the extent possible, the only costs that could be subject to a decrease were the wages for the drivers, who were represented by a union. We met with the union representative, showed him the financials of the company and the projections we had prepared, and advised him that unless the union was prepared to negotiate a substantial wage rate decrease for the drivers, the company would have to close its doors.

Although initially he was adamantly against any reduction in wages, he was well aware of the weakness in the industry (a number of trucking companies had closed), and was very concerned about seeing another 50 or so of his members laid off without other immediate job prospects in the area.

We discussed our proposal at some length, and during the meeting made some modifications in our wage offer that were relatively inexpensive to us and would not materially affect the economics of the business, but appeared very important to him. These modifications concerned compensation for the travel time and expenses of the drivers, uniform allowances, and other details.

The union representative agreed to meet with his members before our presentation to them and to recommend that they accept our new offer. If the vote was unfavorable, we would shut the company down that same day. To ensure that we had made our point, and to prevent any potential vandalism to the equipment, we arranged for all the trucks to be brought into the yard the evening before the meeting and posted a guard.

The meeting took place the following morning as scheduled. The union representative made a presentation which we did not attend. We made our presentation, answered questions, and left. The union representative then conducted a vote that resulted in acceptance of our plan. The drivers went back to work.

This example illustrates a typical process in negotiating a deal. We analyzed the situation and determined that a reduction in the drivers' salaries was required in order to preserve the company. We then made a presentation to the union representative, explaining the situation. The union representative was inclined to go along with us, but required some concessions on our part which we were able to make without seriously affecting the economics of the package. Both sides agreed to support the plan—and it worked.

Using the Threat of Bankruptcy as a Point of Leverage

One of the points of leverage in negotiations with creditors is the implied threat that if the efforts at debt restructuring are unsuccessful, the company (or debtor) may file a voluntary bankruptcy petition, and place the entire matter under the jurisdiction of the bankruptcy court. The bankruptcy weapon is a double-edged sword, and it is important to recognize its benefits and limitations.

We have discussed at some length the advantages that bankruptcy affords to the failing company: the ability to confirm a financial restructuring without 100 percent agreement of creditors; the ability to reject onerous contracts and leases; and other advantages. However, the bankruptcy process involves some inherent risks for both the company and its creditors.

First, bankruptcy will have an adverse impact on the company's distributors, customers, suppliers, and employees, who will see it as a threat to their long-term interests. This is especially true of companies whose customers have long-term relationships and depend on the company for warranty support, guarantees, technical support and service, replacement parts, and advanced technology.

The mere hint of failure of a manufacturing company whose customers depend on it for high-technology components or systems that are not readily available from other suppliers on short notice will cause purchasing agents sleepless nights, and you can depend on the fact they they will immediately start to develop alternative sources.

There is substantially less risk to existing business in the case of companies that do not have long-term or mutually dependent relationships with their customers, such as retail establishments, low-technology manufacturing firms, and service companies.

Second, the hoped-for orderly process afforded by the bankruptcy system can prove to be anything but orderly. It provides an opportunity for the lawyers representing the various groups to engage in very expensive maneuverings, ploys, and counterploys as they attempt to advance the interests of their particular constituency.

Third, the process can be very expensive. Every special-interest group or class of creditors must be represented by an attorney, so you have the attorney for the company, the attorney for the unsecured creditors committee, and the attorneys representing each of the secured creditors if they have not formed a committee. If a principal's interests diverge substantially from those of the company, he will have to have his own attorney, and so on.

Since the majority of the attorneys' fees are typically borne by the estate, the costs of the bankruptcy proceeding consume the funds that would be available to pay back the creditors or rehabilitate the company.

To the extent that the bankruptcy process incurs costs over and above what an out-of-court restructuring would involve (which is quite low in comparison), the process is detrimental to both the creditors and the company.

Finally, management may lose control of the process and the company. This may occur through a successful effort to have a trustee designated to run the affairs of the business, replacing the company's management as "debtor in possession." The petitioning party would, of course, have to show that there has been fraud, dishonesty, incompetence, or gross mismanagement of the debtor's affairs by current management, either before or after the commencement of the case, *or* that the appointment of the trustee would be in the interest of the creditors, any security holders, and other interests of the estate. Whereas it may be difficult to make a case for fraud, dishonesty, or mismanagement, it is easy to make the argument that replacing the current management (who dug the company into the hole) is in the interest of the creditors.

Management can also lose control of the process if it is not able to propose, and have confirmed, a plan of reorganization within the ex-clusionary period (the period during which only the debtor in possession can propose and confirm a plan). After the exclusionary period runs, *any interested party* may propose a plan. Any interested party can include the unsecured creditors' committee, an individual creditor, the secured creditor, a potential buyer of the majority of the assets, a member of management who is being backed by a venture capitalist, or others.

An example of this situation is the W. T. Grant bankruptcy, where a banker-dominated creditors' committee decided that the creditors would recover more through liquidation than through continued operation under Chapter 11. In this case, the decision to liquidate was made only a month after Christmas, when W. T. Grant, a large retailing chain, was in a low-inventory, high-cash position.

THE IMPERIAL WEAVERS CONTEMPLATE BANKRUPTCY

How does this negotiation process really work? And how does the company, with the help of a turnaround consultant, develop a reorganization plan while keeping creditors at bay? The best way to illustrate the interaction involved is to look at a business that is struggling with insolvency—Weavers, Inc.

The Weavers Get Desperate and Get an Attorney

You remember the story in Chapter 4 about the imperial weavers and the emperor's new clothes. Even before the fiasco of that parade in which the emperor appeared an undressed fool in front of the entire kingdom, the weavers' business was a prime candidate for bankruptcy court.

After that fateful day, when the emperor paraded in nonexistent clothes, the financial situation of the weavers went from bad to catastrophic. True, they had made a deal with the emperor to pay back the money he had advanced, but they had only been able to make a couple of payments. Business had fallen off and creditors were hounding them. They were afraid to open the mail, expecting that any day they would receive notice of a lawsuit from the emperor. They took turns not answering the phone. They were never "in" when the doorbell rang.

As the situation grew worse and worse, they decided they would simply declare bankruptcy, thinking that would solve all their financial problems. They just wanted to get out from under their crushing burden of debt and begin again. Their visit to a bankruptcy attorney made it clear that things would not be quite so simple.

The emperor had made the ex-imperial weavers sign a note and security agreement for the money he had advanced to them. He took a security interest in everything they had: their homes, inventory, accounts receivable, bank accounts, and trademarks. These were stiff terms, but preferable to the beheading that the weavers feared the emperor would order.

Since they had not kept up the payments, the emperor had started sending demand letters through his attorney. The weavers also faced a potential lawsuit from the butcher. Three months behind on their rent, they knew the landlord was preparing to throw them out. The silk merchant had filed a collection action for the money they owed him.

The weavers were indignant. They blamed the emperor for being impatient, their landlord for not having faith in them, the butcher for pressuring them unfairly, and the silk merchant—whom they'd always considered greedy—for starting all their trouble.

Given the sorry state of the weavers' financial records, their attorney referred them to a management consultant who could help them put together the information they needed to proceed and suggest a strategy for saving their business and their heads.

"Better get some cash together," said the attorney. "The consultant will want to be paid up front—and you'll have to give me a retainer, too."

With great reluctance, the old weaver agreed to pawn his gold watch to finance the retainers.

"With some luck," said their attorney sympathetically, "you may be able to buy it back later. Right now, though, I don't see that you have any other choice. And unless you get some expert help now, soon you won't own anything at all."

Enter the Turnaround Consultant

The next day, the weavers met with a consultant who was an expert in working with financially troubled companies and insolvent debtors. He interviewed them and reviewed their records. He asked to tour their small shop and made phone calls to some of their customers. When he finally left, late in the afternoon, it was with a bulging briefcase and a retainer check.

When he met the following week with the weavers and their attorney, he gave them his realistic assessment.

"As I see it," said the consultant, "your business was doing quite well until approximately two years ago.

"You were paying yourselves decent salaries and had sufficient profit to finance the 10 percent annual growth you were experiencing. However, three events occurred shortly thereafter which formed the genesis of your present crises. Sales started to decline at an annualized rate of 25 percent; you increased your salaries by 20 percent; and you purchased two computer-controlled looms. You financed the purchase of the looms by using $10,000 of your working capital for the down payment, and you obtained a loan for $30,000 from Imperial Savings, the emperor's personal bank.

"As a result," continued the consultant, "during the period starting two years ago until the parade, you lost approximately $50,000. This loss was financed by stretching the payables owed to your unsecured creditors (the butcher, the silk merchant, the goldsmith, the landlord, and so forth) and the funds advanced by the emperor. As a result of the bad press following the parade, sales decreased by an additional 20 percent. Although you have both struggled valiantly to keep your business afloat, and have sacrificed by cutting your salaries and perks, your situation is hopeless . . . unless you can drastically increase sales.

"Is there anything you guys can do," he asked, "to get your sales back up to the $90,000 per year rate, where you were profitable?"

They thought and thought. They suggested dream schemes and unworkable theories. Finally, grabbing at straws, the young weaver hesitantly suggested they might restart their "Hong Kong Weaver" operation.

"You mean the traveling road show?" asked his partner.

"Remember when we booked shows that brought in $10,000 in one week?" said the young weaver, getting excited.

"That much in one week?" asked the consultant, with great interest. "What is this 'Hong Kong Weaver' deal?"

The weavers explained. In the provinces, there was a great demand for fine clothes. In the early days of their business, they had toured the various villages and cities, allowing customers to choose materials and patterns of the latest fashions. With deposits in hand, they returned to their shop to make the clothes, which were later delivered and paid for. They had discontinued this program because they spent too much time on the road, away from their families—and it was grueling work.

"What would it do for sales, if you did it again?" asked the consultant.

"Oh, we could probably add about $100,000 a year to the $50,000 a year we're doing now," said the young weaver.

"Well, will you do it if it will keep your business out of liquidation and your heads off the block?" asked the consultant.

"You bet!" said the weavers in unison.

The consultant gave a sigh of relief. "Maybe this case won't be that tough after all," he said.

He went through the rest of his report and summarized the assets, the debt structure, and the security interests in each item of equipment that the weavers owned. He provided his estimate of the liquidation value of the assets based upon a brief appraisal.

After some discussion, the consultant and the weavers' attorney determined that the most effective and economical course of action was to attempt to achieve a creditors' agreement outside of bankruptcy. They outlined the elements of the plan to the weavers, who quickly agreed with the concept.

Finally, the weavers' attorney explained to his clients the bankruptcy process and procedure, should the filing of a Chapter 11 petition be necessary.

A petition filed under the bankruptcy code would effect an automatic stay, or cessation, of all collection, foreclosure, eviction, or other actions on the part of creditors, and no creditor holding any claim against the weavers would be able to interfere with them. The attorney explained that a Chapter 11 petition would only make sense if they could secure the emperor's cooperation; in addition, approval of the plan would require an affirmation note of the unsecured creditors comprising two-thirds of the claims in amount and one-half in number.

The Emperor (Secured Creditor) Rages

Meanwhile, across town, a very angry emperor paced the floor of his imperial office, waiting for the arrival of the imperial attorney. He was in quite a state, and had been ever since the parade. He was not a man who took kindly to being made a laughing stock. How could his trusted ministers and court attendants have failed him so? He had fired the lot of them, not wanting to be surrounded by fools. It never would have happened if he hadn't forgotten his glasses, so he could have seen for himself that there were no clothes at all. This was how he consoled himself.

With the arrival of the imperial attorney, the emperor exploded.

"I've had it with those weavers," raged the emperor. "I should have beheaded the bastards for making me a laughing stock. Now I can't get the deadbeats to pay the small payments that I, in my charitable munificence, agreed to." He paused to take a deep breath. "And what's more," he said, getting angrier, "they are not even paying Imperial Savings for the looms."

"Now emperor, try not to get so upset," said his attorney.

"Don't get upset, you say!" fumed the emperor. "Who's upset? *I want my money*! That's the least they can do for me after humiliating me in public. And don't give me that 'poor weavers' story. I know they have the money to pay me. They're probably holding it in a numbered account with the gnomes of Zurich. You're my lawyer, can't you do *something*?"

"Well," said the imperial attorney with a sigh, "we could foreclose on the security. You have a secured interest in all the assets of Weavers, Inc., and we could sue them personally under the guarantees."

"Well, why don't we?" asked the emperor.

"It's not as simple as it sounds," said his attorney. "First, the assets are probably worth a lot less than you are owed. I don't think the computer-controlled looms would bring much at an auction—you know how fast those things go out of date. Their sewing machines, tables, racks, and steamers are all ancient. The receivables are probably O.K., but I understand that their business is down, so they will be minimum. And our experience is that bolts of fabric, which constitutes most of their inventory, will bring under 10 cents on the dollar of original cost."

"Is that all?" asked the emperor, startled.

"Second," continued the attorney, "it's academic anyway, because they will undoubtedly file a bankruptcy petition for the company, Weavers, Inc., which would stop our foreclosure process, and file a personal bankruptcy which would stop the lawsuit against the weavers. Then we would have to fight the whole thing out in the bankruptcy court."

"I knew I should have had them beheaded," fumed the emperor. "What do we do if they file for bankruptcy?"

"Actually, your position isn't too bad," explained the attorney with a bit of enthusiasm. "You're a lot better off than the goldsmith, the silk merchant, the landlord, and the butcher."

"Yes, I know, my loans are secured." said the emperor. "But how does that help me in a bankruptcy action?"

The imperial attorney explained that since they had security agreement on all the property of Weavers, Inc., and had recorded their lien, the emperor's claim had a priority over all the funds that are received from the liquidation of those assets. In much the same way, Imperial Savings had a secured interest in the computer-controlled looms, and they had a priority over any funds received in the liquidation of the looms.

However, there was the problem of the deficiency. The deficiency is the difference between the value of the loan and the value of the secured claim's collateral. If, for example, the weavers owned $22,500 on the looms and Imperial Savings were able to foreclose and sell the looms at auction for $10,000 net of all costs of sale—which was a likely price, considering the advances in the technology of computer looms that had occurred since that model came out—it wouldn't cover the cost of the looms. The deficiency would be $12,500.

To the emperor's dismay, this deficiency would become an unsecured claim on the estate of Weavers, Inc., similar to the claims of the goldsmith, butcher, and other unsecured lenders. It would be paid to the extent that there is enough money in the estate to pay the general unsecured creditors. Since the emperor didn't have a signed personal guarantee from the weavers for the loan on the looms—an oversight of the loan officer—there was no way he could sue the weavers for the deficiency on that debt.

"What difference does all this make," the emperor finally said, "if they file bankruptcy and I can't foreclose anyway?"

"Well, your majesty," replied the attorney, "you and Imperial Savings, as secured creditors, have quite a bit of leverage in this situation.

"They are going to have to pay you something to use your looms, or you can get permission from the court to foreclose. And they can't use the proceeds of the receivables or the inventory, or the money in the bank without a court order.

"This means," the attorney summed up, "that you are in a very strong position vis-à-vis Weavers, Inc., and you can force them to accommodate your interests if they wish to enjoy any prospect for effective reorganization of their business.

"The key issue is," cautioned the imperial attorney, "if you work a deal can they, in fact, stay in business? I hear that the landlord has served them with a notice to pay rent or quit the premises. We're going to have to find out more about their situation. Let me take a few days to review the matter and perhaps call the weavers' attorney."

The Weavers Strike a Deal with the Emperor

Several days later at the offices of the imperial attorney, the various players in the drama assembled: the emperor's attorney, the weavers, their attorney, and their turnaround consultant.

"Let me assure you, sire," began the weaver's attorney, whose first task was to placate the emperor, "that my clients, however naive, inept, and financially incompetent they may be, appreciate the seriousness of their situation and the extent to which you have accommodated them. And they have every intention of paying you in full."

"I should hope so!" said the emperor. Nevertheless, he was pleased with how things were going. Maybe he was right, after all, in not having them beheaded.

"However," the weaver's attorney continued, "we need your cooperation. My colleague, a consultant retained by my clients, will explain the situation."

The turnaround consultant reviewed the financial history of Weavers, Inc., the present debt structure of the corporation, and the liquidation values of the assets. Then he explained the sales projection for the weavers' business, based upon their reactivating the "Hong Kong Weavers" marketing approach. He also presented a thumbnail sketch of the weavers' personal financial situation: the assets that they owned outside the business, such as the equity in their houses, their cars, furniture, and savings accounts.

He carefully explained that in order for the weavers to rehabilitate their business, he proposed that Weavers, Inc., enter into a creditors' agreement with the emperor and the unsecured creditors that would include the following provisions:

1. All claims would be paid over a five-year period, with interest.

2. The weavers would pay a fixed amount per month divided between the emperor and the unsecured creditors. The emperor's note would be revised to extend for a full three years, and all the delinquent interest and principal would be added to the note and amortized over the full three-year term. The unsecured creditors would get only interest payments during the three-year period that the emperor's note was being paid, and would receive their principal back over the last two years of the plan.

3. The loan with Imperial Savings would be revised to extend the terms and decrease the monthly payments, but would carry a slightly higher interest.

4. In order to deal with the landlord, no principal payments against either the secured or the unsecured debt would be made until the default in the rent was cured and the rent was brought current, which he estimated would take about two months.

He then pointed out that considering the weavers' reputation and the condition of their business, it was unlikely that any of the banks in the realm would want to buy out the emperor's position, even at a deep discount. Therefore, without the emperor's cooperation, the weavers would be forced to file a Chapter 7 bankruptcy petition. The consequences for the emperor in the event of a Chapter 7 liquidation would be a recovery of less than 30 cents on the dollar for the emperor's claim and about 50 cents on the dollar on the claim of Imperial Savings. Of course, he added, the unsecured creditors would receive nothing.

Once he understood the situation, the emperor agreed to consider the proposal. After a conference in private with his attorney, the emperor decided to accept the plan. There were smiles all around.

Trouble in the Unsecured Creditors' Corner

In the office of another attorney—this one retained by the unsecured creditors—the goldsmith, silk merchant, landlord, butcher and grocer gathered together to see what they could do. Each had received a copy of the proposed agreement from the weavers' attorney. They were not interested in any such plan. They wanted their money back—all of it—and they were afraid they wouldn't see a penny. Each of them wished he had never extended credit to those untrustworthy weavers. How could they have been so taken in!

Their attorney explained some of the basic elements of the bankruptcy code to them and then he got down to the business at hand.

"Have any of you received any money, any payment on the old debt from the weavers during the 90 days immediately prior to their filing the petition? That would be," he paused, looking at his calendar, "since September 7?"

"I extracted $1600 out of them about two months ago," said the goldsmith.

"You did a lot better than I," said the silk merchant. "I only got $900."

"I'm obviously the piker," said the butcher, "I only got $400."

"Well, this is going to come as bad news," said their attorney. "You might all have to pay it back."

"You're kidding, aren't you?" said the goldsmith.

"I'd rather die than pay them back a nickel," said the silk merchant.

"Over my dead body," said the butcher, flexing his considerable muscle.

"Let me explain," said the unsecured creditors' attorney, with sympathy. "It really has little to do with the weavers. According to the bankruptcy code, the payments you received were preference payments. Any payment made for old debt that took place within 90 days prior to the date of filing may be reversed. If Weavers, Inc., files bankruptcy, the trustee of their estate could file suit against each of you to recover those funds."

They were all speechless. This wasn't something they had expected to hear. They had come to the attorney to get more money from the weavers, not to hear that they might have to give back what they'd already been fortunate enough to get.

"What about my attachment lien?" asked the butcher.

"If they file, it's history," said the attorney. "A bankruptcy petition would extinguish all liens that have not matured."

"What about my notice to pay rent or quit the premises?" asked the landlord.

"You would have to deal with that in the bankruptcy court," replied the attorney. "Either they will have to accept your lease, cure the non-payment of rent to your satisfaction, and begin paying rent, or they will have to reject the lease and move out."

"What about my lawsuit?" asked the silk merchant, without much hope.

"Sorry," said the attorney. "If they file, it is stayed. Your claim would be handled as another unsecured claim."

"I can see now that the emperor has cut himself a fat deal," said the goldsmith.

"What if we reject the proposal?" asked the butcher.

"Yes," said the landlord, excitedly. "Suppose we all say no! Then we'd show who has the leverage."

Their attorney shook his head. "While it's true that all of you in this room control 40 percent of the debt, and can block and 'rain on the weavers' parade,'" he smiled, obviously enjoying the metaphor, "that doesn't make a lot of sense. First, the information their consultant provided clearly shows that if the proposed plan is rejected and the weavers file Chapter 7, the unsecured creditors will not get anything."

"I don't care about the money anymore," said the butcher. "I just want the weavers to rot in hell."

"Let's be reasonable," said the goldsmith, "we certainly don't want to pay money back, do we?"

"No, I agree with the butcher," said the landlord. "To hell with the weavers and their damn plan."

But it wasn't so simple, of course. Nothing in the bankruptcy process is. Their attorney explained that the weavers could, with the cooperation of the emperor, file a Chapter 11 plan. Given the "cram down" provision of the code, the judge could still confirm the plan even if all the unsecured creditors voted against it. And this plan had all the right elements. The plan was fair to all creditors, and everyone would be paid in full and with interest, a much better result than if the weavers filed under Chapter 7. With the weavers' willingness to reactivate the "Hong Kong Weaver" operation, the plan had a good chance of being successful.

Also, he knew the judge hearing the case to be very pragmatic and he speculated that the judge would probably confirm the plan.

"Isn't there anything we can do?" pleaded the goldsmith. "You're our lawyer, can't you think of something?"

"Well, we might up the interest rate," said the attorney. "They're offering 7 percent. We could push for 10 percent as a condition for agreeing with the plan. I know the weavers' attorney very well. He is a cautious man, not prone to take chances. I'll talk with him. Are we in agreement that if he'll go the 10 percent interest we'll support the plan?"

After a long pause, each one nodded agreement.

Resolution in the Hallway of the Bankruptcy Court

One week later, in the hallway outside the courtroom, the weavers' attorney and the unsecured creditors' attorney ran into each other while they were waiting for a hearing in another case.

"Did you check the calendar?" asked the attorney representing the unsecured creditors.

"Yes, we're way down on the list," replied the other. "It will probably be 30 minutes until they call us."

"Good, I'm glad we have some time," said the unsecured creditors' attorney. "I wanted to talk with you about the Weavers, Inc., proposal."

He explained that his clients were furious with the weavers, and felt that the weavers had demonstrated themselves repeatedly to be unscrupulous, untrustworthy, undependable, and unpredictable. His clients, he said, didn't see any reason to go along with the plan.

"Come on," said the weavers' attorney. "The emperor has even more reason to feel that way, and he's agreed to the plan. We've proposed a great plan, with 100 percent payoff to all creditors with interest."

"Look," said the unsecured creditors' attorney. "My clients are very unhappy. They are urging me to reject the proposal."

"Both you and I know that they will get nothing in a Chapter 7 proceeding," said the weavers' attorney.

"That may be true," agreed the other. "But at least they won't have to ever think about the weavers again. They'll take their lumps and move on. You know that an angry client is not a rational client."

The weavers' attorney nodded understandingly, but said he didn't see what else they could offer, since they had proposed a 100 percent payback.

"They want more interest," said the unsecured creditors' attorney, "12 percent."

"But they'll settle for . . . ?" asked the weavers' attorney.

"10 percent," replied the other.

"And they will accept the proposal if we modify the plan to pay 10 percent interest?" asked the weavers' attorney. The other attorney nodded, and they shook hands on the deal.

The weavers' attorney called his clients and advised them that the creditors would support the plan if the interest was raised to 10 percent. The weavers were ecstatic and quickly agreed. One week later the agreement was signed by all the creditors.

The old weaver and the young weaver packed their bags and hit the road to the provinces.

FOLLOWING THROUGH: IMPLEMENTATION OF THE PLAN

Once the plan has been accepted by the company's stakeholders, the turnaround consultant's next task is to implement the plan, with the assistance of the company management. In this endeavor he will use his professional management and entrepreneurial skills to assist in the organization, staffing, implementation of control systems, and motivation of personnel to carry out the plan.

His role in this effort will be determined by the capability of the existing ownership and management; the ability of the company to hire the management staff that the company needs; and the ability of the existing chief executive to perform the professional management skills the company had previously lacked. If the present management is considered incapable of leading the company, and the company cannot afford the risk of a new chief executive, it may be appropriate for the turnaround manager to function as an interim chief executive until the situation is stabilized to the point where either the owners or a new chief executive could successfully fill the leadership role, or until the company is showing performance that could attract a buyer.

The implementation task of the turnaround effort includes the initiation and accomplishment of the specific action items that have been defined in the plan and negotiated with the stakeholders. Typical actions may include any of the tactics discussed in the previous section on formulating the plan. The actions taken during the implementation phase are focused on improving margins, profitability, and return on investment, as opposed to the actions taken during the emergency phase, which were focused on eliminating cash drain, creating a cash hoard, and saving the company.

Actions taken during the implementation activity are a result of careful deliberation, analysis, discussion, and negotiations, and are designed to be consistent with the company's strategic plan. The types of actions that are taken as part of an implementation task are:

1. Sale or liquidation of a strategic business unit

2. Major change in the way a product line is marketed

3. Redefinition of the manner in which certain departments will be managed with the attendant change in management personnel

4. Commencement of periodic payments to unsecured creditors

5. Auctioning off of surplus capital equipment

6. Hiring of new executives

7. Announcing of a new product line

8. Investing in a new computer system

The turnaround manager must concentrate on setting priorities and on applying steady pressure to all critical functions and areas of the firm.

Turnaround programs that are implemented successfully are usually clear and orderly in their action plan and convincing in their demonstration of results. Consequently, the confidence that the stakeholders placed in the company and the turnaround manager is rekindled and enhanced.

When the company implements the plan and starts to tell its various stakeholders and the public what it is doing, it will face a number of challenges. The managers will want to take as upbeat an approach as the facts allow, because of the company's need to reestablish creditability. Management must act "as if" the plan will be a success, even if it may have doubts. If management is tentative and its doubts begin to "bleed through" the veneer of its positive attitude, prospects for success will be greatly diminished.

Management will have to contend with the adverse comments about its prospects, which its competitors will broadcast at every opportunity. It will have to contend with the skepticism of its lenders, the caution of its suppliers, the anxiety of its employees, and any tendency that it may have to become depressed or discouraged over the enormity of the tasks that face it.

Simultaneously, management will have to create support and understanding for some of the very negative aspects of its plan, such as the layoffs of loyal and dedicated employees, the sale or abandonment of successful core business, wholesale salary cuts, a reduction of fringe benefits, and the implementation of rules and procedures to increase employee conformity.

> It (the company) must reassure lenders and trade suppliers that the company will ultimately succeed, yet convince them to make painful concessions. Essentially, executives must achieve a careful and cultivated ambiguity as they address the divergent concerns of the many groups with a keen interest in the company.

Charles M. Williams

16 | A BUSINESS FITNESS KIT

The difference between failure and success is doing a thing nearly right and doing a thing exactly right.

EDWARD SIMMONS

This chapter is designed for anyone thinking of starting a business who wants to minimize the risks and increase the chances of survival. It is intended to be useful to those who are considering starting a new business venture based upon the ruins of one that failed, as well as to the hopeful entrepreneur who is planning a first venture into the challenging, yet risky, world of business. The thinking and planning processes are the same.

THE DOZEN QUESTIONS TO ANSWER BEFORE STARTING YOUR BUSINESS

There are 12 questions that you should be able to answer before quitting your job, taking your money out of the bank and from your relatives, and placing a bet on a new business venture.

1. Have I considered the risk of the business venture?

2. What benefits do I hope to achieve from the business?

3. How do I plan to exit the business?

4. What business am I going into? What products and services will I offer?

5. How will the business be organized?

6. If I'm considering having a partner, have we discussed all of the issues involved?

7. Do I have a written business plan?

8. Is the business venture a good deal for me economically, taking into account my present situation?

9. Do I have the discipline to manage my personal desires in light of the demands the business will make on my resources?

10. Are my beliefs, values, attitudes and personality consistent with those required to succeed in business?

11. How will the business be financed?

12. How will I handle the management tasks of the business?

If you can answer these questions, in a detailed way, then you have already increased your chances of success in your business venture. Planning and careful thinking are the best ways to stack the odds in your favor—and give your business the best start it can have. This chapter will discuss these 12 areas of concern.

PUT YOUR BRAIN IN THE DRIVER'S SEAT: THINKING THINGS THROUGH

We have discussed the lure of business repeatedly in this book. There are many benefits to going into business—it can be one of the most satisfying experiences of your life. But there are also many pitfalls that must be avoided if you are to have a successful business operation. Many a business is doomed to failure before it even opens its doors, because it failed to plan. There is an old saying, "Failure to plan is planning to fail," and it is doubly true in business.

In this chapter we pose some of the really hard questions that most entrepreneurs never consider in their optimistic, eager, and anxious lurch to the starting gate for their career. We're going to pose these questions because we believe that failure to consider them is equivalent to driving the first nail in the coffin of a business enterprise.

When I was going through college in the 1950s, IBM was one of many companies jostling for a position in the emerging computer business. The motto that was being promoted by IBM's then president Thomas Watson, Jr., and which came to be synonymous with IBM, was one word: *think*.

This word was on placards on every wall, every hallway, everywhere you looked. That's a powerful suggestion: *think*. It would be hard to find a motto more appropriate for the entrepreneur.

> Anyone considering starting his own business enjoys a marvelous and paradoxical quirk of fate. The asset most valuable to this enterprise comes free of charge. It is the power to think. It is also a paradox that this key ingredient is far too often not put to use. Your greatest risk in starting a business is that you will not stop and think through certain decisions. Failures are caused by mistakes and mistakes happen when we do not think.
>
> Phillip Holland

Phillip Holland, creator of Yum Yum Donuts, is the author of one of the most interesting and insightful books about the process of starting a business: *The Entrepreneur's Guide*. He discusses an important concept in his book: some people are more inclined to act than to think, because it's easier. He states that if there is ever a time in your life when you need to think things through and resist the urge to act, it is before going into business.

The consequences of failing to do so can be years of unhappiness, frustration, and penury. This has been our experience from dealing with far too many people who are at the end of an ill-planned business venture that they rushed into at full speed. Too many entrepreneurs create their own private hell as a consequence of an impetuous leap of faith into their own business.

WORST-CASE SCENARIOS: WHAT YOU CAN STAND TO LOSE

As we discussed in some detail in Chapter 1, starting a new business is inherently a risky venture. The chances that a new business will fail

are incredibly high, yet many people rush into business with less preparation than they spend to go on vacation. Before beginning a new
venture or expanding an existing one, the risks involved should be given
serious attention—and plans made to minimize those risks as much as
possible.

I recently met a very young businessman who was in serious financial
difficulty because he had attempted to expand his single retail stationery
business by opening a second store on the other side of town without
the necessary start-up capital. He explained, in minute detail, all of the
things that had gone awry in his plans: the fixtures had arrived late; the
leasehold improvements were not completed in time to accept the Christmas inventory; and a check had gotten lost in the mail so some of the
office stationery products had not arrived. He attributed the low monthly
sales and inevitable large losses in his new store to these and a myriad
of other factors.

Knowing, from my experience, how often business expansions fail,
I asked him how he had predicted the expected success of the new store.
Did he have market surveys, analytical information, or, at least, a fortune
teller's prophecy? No. He based his expectations or hopes on the sales
level he was experiencing in his original store—which, incidentally, was
located about 10 miles and five neighborhoods away.

He hadn't given a thought to the fact that opening a new store in a
brand-new shopping center was a risk. I told him that there is a question
I ask clients who are considering a business venture: How much money
are you willing to lose if it doesn't work out? And I asked him what his
answer would have been, as he was thinking about opening the second
store.

After a pause, he replied that he would have said, "Nothing, I'm not
prepared to lose anything." Given that, I told him, my advice would
have been to forget the whole thing. If we could all guarantee success
in a business venture, we would all be multimillionaires. Risk is part of
the formula for success.

Before beginning a business, you should ask yourself how much you
are prepared to lose if the venture doesn't work out. What you put at
risk you may never see again. As any gambler knows, you only put at
stake the amount you can afford to lose.

When starting a business, remind yourself that it is a risk that cannot
be accurately estimated. You should decide how much money you are

going to place at risk, limit your exposure to just that money, and be mentally prepared to lose what you have placed at risk.

HONORABLE INTENTIONS: EXAMINING YOUR MOTIVES

It is important to clearly define the benefits you hope to gain from the business. You need to ask yourself *why* you are going into business. Is it for money, power, or status? Do you just want to be independent? Are you tired of working for others and want to work for yourself? Do you need to buy yourself a job after being laid off by a company in a declining industry, such as oil or agriculture?

Two of the most important reasons to decide why you are going to go into business and to be clear about it are:

1. If you reach your objective, whether it be in terms of money, power, status, or some other measurement, you can decide to get out of business, cash in on the fruits of your labor, and enjoy the rest of your life doing something else, rather than collecting receivables, fighting with payables, or other operating headaches.

2. If you decide for any reason that you simply cannot reach your goal in your present business, you can also decide to quit, get out, and try again in another forum, perhaps in another industry, before you burn out.

Failure to think through both issues results in the following situations, which we see all too often.

A businessperson starts out with nothing except mortgages, his wife, house, and kids. After 15 or 20 years he has a successful business, a big house, membership in a country club, a small airplane, a beach house, one child in law school, and one child in medical school. He is sought out by political candidates for contributions, and he is a highly regarded benefactor of various charities. He believes that the music will never stop, so he never cashes out. He stays in the business but delegates most responsibility to employees or children—and is found to be fully at risk when the industry crashes.

Alternatively, a businessperson starts out with nothing, has some early successes, but barely gets out of the starting gate on the road to riches. He is just successful enough to keep the business alive. As he struggles to keep the business afloat, he may have to sacrifice his family life, his religious life, and his community life to the business.

Each year the business extracts its toll in stress, anxiety, and depression. He works and works, hoping against hope that the next year, the next deal, or the next customer will finally get his enterprise going—but it never does. He operates in a financial purgatory. Since he loses sight of what he wanted to achieve and how much he was willing to "pay," he fails to take stock, cut his losses, sell out (or liquidate), and do something else. He merely gets old "dreaming the impossible dream" and "reaching for the unreachable star."

If you don't start out with some specific goals, you never know when you've reached them, or whether you want to continue toward something which may be unreachable.

EXIT LINES: PLANNING THE END AT THE BEGINNING

A question that should be asked during the start-up phase of a business is: how do you plan to exit the business?

Assume that you've started the business, you've put your effort and your money into it, and it is rocking along, providing you and your family an acceptable standard of living. After many years, this business may constitute a significant portion of your net worth.

There will come a time at which you decide the business has outlived its usefulness or benefits to you. You and your family may have tired of the long hours and weekends. Your health may no longer be able to tolerate the stress that is ever present. Your interests may have changed, and now lie in other areas. You may decide you want to do something else with your time, effort, and money. What do you do now?

You will always have a number of choices, but surprising as it may seem, sometimes the choices are not *that* attractive. Recognize that your investment in the business is not represented by cash in the bank: it's represented by inventory, capital equipment, receivables, leasehold improvements, vehicles, and notes receivable. There may be nothing at hand that you can cash at the bank or use on your vacation to the Bahamas. You have your stock certificates evidencing your ownership, which can be very valuable if the business is very successful—and someone wants to buy it. But suppose that at the time you decide you want to do other things, the business is only moderately successful, or worse, operating at a loss.

What are your alternatives?

1. You can turn it over to your son or daughter and sell it to them— if you have a son or daughter, if they are interested in the business, and if they are capable of running it.

2. You can turn it over to professional management and derive consulting fees and dividends for your ownership—if you can find professional management that is capable, that you trust, and that will work for what the business can afford to pay.

3. You can sell the business intact—if you can find a buyer willing to pay your price.

4. You can liquidate the business, collect the receivables, sell off the capital equipment inventory, sublease the building—if you can find buyers for the hard assets at prices that you can live with.

Surprising as it may seem, in many instances none of the above options is either feasible or acceptable to the owner, and he cannot get out. There simply is no key to unlock the prison that the business seems to have become. More than one businessperson itching to get out of his business has felt as trapped as Charlton Heston in the movie *Ben-Hur*, when he was chained to a spot in the galley, rowing to the beat of the drum, without any prospect of relief, rest, or escape.

FRANKENSTEIN OR PYGMALION?: CREATING THE BUSINESS STRATEGY

The strategy of a business is determined by a number of issues and questions that must be addressed by the entrepreneur. These are as follows.

1. What products and/or services will the business offer and what markets will it serve? Who are the customers and what is it that you

will offer to sell to them? Do the customers that you have identified have a need for the product or service you will be offering? Do you know how serious that need is? Do you know how many customers have some level of interest in your product or service?

2. How will you establish and sustain a competitive advantage in the product-market area you will service? Why will customers buy from you rather than from your competitors? How will you tell your customers about your competitive advantages? Unless such advantages can be created and maintained, profits will be short lived, if they exist at all.

3. What distinctive competences or valuable resource will the business rely on to generate and maintain the sustainable competitive advantage? A distinctive competence is something a business unit does exceptionally well and that has strategic importance to the business, such as the maintenance at Disneyland, the meal consistency at McDonald's, or the route servicing of Frito Lay. Will the business rely on a valuable resource to maintain the competitive advantage, such as a patent, a leasehold interest, or a location?

4. Will the profitability per unit of product or service sold (g = gross profit) and the anticipated number of units that will be shipped once the business is stabilized (N = number of units) be such that the gross profit during any period ($g \times N$) will cover the fixed operating costs of the business (F = fixed costs), the cost of capital that is funding the business (I = cost of money, that is, debt service on the loan), and the earnings required to sustain your personal lifestyle (E = earnings)?

In other words, will this equation work?

$$g \times N > F + I + E$$

You will remember using this equation in Chapter 15 to determine whether the company has a viable core business. It can also be used in your planning stages when setting up the business, as you project whether you actually have a viable core business from the start. The key question is, then: are there enough customers for the product that you offer so that the business will sell enough products in a month so as to cover $F + I + E$?

If the answer is a resounding *yes*, and it is supported by market studies indicating that you can maintain the price and the market share against the competition, you *may* have a business.

If the answer is a hesitant "Gee whiz, I don't know. I think I may, I think I might . . .," then it's time to go back to the drawing board and rethink the business idea.

GETTING DOWN TO BRASS TACKS: THE ORGANIZATION OF THE BUSINESS

Once you have a solid business strategy in mind, it is important to take time to consider precisely how your business is going to be structured.

Legal Organization

An important step in starting a new business venture is to decide how you are going to "organize" the business in the legal sense, and how to determine whether that organization is going to achieve your objectives. While every business has some legal organization that is devised, presumably, to protect the interests of the owners, actually very little thought is devoted to the issue of how the organizational structure will affect the financial risks to which the principals are exposed.

The basic organizational structures are proprietorship, general partnership, limited partnership, and corporation. The risks for the investors for each of the organization types are quite varied. A brief description of the risks inherent to each legal organization structure follows.

Proprietorship: All liabilities go directly to the principal. There is no shield. He is at risk for his total investment plus all of the debts the business incurs.

General Partnership: The partnership agreement may specify different types of partners (capital, junior, and so forth) who are liable in different degrees. However, the partners as a group are at risk for their entire investment, and are jointly and severally liable for all the debts of the business.

Limited Partnership: The partnership agreement will usually provide that the limited partners are at risk for their entire investment but have no risk for the debts the partnership incurs; the general partners are at risk for their investment and all the debts of the partnership.

Corporation: The investors in a corporation are at risk only to the extent of their investment. The corporation serves as a shield, protecting the investors from the debts of the corporation. This shield, however, does not protect the principals from obligations owed to tax trust funds, such as payroll taxes, and in practice the principals of the firm might execute guarantees to banks to secure funds and make themselves personally liable for the debt if the corporation cannot pay.

Frequently individuals who go into business do not think through the benefits that the various organizational structures offer in terms of limiting their risk. They often opt to maximize tax losses during the early years, assuming that the business will be an unqualified success, and that a shield against unsecured creditors is not required.

Lease Agreements: Security Trap?

A good example of the failure to think through organizational issues is offered by the problem of leases. One of the biggest decisions a businessperson makes during the early days of his or her efforts is where to locate the business. If the business is a retail establishment, that decision might be the most crucial one, which determines its success or failure. There are always trade offs to consider, such as the cost per square foot versus potential customer traffic patterns and the proximity to stores where your customer base can shop.

Over the years, several clients experiencing severe difficulty in their business presented the following scenario to me.

1. The business was a start-up. It had never made money.

2. The owners were new to the business. Prior to this business he had worked as a middle-level executive; she had been a housewife.

3. They had poured all their savings into this business; they had no resources left.

4. They were not taking any significant salary—just enough to make their house payment, pay utilities, and buy food.

5. Their creditors were clamoring for payment and threatening to sue.

6. *The business was incorporated, but the owners had personally signed a five-year lease for the store.*

You can now recognize that this is a scenario for disaster. Why would anyone without any business experience commit to lease a location for five years for a business idea that had never been proven? By signing personally on the lease, the owners deprived themselves of the protection of the corporate shield. If the business fails—not an uncommon experience in this sort of situation—the owners must file personal bankruptcy to discharge their lease obligation.

Once the principal executes this type of lease, his entire net worth is at risk. If the business is not successful at that particular location, there is no way that the owner can "walk away" from the space: it is stuck to him like glue. As a group, landlords are not prone to be "flexible" if they have anybody with a sizable net worth on the hook.

Landlords with good space (or potentially good space) want their tenants to be committed, and often insist that the tenant sign a long-term lease personally, or guarantee the lease of his corporation, thereby making the principal personally liable for all the monthly and common area payments for the duration of the lease term.

Signing such a lease as part of the purchase of an existing business with an established client base and traffic pattern might be an optimistic or even risky venture; to do so with a new business in a new shopping center is just slightly short of insane.

PARTNERS: PROS AND CONS

Partners are people who will share the business with you in much the same way that a spouse shares his or her life with you. Note that the term "partner" refers to both legal partners and joint investors/workers/managers in a business that can take the form of a partnership or corporation.

A partner will contribute capital, expertise, collateral, hard work, and creativity. However, partners can develop into huge liabilities and may bring more trouble than everything positive that they have brought to the business. Given the potential risks involved, should you solicit partners in a business? Why would you? Because they may offer something that you and the business need.

1. *Help:*   Provide distinctive competences that the business needs and you do not possess and cannot afford at the time. For example, when an R&D engineer teams up with a salesperson.

2. *Money:*   Provide the cash and financial strength to secure bank loans to fund the enterprise.

3. *Moral Support:*   Provide support as well as judgment, creativity, and ideas, or help overcome the fear you will probably experience in launching a new enterprise.

Issues and Problems with Partners

There are certain problems which, if not addressed directly, frequently develop from a partnership and may ultimately lead to resentment, animosity, the breakup of the partnership, and loss of either capital or opportunity.

1. **Unequal work for equal sharing in the rewards.** It is difficult for partners to provide exactly "equal effort," and the detection or perception by one partner of the "shirking" of the other invariably leads to feelings of anger and resentment.

2. **Partners are jointly and severally liable for the debts of the business.** This means that if the enterprise crumbles and two partners are sued by their creditors, they will both be liable for all of the debts. So if partner A files bankruptcy and has no assets, partner B, who may be wealthy, will be liable for all the debts of the business.

If a business deal crumbles for which partners are personally liable, it is an axiom that the partner with the "deep pockets" usually winds up with the obligations.

3. **The partners either have or develop different goals for the business.** In his book *Taking a Chance to Be First* Warren Avis tells the story of two men who formed a partnership to produce a business information publication. They both had excellent credentials, and the business idea appeared sound—but they had different ideas of the mission.

One of the partners wanted to use the business as a stepping stone to build a major financial empire. He wanted to maximize profit and always was pressing to cut back on any expense that could increase the bottom line, such as editorial expenses and travel costs. The other partner wanted to establish a top-drawer advisory service for the average investor who could not get adequate advice from other professionals. To him, profit was not that important, while spending to improve the quality and scope of the service was.

As a result of their different views of the business, they continuously disagreed, could not get along, and regularly ran into impasses in attempting to make decisions. Their relationship disintegrated into constant bickering and the business eventually failed.

4. The partners differ in the levels of financial commitment that they are willing to make (cash that they will invest) and of risk that they will assume (guarantees that they will sign).

If a business is very successful and sales and profits continue to grow, the business will invariably need more working capital. Similarly, if the business experiences hard times and incurs substantial losses, the business will need working capital to replenish that which has been lost. In order for the business to receive its needed infusion of working capital, the partners will have to agree to either provide it out of their own resources or obtain additional loans from their banks.

Frequently the partners either will not be at the same stage in the decision process, or will have different financial abilities, or simply will not be able to agree. Consequently the business will suffer if not falter from this paralysis of management.

It is very important to consider these issues before committing to a business partnership. It can be one of the most painful mistakes to make, especially for friends who enter business as partners, and all because of not understanding or thinking through how the partnership will work, how the efforts will be shared, how the rewards and benefits will be allocated, and what each partner's commitment to the business will be in terms of time, effort, and financial support.

PUTTING IT IN BLACK AND WHITE: THE BUSINESS PLAN

There are several misconceptions about the purpose of business plans. Some consultants promote business plans only as a vehicle for raising money from banks, insurance companies, and venture capitalists. Others promote business plans as a vehicle to coordinate the objectives and goals of various levels of management and departments in a large organization. Both are valid uses and are subsumed within the larger purpose of a business plan: to serve as a blueprint for building a business.

> What is consciously in an entrepreneur's head is not as complete, as good, as promising as he or she pretends it is. Until committed to paper, intentions are seeds without soil, sails without wind, mere wishes which render communication within an organization inefficient, understanding uncertain, feedback inaccurate, and execution sporadic. Without execution, there is no payoff. The process of committing plans to paper is easy to postpone under the press of day-to-day events. In the absence of a document, fully coordinated usage of the resources of the business is unlikely. Each participant travels along a different route toward a destination of his or her own choosing. Decisions are made independently, without a map. Time is lost: energy squandered.
>
> Steven C. Brandt

Who needs a business plan? Everyone who is planning to go into business, is in business, or is planning to exit a business. Why? Because it forces the owners to define what it is that they are trying to do, how they are going to go about it, and what resources they are placing at risk.

The plan guides the operations on a day-to-day basis. It keeps everyone's eyes focused on the objectives, ensuring its viability and growth. It defines the strategy and tactics for growth and helps the executives communicate with others that have to help the business, such as bankers and other investors. Last, but far from least, it gives the entrepreneurs who are assuming the risk a way to stand back and evaluate their own business objectively—in much the same way as professional investors evaluate businesses—and allows them to assess whether the opportunity for reward is justified by the risk.

The process of writing the business plan provides the entrepreneur the opportunity to demonstrate to himself whether he is clear on the business mission and goals, whether he understands the economics on which the business is based, the competition it will face, and the financing he will require.

Moreover, if a business does not have a plan, it is hard—if not impossible—for the entrepreneur to evaluate how the business is doing. Is the business on target or off target? How will he know if he hasn't formulated a plan?

A typical business plan will describe the following aspects of the business in considerable detail and will be prepared in a manner presentable to bankers, investors, and prospective key employees.

1. Business concept, with the overall strategy and both short-term and long-term objectives.

2. Market analysis, including customer needs and wants, competitive situation, and general conditions within the industry

3. Marketing plan

4. Manufacturing plan

5. Technology plan

6. Financial plan, including profit and loss projections and cash flow projections

7. Organizational system, including key executives

8. Human resource plan

WHAT'S IT WORTH TO YOU: IS THIS A GOOD DEAL ECONOMICALLY?

What is the businessperson going to have to put into the business and what is he going to be able to take out? Is it worth it?

If you are buying an existing business and you can believe the books and records you are being shown, you have a pretty good idea what you're going to put in and what you are going to be able to take out.

For example, if the business had sales of $1 million per year, paying its prior owner $50,000 and making an additional $50,000, which was being plowed back into inventory, you could reasonably expect that, all things being equal (economy, industry, competitive situation), you should be able to take out about the same amount in salary, perks, or debt service. So if the previous owner was willing to sell for $250,000 and finance $150,000 over five years at 10 percent, you could make the following rudimentary calculation:

Your present situation:

Your annual salary	$ 35,000
Interest income (from $100,000 savings @ 7.5%)	7,500
Pretax spendable income	$ 42,500

Your situation should you buy the business:

Business income (before owner's draw)	$100,000
Less debt service ($150,000 amortized over 5 years @ 10%)	66,000
Net available income from the business	$ 34,000

Note that the income from your $100,000 savings will no longer be available because it has been used as a down payment for the business. Therefore, you and your family will have to get by on $8,500 per year less income, and you will not be able to continue the previous owner's program of investing $50,000 per year of profits back into the business for at least five years.

Your decision would be influenced by several factors including your assessment of how hard you and your family would have to work and the other opportunities for employment you had available. For example, if you were suddenly offered a position with an annual salary of $50,000, with a 50 percent probability of a bonus of $25,000, you might make the following calculation:

Situation: Should I accept new job offer?

Annual salary	$50,000
Projected annual bonus ($25,000 × 50% probability)	12,500
Interest income	7,500
Total annual income	$70,000

This income is $27,500 more than you are presently earning and more than twice what you would earn for the next five years should you buy the business. Would this cause you to reevaluate your tentative decision to buy the business?

Suppose, on the other hand, you are like many of those starting new businesses, or starting over in a new business venture. You can't afford to buy an existing, predictable business, so you must start from the ground floor and create one.

These are questions you should ask yourself. What are you going to put into it? What are you going to get out of it? How much does it cost? What if it fails?

What you might put into it is problematic. It may be your heart, soul, and most of your money. What you get out of it is even more problematic. How do you know what the business will do if it's never done it? You might not be able to take out any salary at all, especially in the beginning.

Just because you've been earning $6000 a month as an executive in a large firm doesn't mean that you'll earn that much in your "new" business. The business is remarkably indifferent to your past financial performance. It doesn't care what you've been earning.

Sometimes people who want to "get into their own business" pay dearly for the privilege, and do not think through how much it is really costing them. A young, recently married couple decided to go into the automobile window tinting business. This business did not require any sophisticated capital equipment or facilities. Total start-up costs were in the vicinity of $25,000. Neither of them had been in business before: she had been a merchandising manager for large department stores and he had been a stockbroker. They did not incorporate. All of their "business advice" was coming from their CPA.

Their initial year in business was plagued by employee problems, since neither had any supervisory experience. The business didn't ever really pass through the start-up phase. They did experience a few good months in the summer and operated over break-even. However, the auto glass tinting business was getting more competitive, and they were no longer able to attract customers consistently. The owners drew no income from the business for a year and were living off their savings, which were almost exhausted.

When they came to see us, they were $40,000 behind in their payroll taxes, owed their trade creditors $35,000, and were losing about $2000 each month on meager sales of $6000. We estimated their cost of sales at 65 percent and their minimum selling, general, and administrative expenses to compete in the market at about $4000 per month. Required sales to achieve break-even before owner's draw was therefore almost twice their present sales level (sales at break-even = F/g = $4000/0.35 = $11,428).

They felt they needed an income of $3500 per month for their draw, which would raise the monthly expense burden of the business to $7500 per month and the required sales break-even level to = $7500/0.35 = $21,428.

Finally, if they stayed in business via a turnaround, or a dump and buy back strategy, they would, at a minimum, have to work out a repayment program with the IRS that would require payment over six years with interest. This would add about $800 to their monthly expenses, raising the break-even sales level to $23,714, or about four times their present sales level.

We all agreed that the probability of the business generating four times its current sales level in the immediate future was nil, and that the only viable strategy at this point was to shut down the business and liquidate through Chapter 7 proceeding. They would then both seek jobs consistent with their experience and skills.

It's worth taking a moment to calculate what their entrepreneurial experience cost them.

Cost of the business venture

Their initial investment (supplies, space, telephones, advertising, and so forth)	$ 25,000
Their subsequent cash investments over the year to fund their losses	36,000
The salaries they gave up to start the business	
Her salary	40,000
His salary	48,000
Nondischargeable IRS and state obligations	30,000
Total cost	$179,000

It's amazing how quickly you can lose money in an unsuccessful business! If you are considering entering a business deal, you should determine whether the business you are entering is a good deal for you economically, under the worst-case scenario. Are you better off by being in this business as opposed to other things you might do with your talents?

THE CASE OF THE DISAPPEARING MONEY: EXPENDITURES OVERTAKING INCOME

C. Northcote Parkinson is a prolific writer who has, in a number of books, focused attention on the nonproductive aspects of the business world. In his first book, published in 1957, he formulated the "Parkinson's law," which is: *Work expands to fill the time available*.

In 1960 Parkinson formulated his second law, the law of extravagance: *Expenditures rise to meet income*. This law reflects the tendency of both individuals and businesses not to put something away for a rainy day. Parkinson says:

> Expenditure rises to meet income. Parkinson's Second Law, like the first, is a matter of everyday experience, manifest as soon as it is stated, as obvious as it is simple. When the individual has a rise in salary, he and his wife are prone to decide how the additional income is to be spent: so much on an insurance policy, so much to the savings bank, so much in a trust fund for the children. They might just as well save themselves the trouble, for no surplus ever comes into view. The extra salary is silently absorbed, leaving the family barely in credit and often, in fact, with a deficit which has actually increased. Individual expenditure not only rises to meet income but tends to surpass it, and probably always will.

The phenomenon that Parkinson describes is all too common in businesses that do not have professionally oriented management. A variation of this law in business could be:

Expenditures rise to meet available cash.

The businessperson who is enjoying the heady experience of rising sales and market share and a lot of income usually focuses on what he can easily understand: the cash in the bank. As the available cash increases, he finds new ways to spend it. Company-owned vacation condominiums, airplanes, and boats are frequent repositories for "spare cash."

We've seen owners who have increased their salaries by two and three times, while the company was losing money, simply because there was plenty of cash available. Sometimes executives and major stockholders will have the business support their hobby, such as softball teams, race car development, or foreign travel. But the one place that the cash rarely goes is into savings programs to accumulate reserves for the downturn in business which is more an inevitable than an unlikely event.

Consequently, when the business downturn does come, and there are no reserves to fund the losses, the owner's only recourse is to approach banks and finance companies at precisely the time when the business is not particularly attractive.

DOWNSIDE UP: THE ENTREPRENEUR'S EXISTENCE

When an individual chooses to become an entrepreneur, he buys into a life that has both positive and negative characteristics. On the upside there are independence and freedom to make decisions. Most people stop there, and don't consider the flip side of the deal. On the downside there are the anguish of having to make decisions, ambiguity, and loneliness.

Anguish of Deciding

Every decision that an entrepreneur is faced with will have a number of consequences that he will have to evaluate. The nature of his decisions often causes him to face impossible choices, resulting in the anguish of trying to make the right decision when there is no right answer. Every decision the entrepreneur makes will have consequences in the following dimensions:

Economic/Financial: What is the economic consequence for me? Will I make money as a result of this decision or will I lose money?

Legal: What are the legal consequences of this decision? Will I be breaking the law? Will I be exposing myself to legal action by another party?

Organizational: How will this decision affect my management personnel and my employees? Will the organizational climate improve or will it deteriorate?

Ethical: Is this decision consistent with my values and the things that I stand for, or is it counter to them? To what extent am I willing to bend my ethical standards?

Family: How will this decision affect my relationship with my spouse or my children? Will it bring us closer together or will it alienate us?

Social: How will this decision affect my friends and acquaintances? Will they benefit because of this decision or will they be harmed? Will they think better of me and like me more because of this decision or will they think less of me and shun me?

Reputational: How will this decision affect my standing in the community? Will it increase my stature and status or will it diminish it?

The anguish of the entrepreneur is that virtually every decision he makes has both beneficial consequences and adverse consequences.

For example, posed with the alternatives of pledging an invoice to the bank (for accounts receivable financing) for a product that has not been shipped or not meeting the payroll, he must weigh the positive consequences of getting the money (economic) and meeting the payroll (organizational), paying for supplies shipped by some of his friends (social), and bringing home a paycheck to his wife (family), against the negative consequences of misrepresentation (ethical and legal) and being sued by the bank if his action is discovered (reputational).

Or, posed with the alternative of filing bankruptcy for his business or convincing friends and relatives to lend him money to keep his business alive, he must weigh the positive consequences of getting the money (economic), keeping the organization going (organizational), keeping the paychecks flowing (economic), and not filing bankruptcy (reputational), against the negative consequences of exploiting his friends (ethical), potentially misrepresenting the safety of the loan (legal), and the alienation of his friends if their money is lost (social).

Loneliness

Although entrepreneurs are surrounded by others—managers, employees, customers, colleagues, accountants, and lawyers—and spend a good deal of time in meetings, they are usually isolated from persons in whom they can confide. As a consequence, they must make most of their decisions alone and in isolation.

> Loneliness is my biggest problem. With whom do you talk? I'm supposed to talk with my accountant, I'm supposed to talk with my banker, with my lawyer. Well I can, and I do, but they can't be objective. They all have an axe to grind because they work for me in one way or another.

These are the words of an entrepreneur interviewed for a *Harvard Business Review* article by David E. Gumpert and David P. Boyd. He could have added that colleagues and associates who are not competitors and in whom one could easily confide rarely have sufficient knowledge or interest in your business to be of much help.

Entrepreneurs must learn to live with the reality that they have the ultimate authority and responsibility for every major decision that is made in their business. They will usually make that decision alone, and they alone will be accountable for its consequences.

Ambiguity

Samuel Johnson wrote that "he is no wise man who will quit a certainty for an uncertainty." Entrepreneurs are by that definition not wise men, since all of their decisions and actions are characterized by uncertainty. The economics of business decisions are such that increased certainty is purchased at the cost of money and time, and very often the time that elapses as data are gathered to decrease uncertainty results in additional risk to the enterprise.

For example, when performing research and development in order to bring out a new product, the engineering and marketing decisions that will have to be made will require the expenditure of the funds. Information must be acquired that will result in the optimum product to meet competition. However, the longer the time that it takes to gather sufficient data to make the decision, the greater the risk that the product will be too late in reaching the market. So the entrepreneur soon learns that he never has enough time or enough information to make a decision that he will really feel comfortable with: he must operate in a state of perpetual ambiguity.

Do You Have What It Takes?

Many individuals find, *after* they have plunged into entrepreneurship, that the never-ending loneliness, ambiguity, and anguish around decision making cause them stress with which they cannot cope. It is important to recognize the characteristics and demands that are placed on you emotionally by being the head of a business.

You need to consider carefully whether you have the emotional strength, stability, and self-esteem at the present time to withstand the emotional buffeting that often accompanies business difficulties and setbacks— things that are sure to occur during the start-up of the business.

Review the material presented in earlier chapters that deal with emotional issues. Do you recognize yourself in the "high-risk" client profiles? Or do you have a strong sense of autonomy, integrity, and self-esteem? Are your motives for wanting to start the business based more on emotional rewards than just on making a livelihood? How are you going to protect yourself from not taking business setbacks personally?

These are issues to consider before you commit yourself to a risky financial venture. It may even be a matter of timing. Are you already under a great deal of stress in your life? Do you really want to add another stress?

MONEY, MONEY, MONEY: THE LIFEBLOOD OF BUSINESS

Where is the money going to come from, and what price do you have to pay for it? This is a critical question to ask when considering the start of a business venture. Several aspects of the funding question follow.

Where Will the Money Come from to Fund the Business?

What kind of money comes into the business? The money exists in three forms:

1. Cash that you actually put into the business

2. Guarantees or security you provide to the lending institution to ensure repayment of the money that they lend to your company

3. Guarantees you provide to vendors for the credit that they provide to the business for goods that are purchased

The total of these three forms is the investment an individual makes.

Very often the entrepreneur or his backers forget that the security he provided and the guarantees he signed are every bit as important as the cash investment because the guarantees do not represent immediate cash out of pocket. Unfortunately they don't appreciate that the guarantee represents an investment, until it is being called by the bank or an unsecured creditor.

Who Will Provide the Money?

Money comes from a number of different sources, each of which can provide money in various amounts and each of which has its own unique interest for getting involved in your business.

Source	*Objective/Interest*
Yourself and your spouse	To create your enterprise for future income and security

Source	*Objective/Interest*
Friends, relatives, and acquaintances	To help you and share in your success, to get in on a new and exciting enterprise
Banks, finance companies, leasing companies, and so forth	To earn an income from the money they lend and be secure that it will be paid back either from the profits of the business or by liquidating the collateral
Partners—active, silent, and limited	To earn a greater potential return than available through a conventional investment (bonds or stocks) by participating with you in your venture
Venture capitalists	To take a large risk in the hope that your enterprise turns out to be a "star" and not a "dog"

When an entrepreneur begins soliciting money from these sources, he is always focused on the upside: how terrific everything is going to be once his business gets going and everyone is making a lot of money. He rarely thinks about the downside: what happens if everything turns to garbage and the business fails? Who is going to lose what? How will the loss affect my relationships with my lenders and investors? What effect will that loss have on my social position, my status in the community, my relationship with my family, my spouse's family? These questions are rarely, if ever, thought about by the enthusiastic entrepreneur who has his sights fixed on a single task: *raising the money*.

So let's ask the rarely asked question. If the deal turns sour, who will lose and how will that loss affect me?

1. You and your spouse will lose your money.

2. You will lose your relatives' goodwill (they will remain your relatives but Thanksgiving dinner may be strained).

3. Your friends will be lost with the investment.

4. The banks will attempt to collect on the guarantees and hound you for the money at risk, but they will be professional in their approval.

After all, as Ogden Nash so eloquently stated, "Bankers are just like anybody else, except richer."

5. Partners will engage in mutual recriminations with you, causing the business to remain paralyzed; they will blame you for everything that went wrong, including the things for which they were responsible and accountable.

6. Venture capitalists will write off the investment as one of their "dogs" and will "bad mouth" you to all of their associates, making it difficult for you to raise money in the future.

How Much Money Is Required?

How much money do you need to get this deal going? A lot more than you expect.

In starting a new business you must be sensitive to the fact that the money you will need will fall into five primary categories, only three of which can be estimated.

1. Your soft start-up expense: your organization costs; deposits on telephone service and other utilities; the costs of your checks and business license.

2. Your hard start-up expenses: the cost of your capital equipment such as office furniture, computers, typewriters, production equipment, and warehouse equipment.

3. The costs of building your market image: your initial promotion and marketing costs to tell the world that you've arrived.

4. Working capital: the capital you will require to support your inventory, receivables, and payroll at the level of sales volume that you are planning. The amount of working capital will depend on the inventory level you need to maintain and the turnover rate of the inventory. The funds to support the working capital can be estimated based on projected sales.

5. Money to fund losses: the money you will need to fund the losses until you achieve break-even operation.

Break-even operation is defined as that sales level where your variable gross profit will cover your fixed operating costs and your debt service.

How much money will you need to cover your loss until break-even? There's no answer to this question, other than: it takes as much as it takes. When you start a business from scratch, you have no guarantee you will achieve break-even by any specific time, if ever.

Most people starting new business ventures calculate the soft and hard start-up costs, but ignore the initial market creation costs; or they may think about it, but they do not calculate their working capital requirements, and do not realistically provide for the start-up losses.

Needless to say, if the business runs out of money before it achieves break-even, then a substantial portion of the total investment that has been made up to that date will be jeopardized, since the business will have to be sold at a distress sale or will have to be liquidated.

At the very least, the entrepreneur should make an assumption as to how many months of losses he anticipates or what the total aggregate loss is that he is willing to absorb, and he should fund that amount in his plan. When he reaches that level, he must sell, liquidate, or shut down pending new investment.

EXPANDING HORIZONS: DANGERS OF SPREADING YOUR BUSINESS TOO THIN

A businessperson who has been successful in one enterprise or in one location gets the urge to build a bigger enterprise. Historically, the thinking process goes something like this: I've been successful in X business at Y location and have made good money. Therefore, if I expand to X1 business at Y1 location, I can increase my overall sales, spread my overhead expenses, and make a lot more money.

Or like this: we're using large quantities of X material in our business and it is costing us $Y per pound. If we manufactured X rather than purchasing it, we could save 50 percent of our costs and significantly increase our profitability.

In the former situation the expansion is horizontal and in the latter it is vertical. In both instances, however, a new business is being created.

That thinking is fine if the new business is successful. But if it's not successful, it's just another failing business. The differences between funding a business from a start-up situation and funding it from the profitability of an existing business are twofold.

1. Expanding a business can usually be accomplished with pretax dollars, rather than aftertax dollars. This is always a significant incentive for a profitable business. The owners ask themselves: why should I pay taxes to the government when I can invest this money into the business?

2. An expansion business is in the position to drain the profitable business ad infinitum unless someone shuts off the losses. An unsuccessful business supported by a profitable business can be the mistake that will pull down the successful business. The unprofitable business will drive the profitable business out of business.

RUNNING THE SHOW: MANAGEMENT OF THE BUSINESS

There are many issues to consider once the business idea has become a reality. The day-to-day management of the business requires a variety of skills and makes many demands on the owners. There are a number of questions you should ask yourself about how the management of the business is going to be operated.

1. *Where is the experience coming from that understands this particular business?* Business is not an institution that can be expected to conform to laws of cause and effect. In other words, just because you do something there is no guarantee that the desired result will occur. Business operates on the laws of statistics and probability. Most people in business learn their industry and markets through trial and error, not theoretically. Who understands this business? Are you going to rely on others? Do you as the owner have confidence in the representations that are being made to you?

Learning how to run a business cannot be accomplished through an instructor or a night-school course. A business is a complex institution where the owners and managers must rely on experience, task skills, people skills, judgment, creativity, and their unique knowledge about the industry's processes and markets. They must interact continuously with those many aspects of the business to steer the enterprise.

2. *Does the business have all the right types of players to ensure its success?* For a business to be successful, it requires different skills in its personnel

and managers. All of the skills required by the business must be provided by the management: to the extent they are not, the business will not function properly. The business needs producers to get the work done, salespersons to sell, engineers to design, and so forth; it needs administrators to organize, keep the paperwork up to snuff, file the right forms, and balance the checkbook; it needs an entrepreneur to create ideas, initiate change, and make deals; and it needs integrators to translate the plans and creative ideas of the entrepreneur into assignments for the producers and administrators, so that the personnel and the managers are motivated to carry out the mission of the business.

Most companies that experience significant financial trouble are lacking in one or more of the required management types.

3. *How hard are you and your spouse going to have to work to make this a success and are you willing to do it?* Starting a new business is a difficult, time-consuming venture. You may find yourself working 12 to 14 hours a day, 6 or 7 days a week, and what is worse, you may find that the only way you will be able to manage is to have your spouse, children, or other relatives working right by you. You and your family may both wind up living and breathing the business as if your very lives depended on it. And your economic life probably will.

You need to think about how much you are prepared to give for the opportunity of getting up to bat in the business game. Make sure you have clear agreement and support from those whose help you will be depending upon.

4. *To whom are you going to be accountable?* It is important to have someone to whom the entrepreneur is accountable for decisions, successes, and failures.

A Biblical proverb tells us, "Plans fail for lack of counsel, but with many advisers they succeed." Anyone in business needs advisers. In many small businesses, where there are no outside investors, the entrepreneur is often responsible to no one.

Advisers or boards—someone to be accountable to—often can tell the business where it is deviating from the path it set out to follow, and keep the entrepreneur in touch with reality.

Once the business is established, it is important to keep things working properly, to adhere to a plan, to ensure that the business is functioning the way you think it should. You need to have a way of making sure that there are no potential disasters lurking in the shadows and that you haven't done something foolish to put the business at risk. Mistakes and failures have to be investigated so that they do not reoccur.

> You may put yourself on solid ground and begin to show a profit in your business. But then you slip back into bad habits, because of a failure to follow through, all of your initial efforts at setting mission and goals, and at implementation may have been in vain. You'll merely postpone an inevitable disaster to some point in the future, when it will cost many times more than the cost of follow through in lost hard cash and customer goodwill.
>
> Warren Avis

Lord Acton said that "power tends to corrupt and absolute power corrupts absolutely." Absolute power is the consequence of not having a boss or some other entity that can make sure the entrepreneur is, and stays, grounded. If such an accountability agent is not available, the entrepreneur can literally do crazy and self-destructive acts for years, until their consequences so erode the business that it is doomed to failure. Accountability agents can be boards of directors, outside consultants, mentors, or interested and concerned investors.

Lawyers, CPAs, and bankers, however, do not typically function as good accountability agents. In the case of lawyers, their expertise is the law, not business, and to the extent that they start to offer advice and guidance in your business rather than in your legal affairs, they diminish their value as an advocate of your legal position. What's more, in very rare instances is the lawyer sufficiently sophisticated in affairs of business in general, or in your business in particular, to be of much help. The worst problem with a lawyer giving you business advice is that he provides you a false sense of security: you think you're being "mentored and counseled" and it is more likely that you're not.

CPAs are not much more effective as accountability agents, notwithstanding the movement of the CPAs into the management consulting activities. CPAs, like lawyers, are professionals who serve business in a very specific manner, and when they do that well, they make a very positive contribution to the business. They will, hopefully, help the entrepreneur keep "score." They keep him "honest" in his dealings with the government taxing authorities and ensure that his taxes are prepared accurately.

Bankers, who are often viewed by businesspersons as "friendly advisors" usually have neither the experience nor the time to be of much help to any specific entrepreneur and, more important, they are vendors—renters of money. While they have a stake in the success of the company and are interested in helping it, they must scrupulously avoid the appearance of participating in management. Such activities could result in their being viewed more as investors than bankers. In addition, the banker's interests and the entrepreneur's interests can often be at odds. The banker can become an adversary who just "wants his money back." More than one businessperson has found, as his business fell into trouble, that his status as "favored customer" at the bank had crashed, and he was just a "debtor."

In short, the businessperson must usually go beyond his attorney, CPA, and banker in his quest for an accountability agent.

5. *Who is going to keep score and who is going to make sure that the score is being kept accurately?* We have discussed the problem of accurate accounting records. It is a problem that plagues all businesses, small and large alike.

Regardless of who is doing the books and keeping the score, the result is often the same: the records are not timely, relevant, or accurate. To appreciate what an enormous burden this creates for the entrepreneur, is to imagine what it would be like to be a coach of a football team and be in the fourth quarter without knowing what happened in the first and second quarters. I don't believe too many coaches would stay.

The scope of the problem is illustrated by the case of a client in the construction business that did not distinguish between bookings (orders in hand but not yet completed or billed) and accounts receivable (invoices outstanding for work completed but not yet paid). The client had been keeping his books this way for a period of two years, and monthly statements were being prepared by a well-respected CPA firm. Two banks had reviewed his financials without comment, and both had provided him lines of credit.

As we wrote to him in our report:

> The fact that this method of reporting could continue over a period of time without its being called to your attention either by your CPA or the bank is surprising. This is especially true in light of the fact that an order in hand is not viewed as collateral by a bank, but accounts receivable are considered viable collateral on which a bank could lend. The effect of this "error" for your firm was that you overstated your earnings, overstated your accounts receivable, and therefore the bank's collateral, understated your inventory, overpaid your taxes, and you overstated your net worth.

I cannot overemphasize how serious this error is: your ability to deal with the banks and creditors, etc., requires that you prepare and be able to periodically issue financial statements that are accurate, reflect reality, and are in accordance with generally accepted accounting principles. If your financial statements are either not accurate or not timely or "highly creative," you will quickly lose the respect of the bankers, and your credibility as a businessman will deteriorate.

For a business to be successful in the long term it must have an accurate and timely accounting system that is maintained by competent and trained personnel and is periodically audited by competent and independent outside CPAs. It is crucial, when starting a business, to make a commitment to and a plan for an accounting system that is timely, accurate, and relevant.

LEAP *AFTER* YOU'VE LOOKED: A FINAL WORD TO THE WISE

So now you know how to create your business in a way that will keep it fit and improve your chances for survival, success, and prosperity. When I discuss the concepts presented in this chapter at a seminar and recite the horrors that can—and do—result from violating these precepts, a member of the audience will typically counter my statements with platitudes about business and risk taking that are tantamount to the well-known aphorisms: "faint heart never won fair lady," "nothing ventured, nothing gained," or "great deeds are usually wrought at great risk."

What they say, in essence, is: "If every potential entrepreneur did what you suggest, *nobody* would go into business."

Wrong! Qualified entrepreneurs, who can adequately answer these twelve questions, *would* start businesses—and would be substantially better prepared to face the challenges ahead. If more people started businesses with a clear idea of what their business was about, aware of the price they would have to pay in loneliness, anxiety, and decision-making anguish, the business survival rate would be higher. Those who decide, after considering the issues in this chapter, to either delay the start of their business or not to start a business at all will be better off having avoided a probable disaster. They can enjoy the wealth they preserve by not embarking on an ill-conceived, inadequately financed, and poorly implemented business venture and can consider themselves fortunate not to have become another business failure statistic.

The point is not that people should never start a business, but rather that preparation and planning are as necessary as courage and ideas.

Go ahead and take the plunge. But first, make sure you know how to swim.

EPILOGUE: LESSONS FROM FAILURE

Economic distress will teach men, if anything can, that realities are less dangerous than fancies, that fact-finding is more effective than fault-finding.

CARL LOTUS BECKER

In this book I have shared with you my experience, and the experience of others, regarding a traumatic event: business failure. The information provided about its cause and prevention may hopefully keep your creditors from breaking down the door. I have also described what kind of help it is possible to get from an experienced turnaround manager, in an attempt to demystify the process and encourage businesses to seek professional help when they are in crisis.

It is an unfortunate fact, however, that sometimes the death of a business is inevitable. The resources and help aren't there, or come too late. There are times when no matter what you do, you cannot keep the business from going under. What do you do then? You learn from your mistakes. You shrug your shoulders and go on. You try to put the experience in perspective, and rather than viewing business collapse as the end of the line, consider it simply the end of a particular phase in your life. Think about what Richard Bach wrote: "What the caterpillar calls the end of the world, the Master calls a butterfly."

IN GOOD COMPANY: JOINING THE RANKS OF SUCCESSFUL FAILURES

Before we look more closely at the benefits and lessons that failure allows, let us first consider the well-hidden fact that many of history's successes were also colossal failures.

One of the most common examples of the successful failure is Thomas Edison, who is credited with inventing the incandescent electric lamp. We think of him as the creator of the light bulb, one of the most widely used inventions in homes and businesses around the world. But to look at his overall success rate, you'd have to say that he failed many more times than he succeeded. He patented more than 1000 inventions, an average of one new patent every two weeks of his adult life. Few of them ever saw the light of day, much less the incandescent glow of his most famous invention.

In the business world, Charles Goodyear struggled as a failure for many years. His obsession was to transform raw rubber into a useful material—one that would stand the test of seasonal changes, and would neither freeze in winter temperatures nor melt in the hot summer sun. His experiments kept him on the edge of poverty, and even put him into debtors' prison for a period of time. Even there, he spent his time trying to figure out how to succeed with his idea of what rubber could be. It is said that he sold everything in sight, from his watch to the dishes off his table to continue in his single-minded determination.

Ultimately, his success came by way of accident. He dropped a piece of rubber that had been treated with sulfur onto a hot stove, and had the first glimmerings of the path he had to take. He ended up developing an entire new industry, yet continued to show bad judgment in business and died in poverty. Was he a success or a failure?

Gail Borden is a more classic example of success from the depths of failure. He had failed miserably and spectacularly through many business ventures, finally focusing his attention on extending the shelf life of milk through a vacuum condensation process. He was 56, with a lifetime of failures behind him, before condensed milk became a fortune maker.

King C. Gillette was another failure whose name has become a household word. He struggled for eight lean years trying to gain a market for the safety razor—his invention—and only sold 51 in the first year.

Rowland Hussey Macy watched, with great dismay, the failure of his dry goods store in the California gold rush—the third such business venture to end up on the rocks. It was 14 years later that he returned to the retail business, opening a dry goods store in New York City in 1858, and finally saw his fortunes start to turn.

If any of these people had been interviewed in the midst of their down-and-out times, they would not have been considered front-page news in the business section, or likely future successes. But they learned from their failures, they continued to try, and in some cases to redirect their energies. They ultimately became known, in the final analysis, as great successes.

So if you have just emerged on the wrong end of a business failure, know that you are in good company. Failure does not have to be a lifelong pattern.

WHAT IS THIS THING CALLED FAILURE?

It is a matter of debate what failure actually is, and when you can positively say that some person or event is a failure. Your perspective changes as events change.

Ernest A. Fitzgerald, in his book *How to Be a Successful Failure*, relates the story about a Chinese landowner. The story suggests that we should not be too quick to judge when a failure has occurred: One day some wild horses wandered onto his property. The horses were worth a fortune. The neighbors gathered to congratulate him on his good luck. The man stoically remarked, "How do you know I am lucky?" Later the man's son was trying to break in one of the horses. The boy was thrown, and his leg was broken. The neighbors tried to console the father on his misfortune. He asked again, "How do you know I am unfortunate?" A while later the king declared war, and the landowner's son was exempted from military duty because of his broken leg. The neighbors came in to say how fortunate the man was. He asked the same question, "How do you know I am fortunate?"

This story offers great insight into the fact that life is a process, and at any point as you measure success or failure, you cannot know what will happen next. Success and failure are merely punctuation points in the story that is unfolding, nothing more and nothing less.

In another book, which discusses the nature of failure, *When Smart People Fail*, authors Carole Hyatt and Linda Gottlieb point out that:

> Failure is a judgment about events. That is all it is . . . How well you cope with that event in large part determines what kind of person you become. The point to remember here is that it is the way you cope with failure that shapes you, not failure itself.

LEARNING FROM FAILURE

Failure provides opportunities to learn which are rarely present in success. People tend to spend a great deal of time analyzing their failures, and very little effort in determining why they are successful. This is because, in part, failure forces you to consider what happened, and provides much more data than success.

Olympic decathlon champion Rafer Johnson, who is interviewed at length in Edward de Bono's book *Tactics: The Art and Science of Success*, explains how he perceives the value of failure:

> To my mind, the great champions are the ones that react to defeat in a positive way. I'd much rather climb into the head of someone who's lost, and see what made that person come back to be a victor, than to climb into the head of a winner. You can probably learn more from failures. That somebody wins all the time does not necessarily mean they are successful.

One of the most valuable gifts of business failure is that it allows you the opportunity to learn what you were doing wrong, and to correct those mistakes. It is far worse to struggle along in a kind of business purgatory, never really succeeding and never totally failing, than to have a halt put to all your activity. Failure permits time for reevaluation, and it provides the opportunity to come to the point of acceptance of the limitations that have kept you from being successful.

Success and failure are linked processes. Contingency planning— what to do if something goes wrong—is an integral part of many business plans. It should also apply to the individual's own strategy. As de Bono puts it:

> Any style of success must also include a style of failure. How does a successful person cope with failure? Failures there will be. Failure takes different people different ways. It can utterly destroy or build a personality's confidence; it can activate a spiral of depression or be a stimulus.

Joseph Sugarman, in his book *Success Forces*, takes this idea one step further. He considers failure to be a very positive force for success:

> One of the most powerful Success Forces is failure. Every time you fail you create a positive force for success. . . . I am firmly convinced that

failure is such a powerful Success Force that it gives me the reassurance to try almost anything, for I know that even if I fail, it will create a force for success later.

The most important thing to keep in mind when examining failure is to keep from the temptation of blaming others for your failures. Blaming others only robs you of the opportunity to learn from your mistakes. Blaming yourself limits your ability to assess objectively what could be done better. The real value of failure is that it allows you the chance to change, to be different, and to move forward.

The best defense against failure is to get on with your life. Consider the words of Josef Pilsudski:

"To be vanquished and not surrender, that is victory."

BIBLIOGRAPHY

Chapter 1: Risk and Reward: Mortality in Business

Augustine, Norman R., *Augustine's Laws*. New York: Viking Penguin (1986).

1986 Statistical Abstract of the United States, 106th ed. Washington, DC: U.S. Department of Commerce, Bureau of the Census.

Peters, Thomas J., and Waterman, Robert H. Jr., *In Search of Excellence: Lessons from America's Best-Run Companies*. New York: Harper & Row (1982).

The Business Failure Record. New York: Dun & Bradstreet (1987).

Wechsler, Jill, "Bringing a Business Back from the Brink of Bankruptcy," *Working Woman*, pp. 39–41 (Mar. 1985).

Yoshihara, Nancy, "Ming the Merciless Is on the Prowl," *Los Angeles Times Magazine*, pp. 11–17 (July 27, 1986).

Chapter 2: How Healthy Is Your Business?

Altman, Edward I., *Corporate Financial Distress: A Complete Guide to Predicting, Avoiding, and Dealing with Bankruptcy*. New York: Wiley (1983).

Chapter 3: A Plague of Errors: The 13 Causes of Corporate Illness

Argentini, John, *Corporate Collapse: The Causes and the Symptoms*. New York: Wiley (1976).

"A Warning Fulfilled," *Forbes*, p. 12 (Mar. 29, 1982).

"Prince Triumphant," *Fortune*, p. 84 (Feb. 22, 1982).

Banaszewski, John, "Thirteen Ways to Get a Company in Trouble," *Inc.* (Sept. 1981).

Bennis, Warren, and Nanus, Burt, *Leaders, The Strategies for Taking Charge*. New York: Harper & Row (1985).

Bibeault, Donald B., *Corporate Turnaround: How Managers Turn Losers into Winners*. New York: McGraw-Hill (1982).

Garfield, Charles, *Peak Performers: The New Heroes of American Business*. New York: William Morrow (1986).

Nelson, Philip B., *Corporations in Crisis: Behavioral Observations for Bankruptcy Policy*. New York: Praeger (1981).

Peter, Lawrence J., and Hull, Raymond, *The Peter Principle*. New York: William Morrow (1969).

Chapter 4: "Give It to Me Straight": Escaping the Trap of Denial

Bettelheim, Bruno, *The Uses of Enchantment: The Meaning and Importance of Fairy Tales*. New York: Vintage (1977).

Untermeyer, Bryna, and Untermeyer, Louis (Eds.), *The Golden Treasury of Children's Literature*. Racine, WI: Western Publ. (1966).

Chapter 5: The Eye of the Beholder: The Outside World's View of the Business

Goldstick, Gary, and Schreiber, George, "An Early Warning System for Bankers: How to Screen New Client Companies and Spot Potential Trouble in Existing Loans" (Seminar Publ.). Los Angeles: Goldstick and Schreiber, Inc. (1982).

Chapter 6: Internal Bleeding: What's Happening Inside the Company

Kets de Vries, Manfred F. R., and Miller, Danny, *The Neurotic Organization*. San Francisco: Jossey-Bass (1985).

Knight, Henry C., "Surviving a Corporate Financial Crisis," *Cost and Management*, pp. 54–55 (May-June 1982).

McBer & Co., "Managing Motivation for Performance Improvement" (Seminar publ.). Boston: McBer and Co. (1976).

Silver, David A., *The Entrepreneurial Life: How to Go for It and Get It*. New York: Wiley (1983).

Whitney, John W., *Taking Charge: Management Guide to Troubled Companies and Turnarounds*. Homewood, IL: Dow Jones-Irwin (1987).

Chapter 7: Out of Their Minds: Executive Experience in Business Distress

Albrect, Karl, *Brain Power: Learn to Improve Your Thinking Skills*. Englewood Cliffs, NJ: Prentice-Hall (1980).

——— , *Stress and the Manager: Making It Work for You*. Englewood Cliffs, NJ: Prentice-Hall (1979).

"Alvin L. Feldman Dead at 53; Head of Continental Airlines," *New York Times* (Aug. 10, 1981).

Beck, Aaron T., *Cognitive Therapy and the Emotional Disorders*. New York: New American Library (1976).

——— , Emery, Gary, with Greenberg, Ruth L., *Anxiety Disorders and Phobias*. New York: Basic Books (1985).

_____ , Rush, A. John, Shaw, Brian F., and Emery, Gary, *Cognitive Therapy of Depression*. New York: Guilford Press (1980).

Boyd, David P., and Gumpert, David E., "Coping with Entrepreneurial Stress," *Harvard Business Review*, pp. 44–59 (Mar./Apr. 1983).

Burns, David D., *Feeling Good: The New Mood Therapy*. New York: William Morrow (1980).

"Depression," *Newsweek* (May 4, 1987).

Emery, Gary, *A New Beginning: How You Can Change Your Life through Cognitive Therapy*. New York: Simon & Schuster (1981).

_____ , *Own Your Own Life: How the New Cognitive Therapy Can Make You Feel Wonderful*. New York: New American Library (1982).

Fieve, Ronald R., *Moodswing: The Third Revolution in Psychiatry*. New York: Bantam (1981).

Hadas, Moses (Ed.), *The Complete Plays of Sophocles* (transl. by Sir Richard Claverhouse Jebb). New York: Bantam (1982).

Holmes, Thomas H. and Rahe, Richard H., "Holmes/Rahe Social Readjustment Rating Scale," *Journal of Psychosomatic Research*, vol. 2, pp. 213–218 (1967).

Horovitz, Bruce, "Suicide: An Executive Suite Hazard?" *Industry Week*, pp. 41ff (Mar. 9, 1981).

Ingrassia, Lawrence, "Executive's Crisis: Aftermath of Failure: The Collapse of a Man, The Agony of a Family (Jerald H. Maxwell)," *The Wall Street Journal* (Mar. 12, 1982).

Kets de Vries, Manfred F. R., "The Dark Side of Entrepreneurship," *Harvard Business Review*, pp. 160–167 (Nov./Dec. 1985).

Kline, Nathan S., *From Sad to Glad*. New York: Ballantine (1981).

Meyers, Gerald C., with Holusha, John, *When It Hits the Fan: Managing the Nine Crises of Business*. Boston: Houghton Mifflin (1986).

Nuernberger, Phil, *Freedom from Stress: A Holistic Approach*. Honesdale, PA: Himalayan Internatl. Inst. of Yoga Science and Philosophy (1981).

Woolfolk, Robert L., and Richardson, Frank C., *Stress, Sanity, and Survival*. New York: New American Library (1978).

Chapter 8: Where's the Fairy Godmother? Change Agents and Processes

Allaire, Yvan, and Firslrotu, Mihaela, "How to Implement Radical Strategies in Large Organizations," *Sloan Management Review*, pp. 19–34 (Spring 1985).

Branden, Nathaniel, *Honoring the Self: Personal Integrity and the Heroic Potentials of Human Nature*. Los Angeles: Jenny P. Tarcher (1983).

Clifford, Donald K., Jr., and Cavanaugh, Richard E., *The Winning Performance: How America's High-Growth Midsize Companies Succeed*. Boston: Boston Books (1985).

Drucker, Peter, *The Effective Executive*. New York: Harper & Row (1966).

Emery, Gary, *Own Your Own Life: How the New Cognitive Therapy Can Make You Feel Wonderful*. New York: New American Library (1982).

Grimm, Jacob and Wilhelm, *Fairy Tales* (transl. by Lucy Crane, Marian Edwards, et al.). Cleveland, OH: World Publ. (1947).

Heller, Joseph, *Catch-22*. New York: Simon & Schuster (1961).

Khandwalla, Pradip N., "Turnaround Management of Mismanaged Complex Organizations," *International Studies of Management and Organizations*, vol. 13, no. 4. M. E. Sharpe (1983–1984), pp. 4–41.

Peters, Thomas J., and Waterman, Robert H., Jr., *In Search of Excellence: Lessons from America's Best-Run Companies*. New York: Harper & Row (1982).

Ringer, Robert, *Winning through Intimidation*. New York: Funk & Wagnalls (1973).

Watzlawick, Paul, Weakland, John H., and Fisch, Richard, *Change: Principles of Problem Formation and Problem Resolution*. New York: Norton (1974).

Chapter 9: Help Is Not a Four-Letter Word: Hiring a Turnaround Consultant

Bibeault, Donald B., *Corporate Turnaround: How Managers Turn Losers into Winners*. New York: McGraw-Hill (1982).

Bolton, Robert, *People Skills: How to Assert Yourself, Listen to Others, and Resolve Conflicts*. Englewood Cliffs, NJ: Prentice-Hall (1979).

Greiner, Larry E., and Metzger, Robert O., *Consulting to Management*. Englewood Cliffs, NJ: Prentice-Hall (1983).

"How to Select a Management Consultant and Get Your Money's Worth," Institute of Management Consultants, Inc., New York (n.d.).

Krentzman, Harvey C., and Samaras, John N., "Can Small Businesses Use Consultants?" *Growing Concerns: Building and Managing the Smaller Business*, David E. Gumpert (Ed.). New York: Wiley (1984), chap. 24.

Kubr, Milan (Ed.), *Management Consulting: A Guide to the Profession*. Geneva, Switzerland: International Labour Organization (1986).

Quay, John, *Diagnostic Interviewing for Consultants and Auditors*. Columbus, OH: Quay Associates (1986).

"Turnaround Manager: More Using Your Head Than Chopping Them Off," Main, Jackson and Garfield, Inc.; republished in *Data Management* (Oct. 1981).

Turner, Arthur N., "Consulting Is More Than Giving Advice," *Harvard Business Review*, pp. 120–129 (Sept.-Oct. 1982).

Wittreich, Warren J., "How to Buy/Sell Professional Service," *Harvard Business Review*, vol. 44, pp. 127–138 (Mar./Apr. 1966).

Chapter 10: The Business Diagnosis: Analyzing a Company in Trouble

Aaker, David A., *Developing Business Strategies*. New York: Wiley (1984).

Goldstein, Arnold S., *How to Save Your Business*. Wilmington, DE: Enterprise Publ. (1983).

Quay, John, *Diagnostic Interviewing for Consultants and Auditors*. Columbus, OH: Quay Associates (1986).

Remick, Carl, "Time for a Turnaround," *Society for Advancement of Management Journal*, vol. 45, no. 4, pp. 4–15 (Autumn 1980).

Rowe, Alan J., Mason, Richard O., and Dickel, Karl E., *Strategic Management and Business Policy: A Methodological Approach*, 2d ed. Reading, MA: Addison Wesley (1986).

Chapter 11: What You Must Know about Bankruptcy Law

Augustine, Norman R., *Augustine's Laws*. New York: Viking Penguin (1986).

Bankruptcy Reform Act of 1978. Chicago: Commerce Clearing House (1978).

Burger, Warren E., "Isn't There a Better Way?" *American Bar Association Journal*, pp. 274–277 (Mar. 1982).

Forer, Lois G., *Death of the Law*. New York: McKay (1985).

Freiermuth, Edmund P., *Revitalizing Your Business: 5 Steps for Successfully Turning around Your Business*. Chicago: Probus (1985).

Harding, Christopher, et al., *Imprisonment in England and Wales*. London: Croom Helm (1985).

Kafka, Franz, *The Trial*. New York: Vintage (1964).

Kibel, H. Ronald, *How to Turn around a Financially Troubled Company*. New York: McGraw-Hill (1982).

Lampe, David R., and Goldstick, Gary H., "The Myth of the Law," unpublished manuscript.

McCormack, Mark H., *The Terrible Truth about Lawyers: How Lawyers Really Work and How to Deal with Them Successfully*. New York: William Morrow (1987).

McLauchlan, William P., *American Legal Process*. New York: Wiley (1976).

Morrison, Rees W., *Business Opportunities from Corporate Bankruptcies*. New York: Wiley (1985).

Nader, Ralph, and Green, Mark, *Verdicts on Lawyers*. London: Thomas Y. Crowell (1976).

Nelson, Philip B., *Corporations in Crisis: Behavioral Observations for Bankruptcy Policy*. New York: Praeger (1981).

Newton, Grant W., and Bloom, Gilbert D., *Tax Planning for the Troubled Business*. New York: Wiley (1984).

Chapter 12: Health Is a Relative Term: Insolvency Objectives, Strategies, and Processes

Bankruptcy Reform Act of 1978. Chicago: Commerce Clearing House (1978).

Goldstein, Arnold S., *How to Save Your Business*. Wilmington, DE: Enterprise Publ. (1983).

Chapter 13: Will the Patient Live? Key Factors in Company Survival

Adizes, Ichak, *How to Solve the Mismanagement Crisis: Diagnosis Treatment of Management Problems*. Los Angeles: MDOR Institute (1980).

Bibeault, Donald B., *Corporate Turnaround: How Managers Turn Losers into Winners*. New York: McGraw-Hill (1982).

Clifford, Donald K., Jr., and Cavanagh, Richard E., *Winning Performance: How America's High-Growth Midsize Companies Succeed*. New York: Bantam (1985).

Freiermuth, Edmund P., *Revitalizing Your Business: 5 Steps for Successfully Turning around Your Business*. Chicago: Probus (1985).

Goldstein, Arnold S., *How to Save Your Business*. Wilmington, DE: Enterprise Publ. (1983).

Chapter 14: Increasing Life Expectancy: Tasks of the Turnaround Manager

Bibeault, Donald B., *Corporate Turnaround: How Managers Turn Losers into Winners*. New York: McGraw-Hill (1982).

Gink, Steven F., *Crisis Management*. New York: Amacom (1986).

Irvine, Peter J., "From a Company Doctor: The Anatomy of a Turnaround," *Executive* (Aug. 1983).

Knight, Henry C., "Surviving a Corporate Financial Crisis," *Case and Management*, pp. 54–55 (May–June 1982).

Meyers, Gerald C., with Holusha, John, *When It Hits the Fan: Managing the Nine Crisis of Business*. Boston: Houghton Mifflin (1986).

Whitney, John W., *Taking Charge: Management Guide to Troubled Companies and Turnarounds*. Homewood, IL: Dow Jones-Irwin (1987).

Chapter 15: Choices for Survival

Bibeault, Donald B., *Corporate Turnaround: How Managers Turn Losers into Winners*. New York: McGraw-Hill (1982).

Hofer, Charles W., "Turnaround Strategies," *Journal of Business Strategy*, p. 1931 (Summer 1, 1980).

McKinley, John E. III, et al., *Problem Loan Strategies*. Philadelphia, PA: Robert Morris (1985).

Oneil, Hugh M., "Turnaround and Recovery: What Strategy Do You Need?" *Long Range Planning*, vol. 19, no. 1 (1986).

Scheel, John, "The Crunch of the Turnaround," *Executive* (June 1981).

Schwartz, Kenneth B., and Krishnagopal, Menon, "Executive Succession in Failing Firms," *Academy of Management Journal*, vol. 28, no. 3, pp. 680–686 (Sept. 1985).

Williams, Charles M., "When the Mighty Stumble," *Harvard Business Review* (July-Aug. 1984).

Zimmerman, Fred, "Turnaround: A Painful Learning Process," *Long Range Planning*, vol. 19, no. 4, pp. 104–114 (Aug. 1986).

Chapter 16: A Business Fitness Kit

Avis, Warren, *Take a Chance to Be First: The Secrets of Entrepreneurial Success*. New York: Macmillan (1986).

Brandt, Steven C., *Entrepreneuring: The Ten Commandments for Building a Growth Co*. New York: Mentor Books (1983).

Fox, Harold W., "Quasi Boards: Useful Small Business Confidants," in *Growing Concerns, Building and Managing the Smaller Firm*, David E. Gumpert (Ed.). New York: Wiley (1984).

Goldstein, Arnold S., *How to Save Your Business*. Wilmington, DE: Enterprise Publ. (1983).

Gumpert, David E., and Boyd, David P., "The Loneliness of the Small-Business Owner," *Harvard Business Review*, pp. 18–24 (Nov.-Dec. 1984).

Holland, Phillip, *The Entrepreneur's Guide: How to Start and Succeed in Your Own Business*. New York: Penguin (1986).

Parkinson, C. Northcote, *Parkinson: The Law*. Boston: Houghton Mifflin (1980).

Rich, Stanley R., and Gumpert, David E., *Business Plans That Win $$$: Lesson from the MIT Enterprise Forum*. New York: Harper & Row (1985).

Sartre, Jean-Paul, *Existentialism and Human Emotions*. Secaucus, NJ: Castle, a division of Book Sales, Inc.

Silver, A. David, *Up Front Financing: The Entrepreneur's Guide*. New York: John Wiley & Sons (1988).

Smith, Geoffrey, N., and Brown, Paul B., *Sweat Equity: What It Really Takes to Build America's Best Small Companies by the Group Who Did It*. New York: Simon & Schuster (1986).

Epilogue: Lessons from Failure

deBono, Edward, *Tactics: The Art and Science of Success*. Boston: Little, Brown (1983).

Fitzgerald, Ernest A., *How to Be a Successful Failure*. New York: Atheneum/SMI (1978).

Gatty, Bob, "Building a Failure," *Nation's Business*, pp. 50–51 (Apr. 1987).

Hyatt, Carole, and Gottlieb, Linda, *When Smart People Fail*. New York: Simon & Schuster (1987).

Jennings, Eugene Emerson, *Executive Success: Stresses, Problems and Adjustments*. New York: Meredith (1967).

Lewis, Robert T., *Taking Chances: The Psychology of Losing and How to Profit from It*. Boston: Houghton Mifflin (1979).

Sugarman, Joseph, *Success Forces*. Chicago: Contemporary Books (1980).

INDEX